STAR WARS

DARTH VADER

SHADOWS AND SECRETS

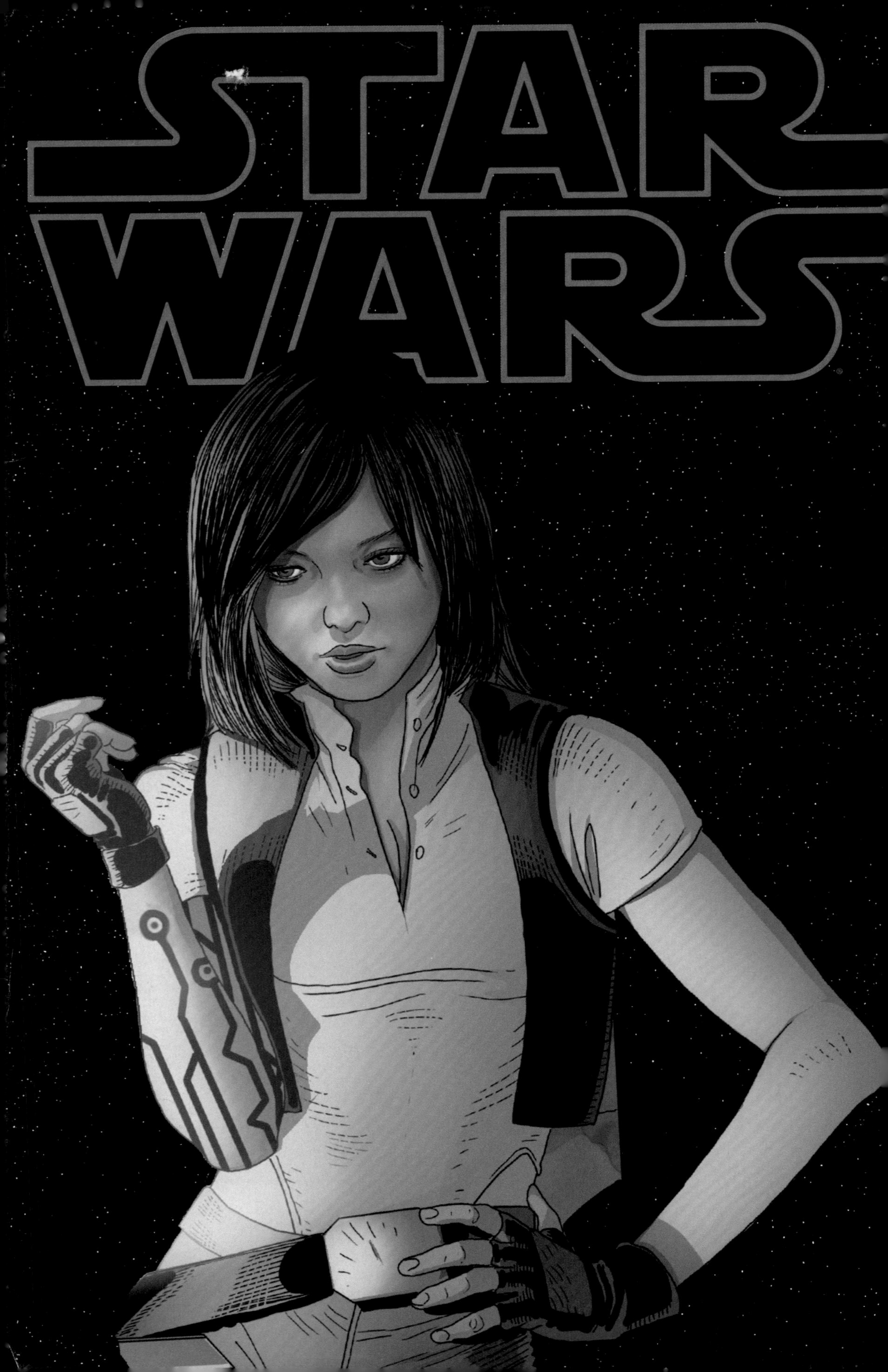
STAR
WARS

DARTH VADER

SHADOWS AND SECRETS

Writer	**KIERON GILLEN**
Artist	**SALVADOR LARROCA**
Colorist	**EDGAR DELGADO**
Letterer	**VC's JOE CARAMAGNA**
Cover Art	**ADI GRANOV**
Assistant Editor	**HEATHER ANTOS**
Editor	**JORDAN D. WHITE**
Executive Editor	**C.B. CEBULSKI**

Editor in Chief	**AXEL ALONSO**
Chief Creative Officer	**JOE QUESADA**
Publisher	**DAN BUCKLEY**

For Lucasfilm:

Creative Director	**MICHAEL SIGLAIN**
Senior Editors	**FRANK PARISI**
Lucasfilm Story Group	**RAYNE ROBERTS, PABLO HIDALGO, LELAND CHEE**

Collection Editor	**JENNIFER GRÜNWALD**
Assistant Editor	**SARAH BRUNSTAD**
Associate Managing Editor	**ALEX STARBUCK**
Editor, Special Projects	**MARK D. BEAZLEY**
Senior Editor, Special Projects	**JEFF YOUNGQUIST**
SVP Print, Sales & Marketing	**DAVID GABRIEL**
Book Designer	**ADAM DEL RE**

STAR WARS: DARTH VADER VOL. 2 — SHADOWS AND SECRETS. Contains material originally published in magazine form as DARTH VADER #7-12. First printing 2016. ISBN# 978-0-7851-9256-5. Published by MARVEL WORLDWIDE, INC., a subsidiary of MARVEL ENTERTAINMENT, LLC. OFFICE OF PUBLICATION: 135 West 50th Street, New York, NY 10020. STAR WARS and related text and illustrations are trademarks and/or copyrights, in the United States and other countries, of Lucasfilm Ltd. and/or its affiliates. © & TM Lucasfilm Ltd. No similarity between any of the names, characters, persons, and/or institutions in this magazine with those of any living or dead person or institution is intended, and any such similarity which may exist is purely coincidental. Marvel and its logos are TM Marvel Characters, Inc. **Printed in Canada.** ALAN FINE, President, Marvel Entertainment; DAN BUCKLEY, President, TV, Publishing and Brand Management; JOE QUESADA, Chief Creative Officer; TOM BREVOORT, SVP of Publishing; DAVID BOGART, SVP of Operations & Procurement, Publishing; C.B. CEBULSKI, VP of International Development & Brand Management; DAVID GABRIEL, SVP Print, Sales & Marketing; JIM O'KEEFE, VP of Operations & Logistics; DAN CARR, Executive Director of Publishing Technology; SUSAN CRESPI, Editorial Operations Manager; ALEX MORALES, Publishing Operations Manager; STAN LEE, Chairman Emeritus. For information regarding advertising in Marvel Comics or on Marvel.com, please contact Jonathan Rheingold, VP of Custom Solutions & Ad Sales, at jrheingold@marvel.com. For Marvel subscription inquiries, please call 800-217-9158. **Manufactured between 10/30/2015 and 12/7/2015 by SOLISCO PRINTERS, SCOTT, QC, CANADA.**

10 9 8 7 6 5 4 3 2 1

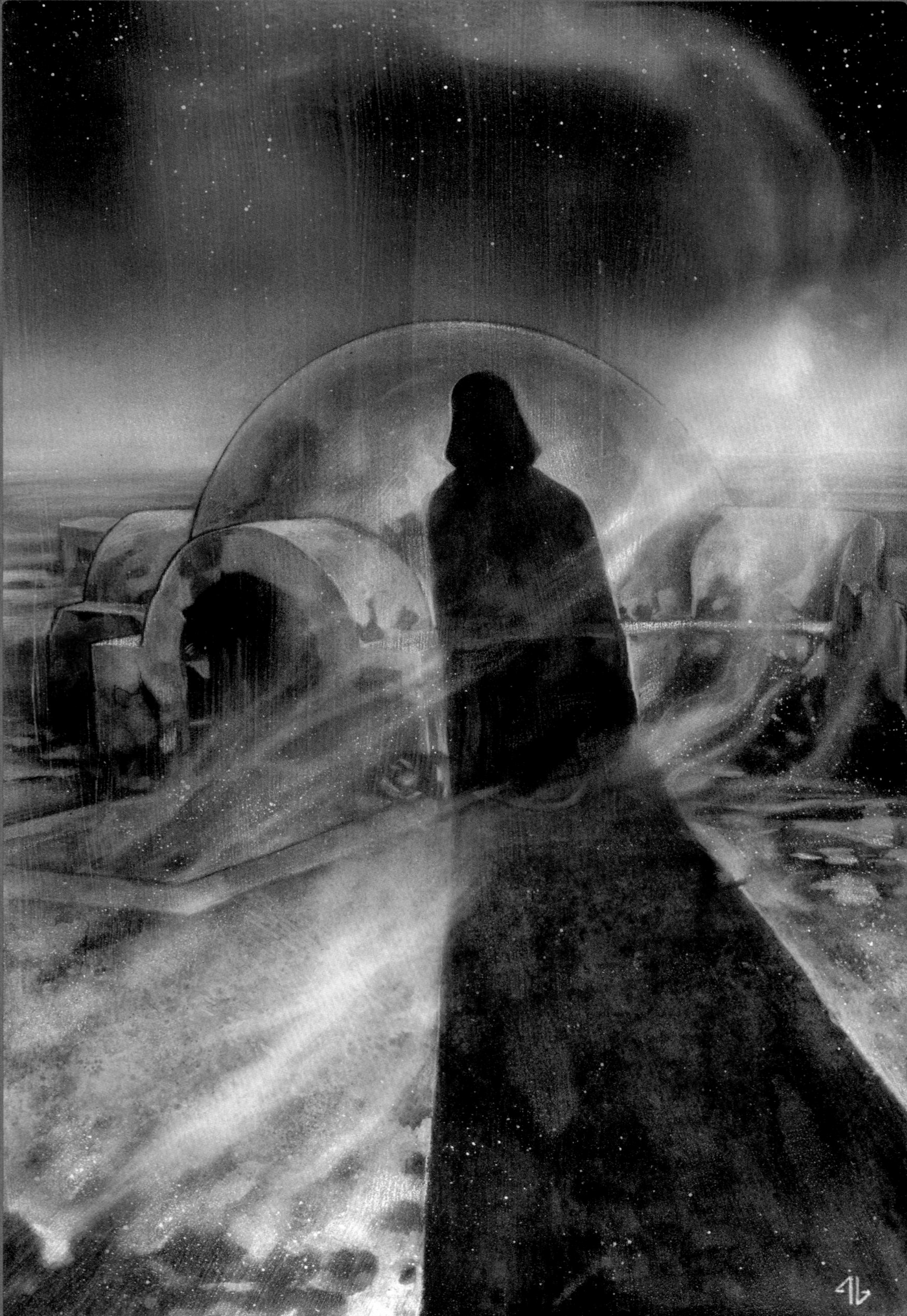

SHADOWS AND SECRETS

Disorder engulfs the galaxy. After the destruction of the Death Star by a mysterious Force-strong rebel pilot, the Sith Lord DARTH VADER was deemed responsible by his master, EMPEROR PALPATINE. Now pursuing his own agenda — the pilot's identity — Vader recruited bounty hunter BOBA FETT and archaeologist DOCTOR APHRA.

Pitted by the Emperor against a new array of rivals for his position in the Empire, Vader's rage at being doubted was compounded by an even more shocking revelation—the rebel pilot he sought was actually the son he never knew he'd had.

Now, alongside Aphra, the Sith Lord returns to his home planet of Tatooine to the former homestead of the pilot, following a trail left behind by Boba Fett and the young Skywalker....

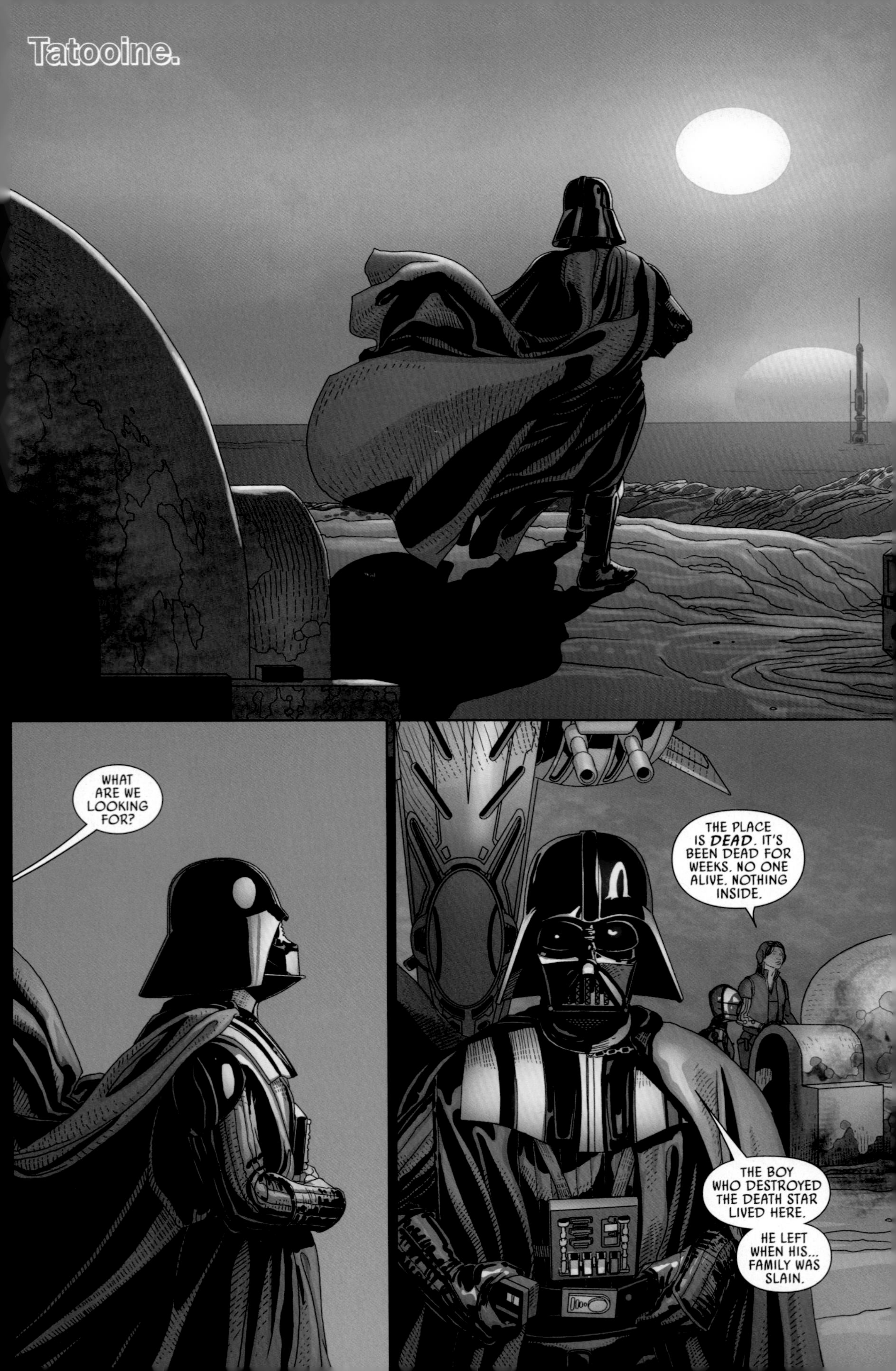
Tatooine.
WHAT ARE WE LOOKING FOR?
THE PLACE IS DEAD. IT'S BEEN DEAD FOR WEEKS. NO ONE ALIVE. NOTHING INSIDE.
THE BOY WHO DESTROYED THE DEATH STAR LIVED HERE.
HE LEFT WHEN HIS... FAMILY WAS SLAIN.

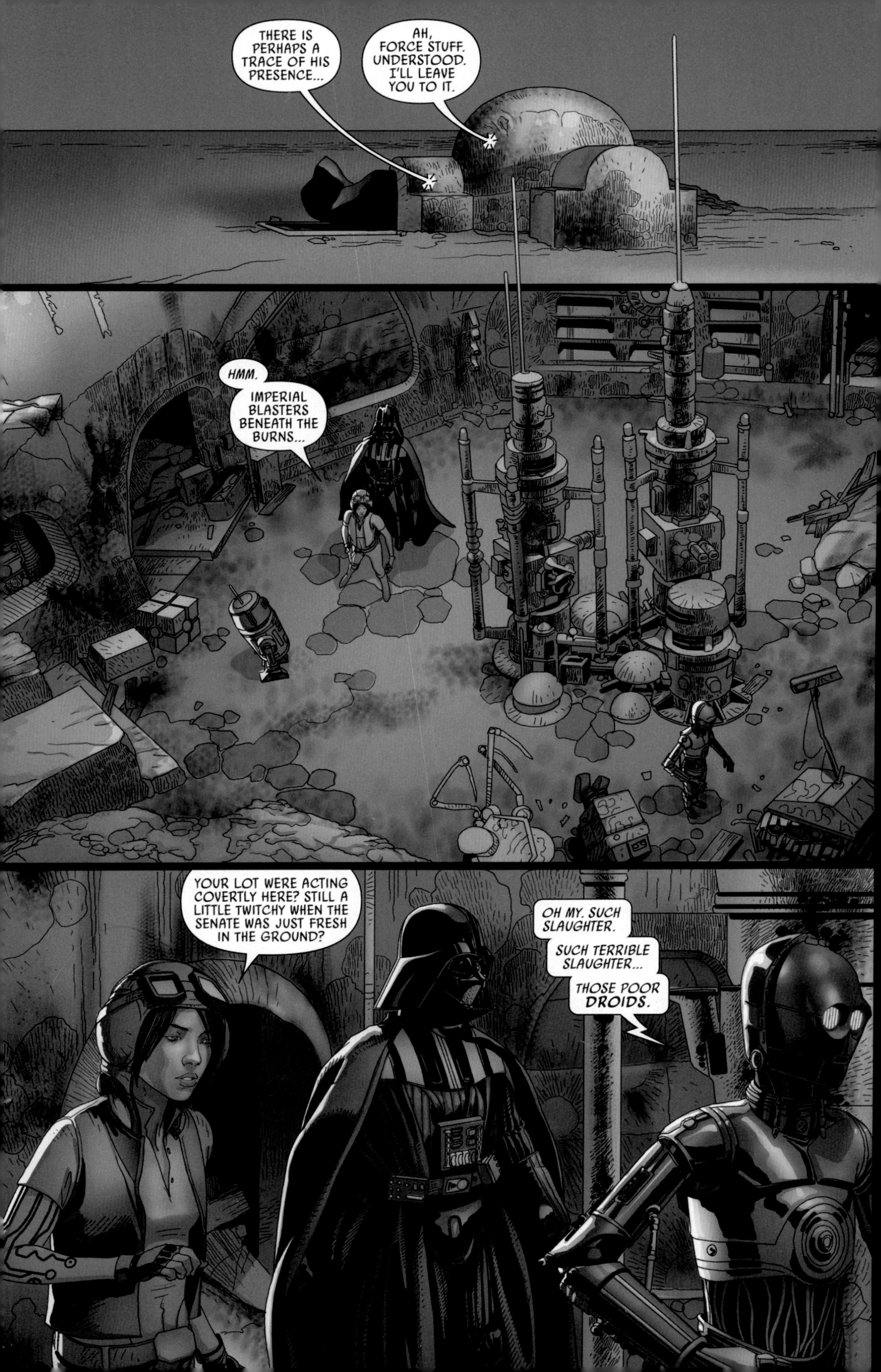
THERE IS PERHAPS A TRACE OF HIS PRESENCE...
AH, FORCE STUFF. UNDERSTOOD. I'LL LEAVE YOU TO IT.
HMM.
IMPERIAL BLASTERS BENEATH THE BURNS...
YOUR LOT WERE ACTING COVERTLY HERE? STILL A LITTLE TWITCHY WHEN THE SENATE WAS JUST FRESH IN THE GROUND?
OH MY. SUCH SLAUGHTER.
SUCH TERRIBLE SLAUGHTER...
THOSE POOR DROIDS.

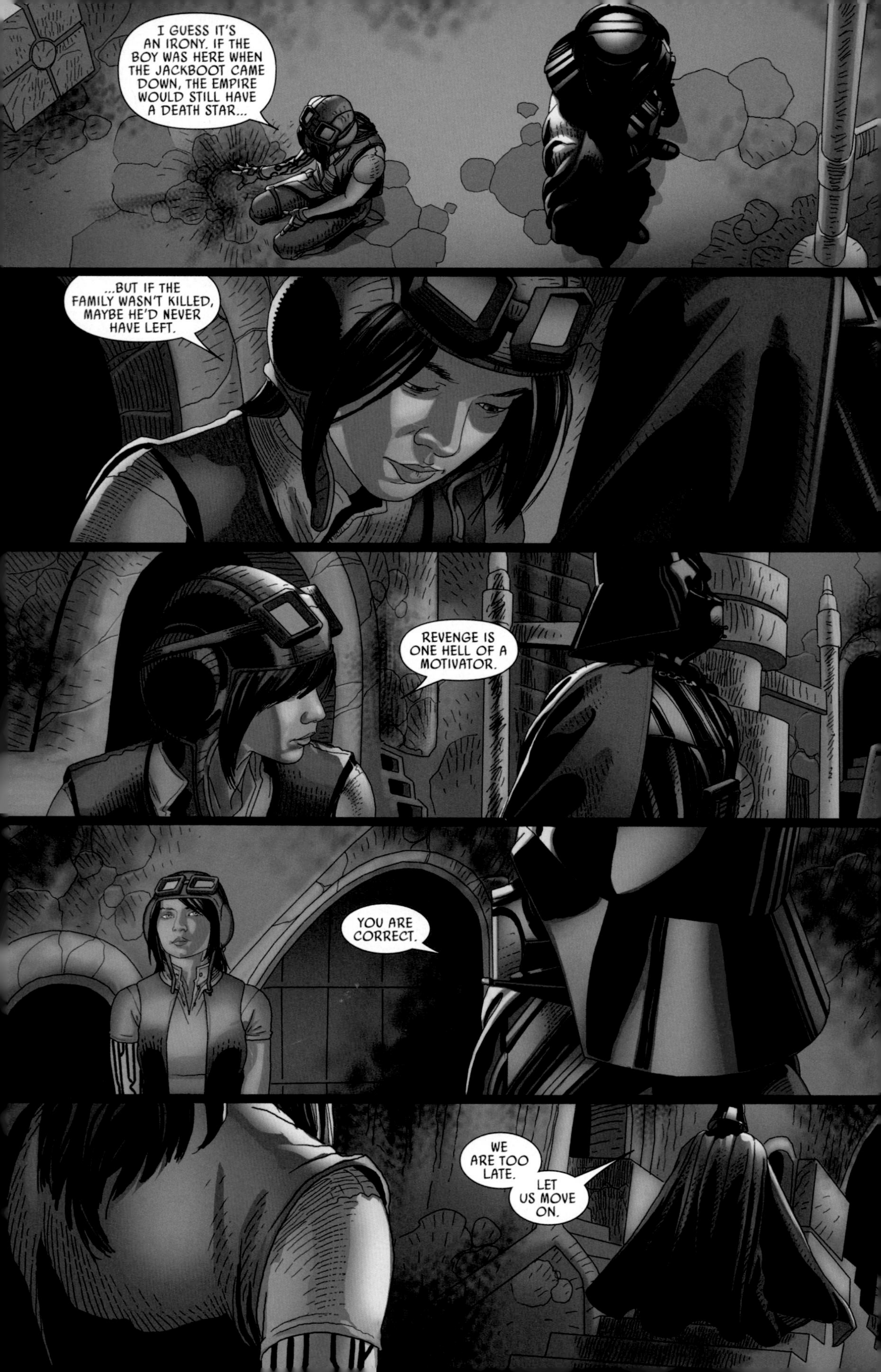
I GUESS IT'S AN IRONY. IF THE BOY WAS HERE WHEN THE JACKBOOT CAME DOWN, THE EMPIRE WOULD STILL HAVE A DEATH STAR...
...BUT IF THE FAMILY WASN'T KILLED, MAYBE HE'D NEVER HAVE LEFT.
REVENGE IS ONE HELL OF A MOTIVATOR.
YOU ARE CORRECT.
WE ARE TOO LATE.
LET US MOVE ON.

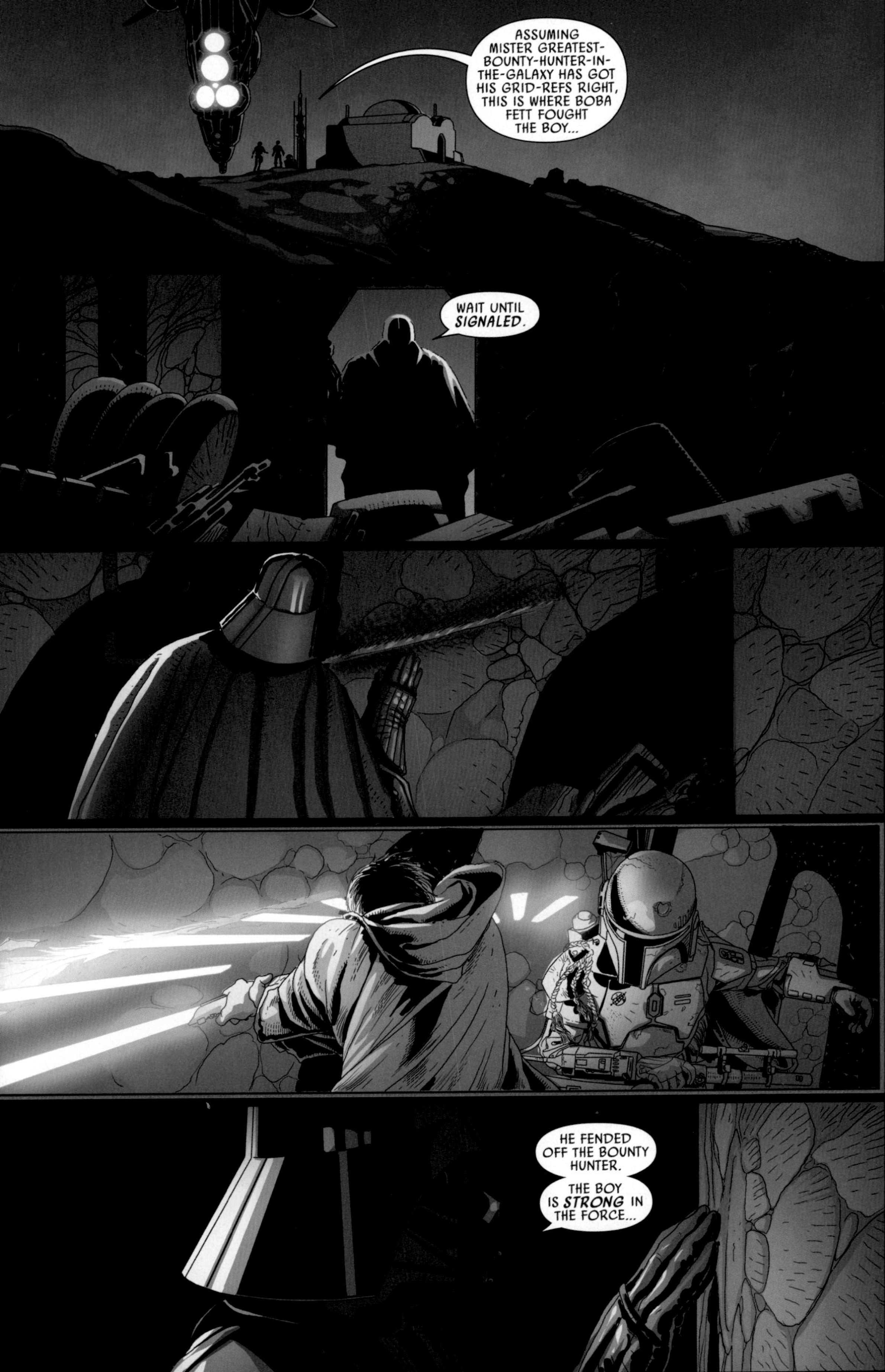
ASSUMING MISTER GREATEST-BOUNTY-HUNTER-IN-THE-GALAXY HAS GOT HIS GRID-REFS RIGHT, THIS IS WHERE BOBA FETT FOUGHT THE BOY...
WAIT UNTIL SIGNALED.
HE FENDED OFF THE BOUNTY HUNTER.
THE BOY IS STRONG IN THE FORCE...

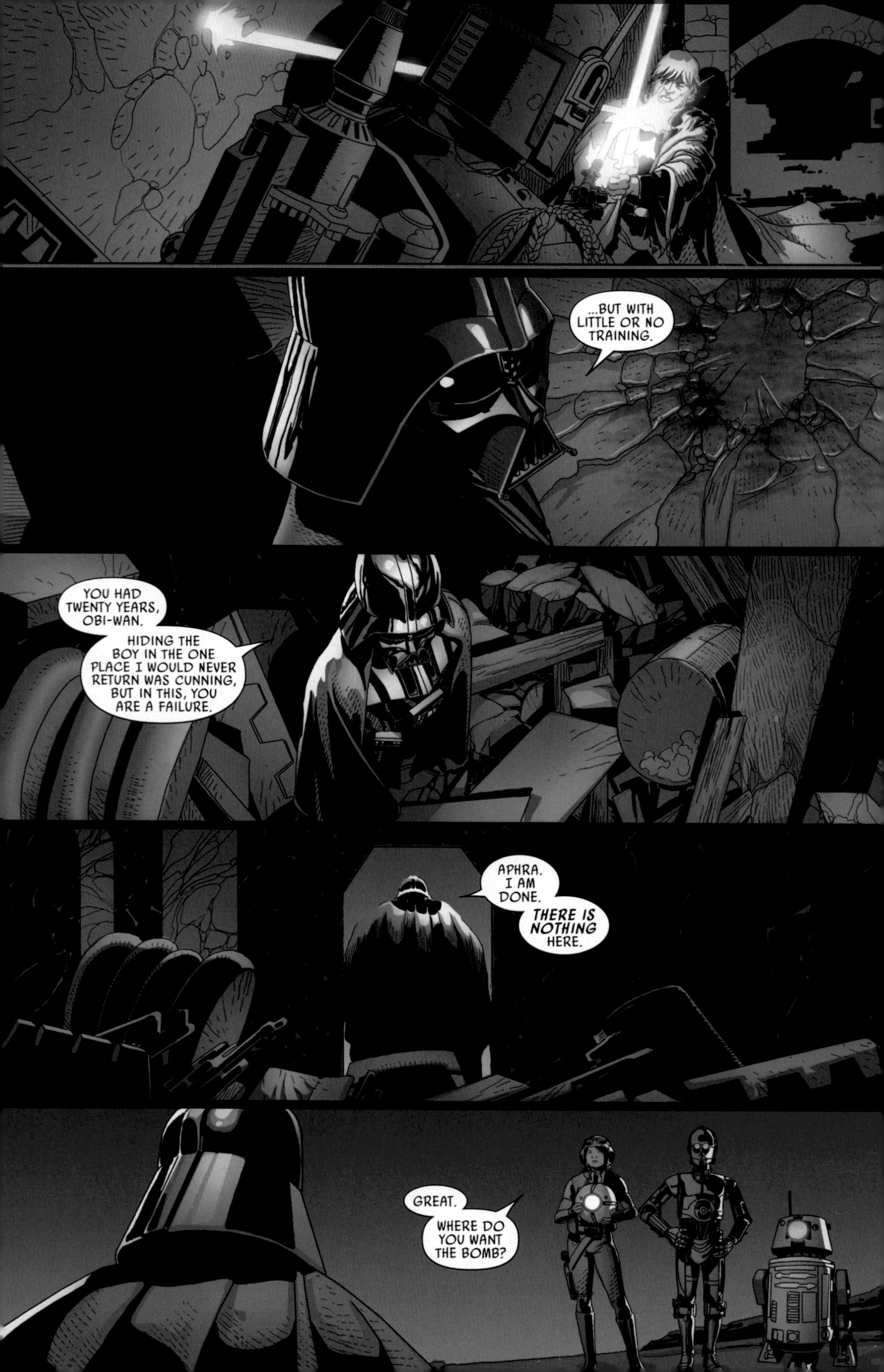

...BUT WITH LITTLE OR NO TRAINING.
YOU HAD TWENTY YEARS, OBI-WAN.
HIDING THE BOY IN THE ONE PLACE I WOULD NEVER RETURN WAS CUNNING, BUT IN THIS, YOU ARE A FAILURE.
APHRA. I AM DONE.
THERE IS NOTHING HERE.
GREAT.
WHERE DO YOU WANT THE BOMB?

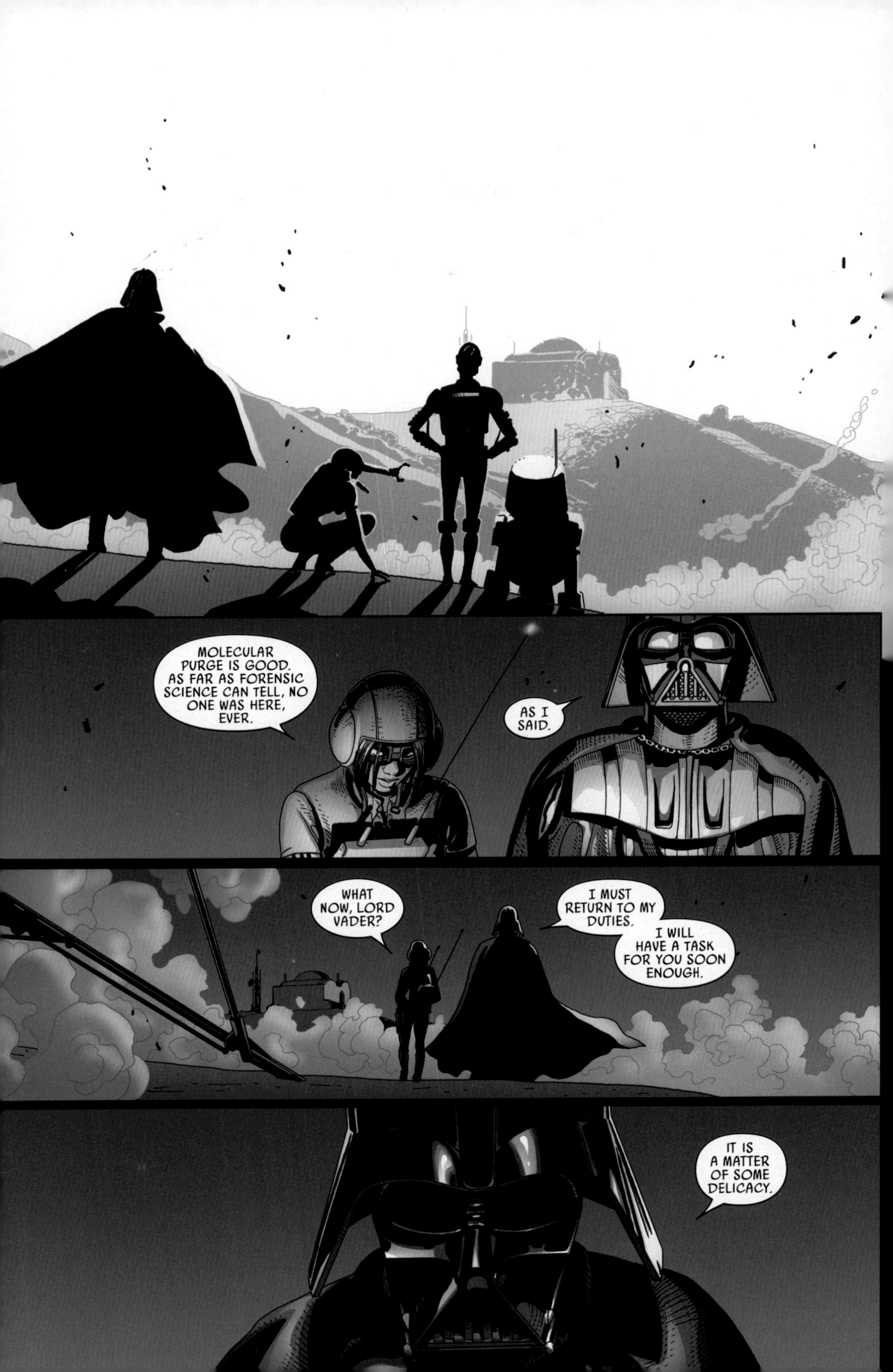
MOLECULAR PURGE IS GOOD. AS FAR AS FORENSIC SCIENCE CAN TELL, NO ONE WAS HERE, EVER.
AS I SAID.
WHAT NOW, LORD VADER?
I MUST RETURN TO MY DUTIES.
I WILL HAVE A TASK FOR YOU SOON ENOUGH.
IT IS A MATTER OF SOME DELICACY.

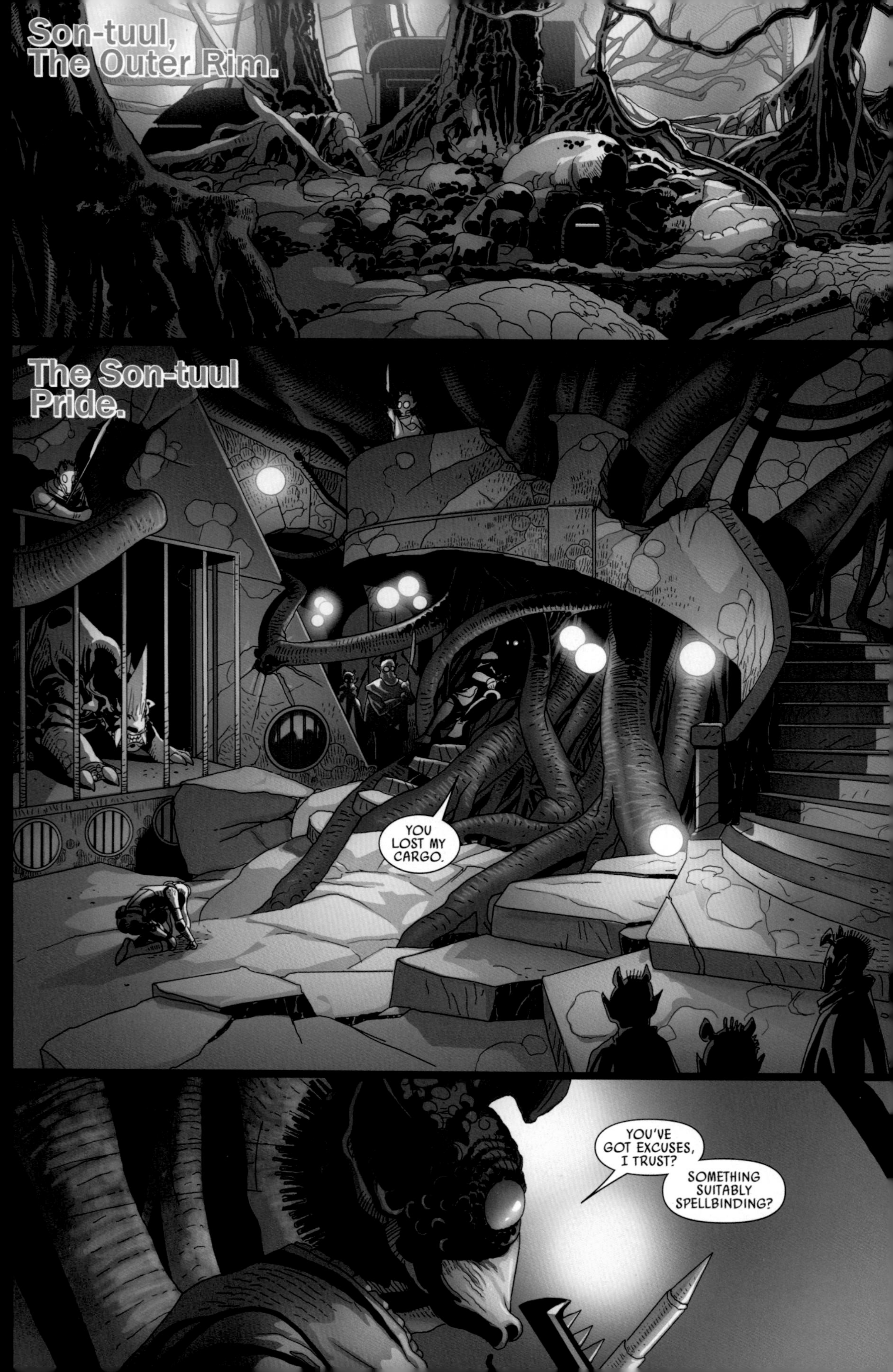
Son-tuul,
The Outer Rim.
The Son-tuul
Pride.
YOU LOST MY CARGO.
YOU'VE GOT EXCUSES, I TRUST?
SOMETHING SUITABLY SPELLBINDING?

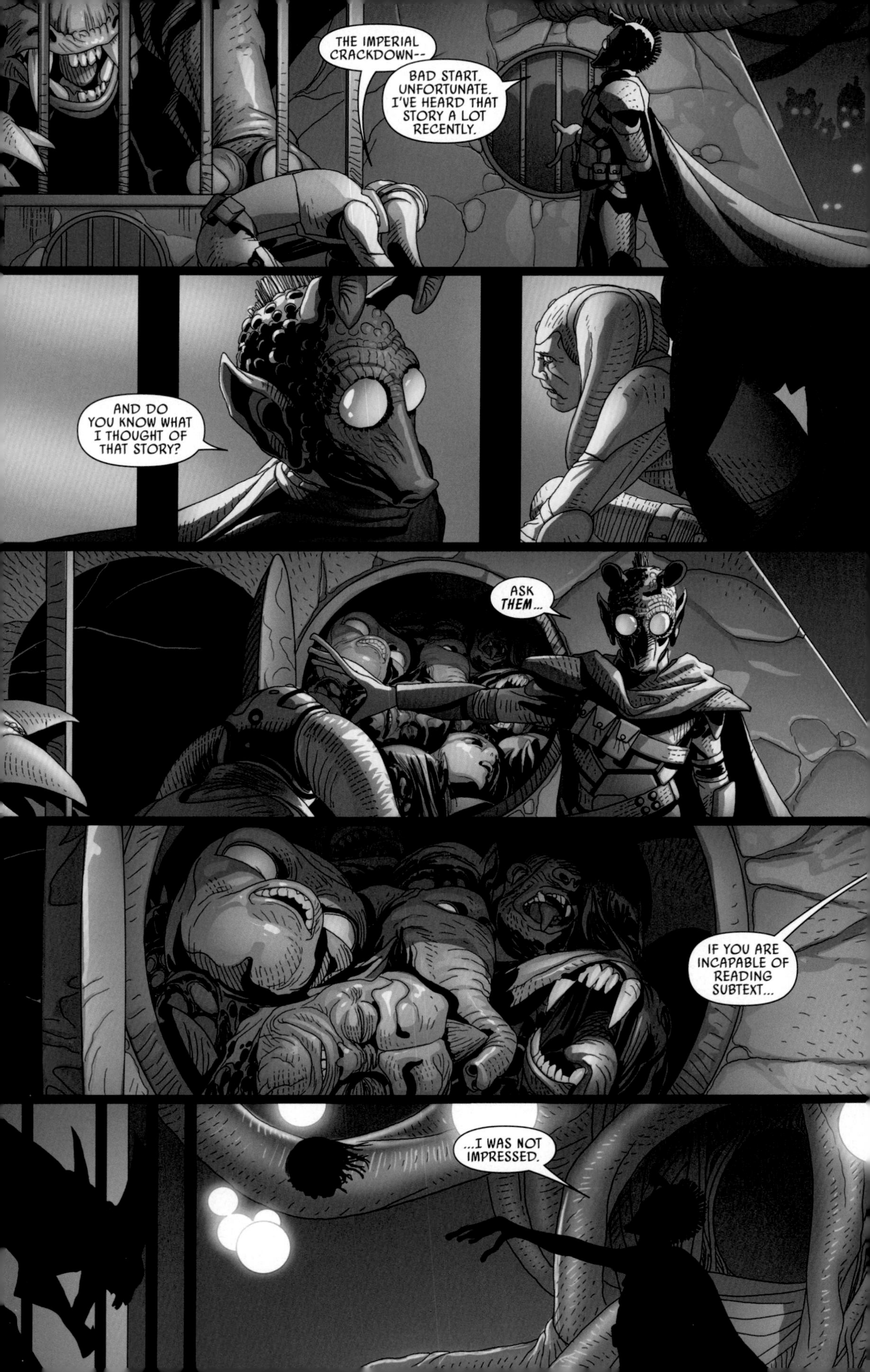
THE IMPERIAL CRACKDOWN--
BAD START. UNFORTUNATE. I'VE HEARD THAT STORY A LOT RECENTLY.
AND DO YOU KNOW WHAT I THOUGHT OF THAT STORY?
ASK *THEM*...
IF YOU ARE INCAPABLE OF READING SUBTEXT...
...I WAS NOT IMPRESSED.

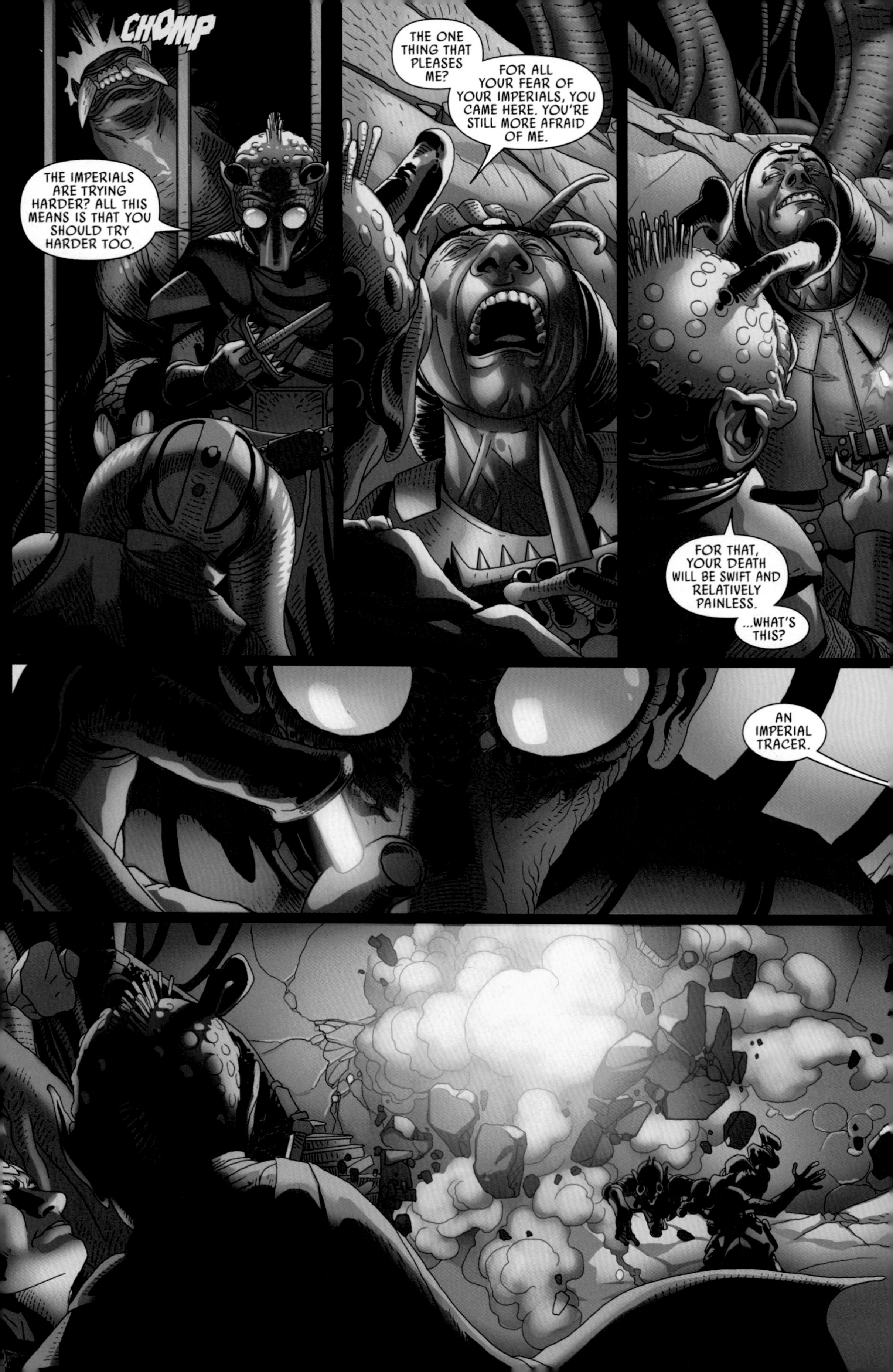
CHOMP
THE IMPERIALS ARE TRYING HARDER? ALL THIS MEANS IS THAT YOU SHOULD TRY HARDER TOO.
THE ONE THING THAT PLEASES ME?
FOR ALL YOUR FEAR OF YOUR IMPERIALS, YOU CAME HERE. YOU'RE STILL MORE AFRAID OF ME.
FOR THAT, YOUR DEATH WILL BE SWIFT AND RELATIVELY PAINLESS.
...WHAT'S THIS?
AN IMPERIAL TRACER.

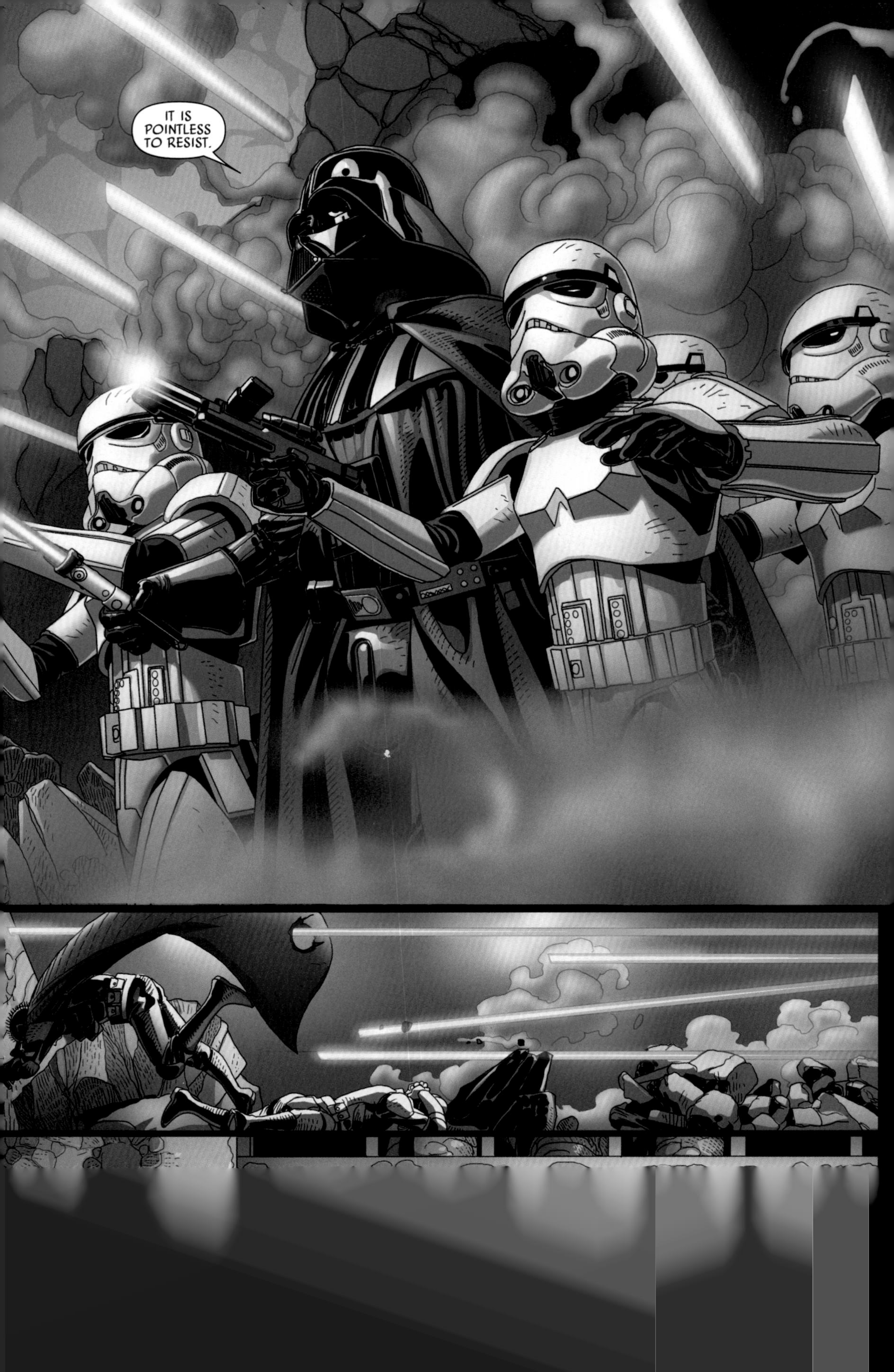
IT IS POINTLESS TO RESIST.

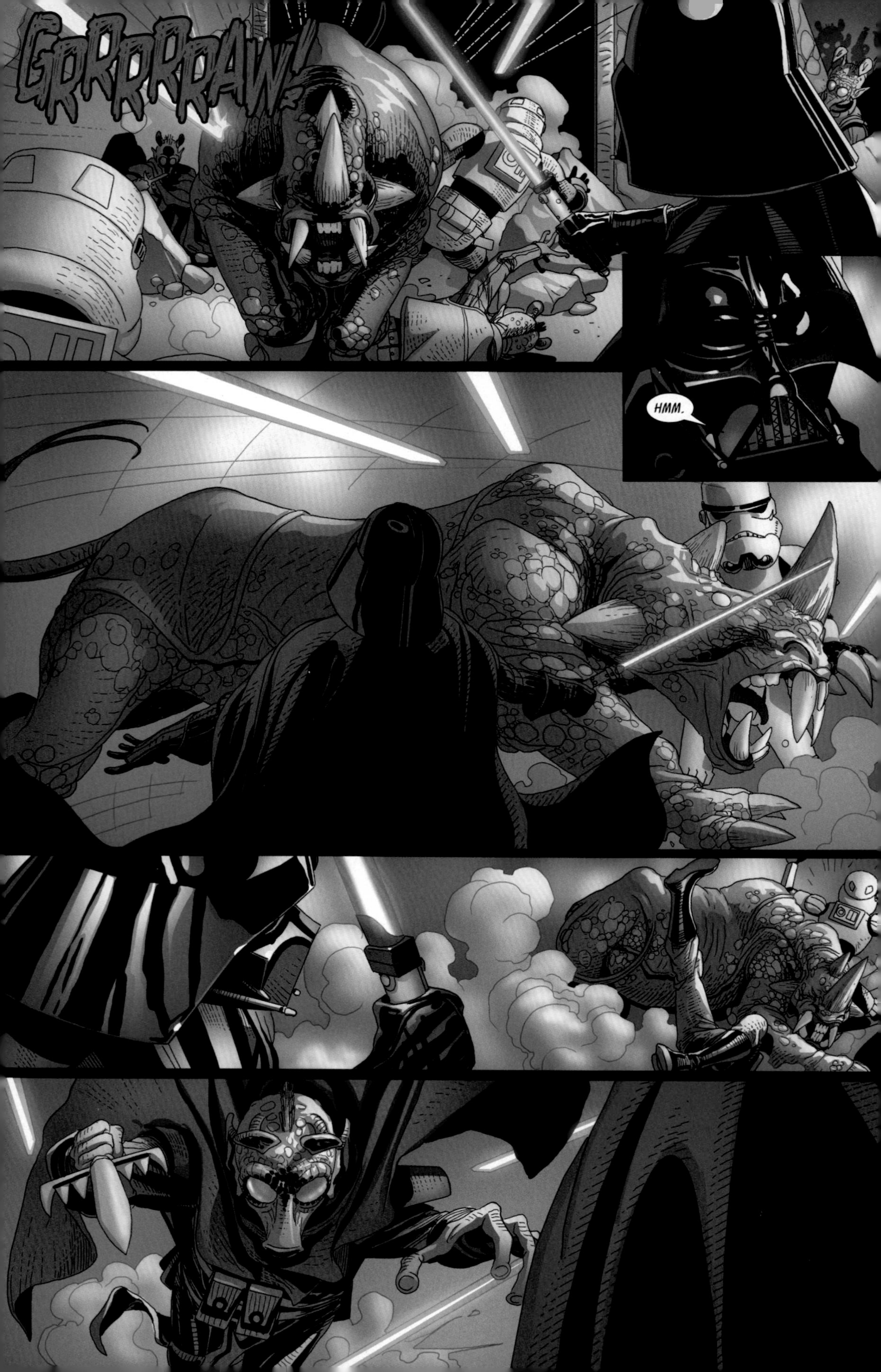
GRRRRRAW!
HMM.

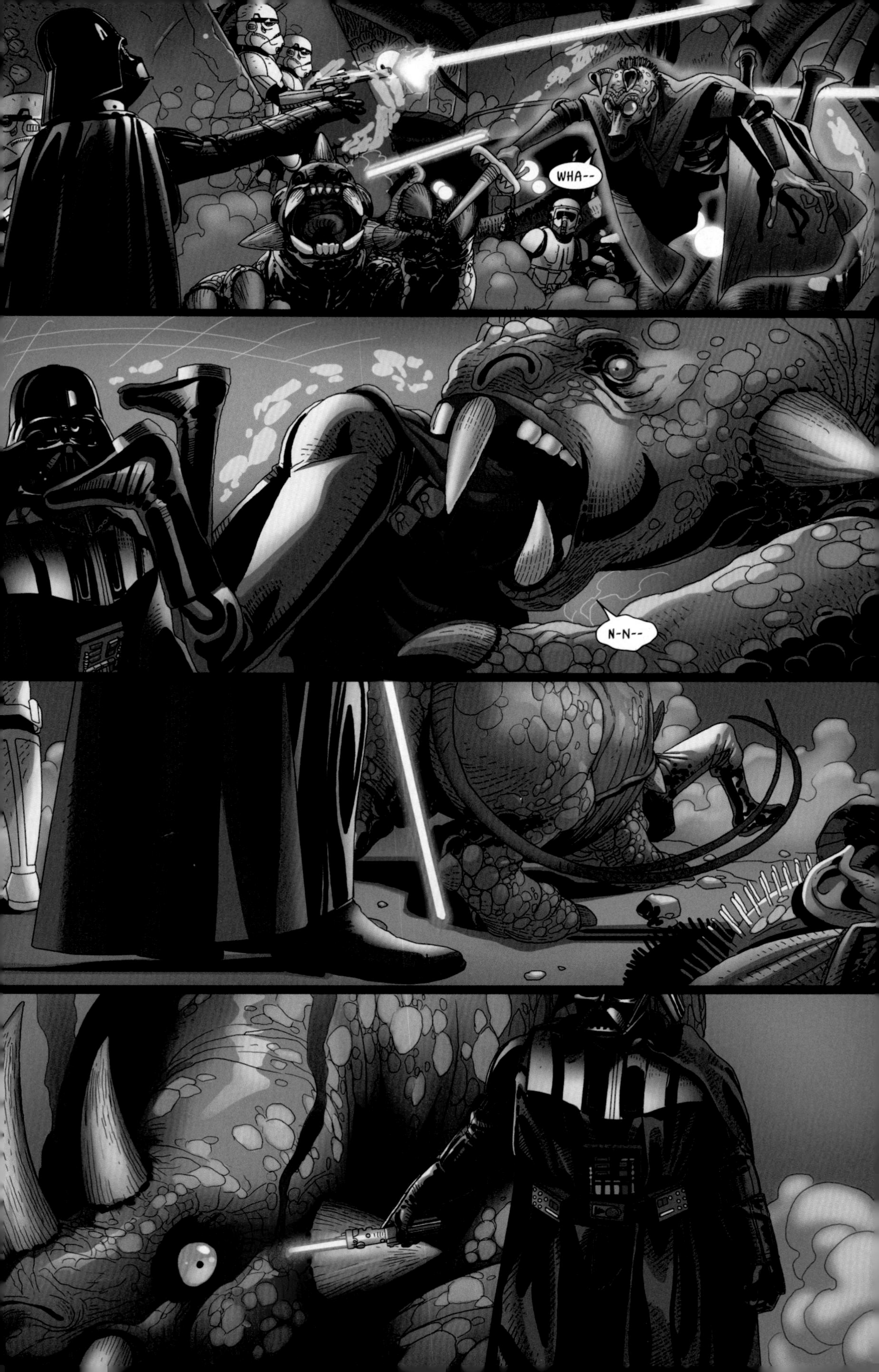
WHA--
N-N--

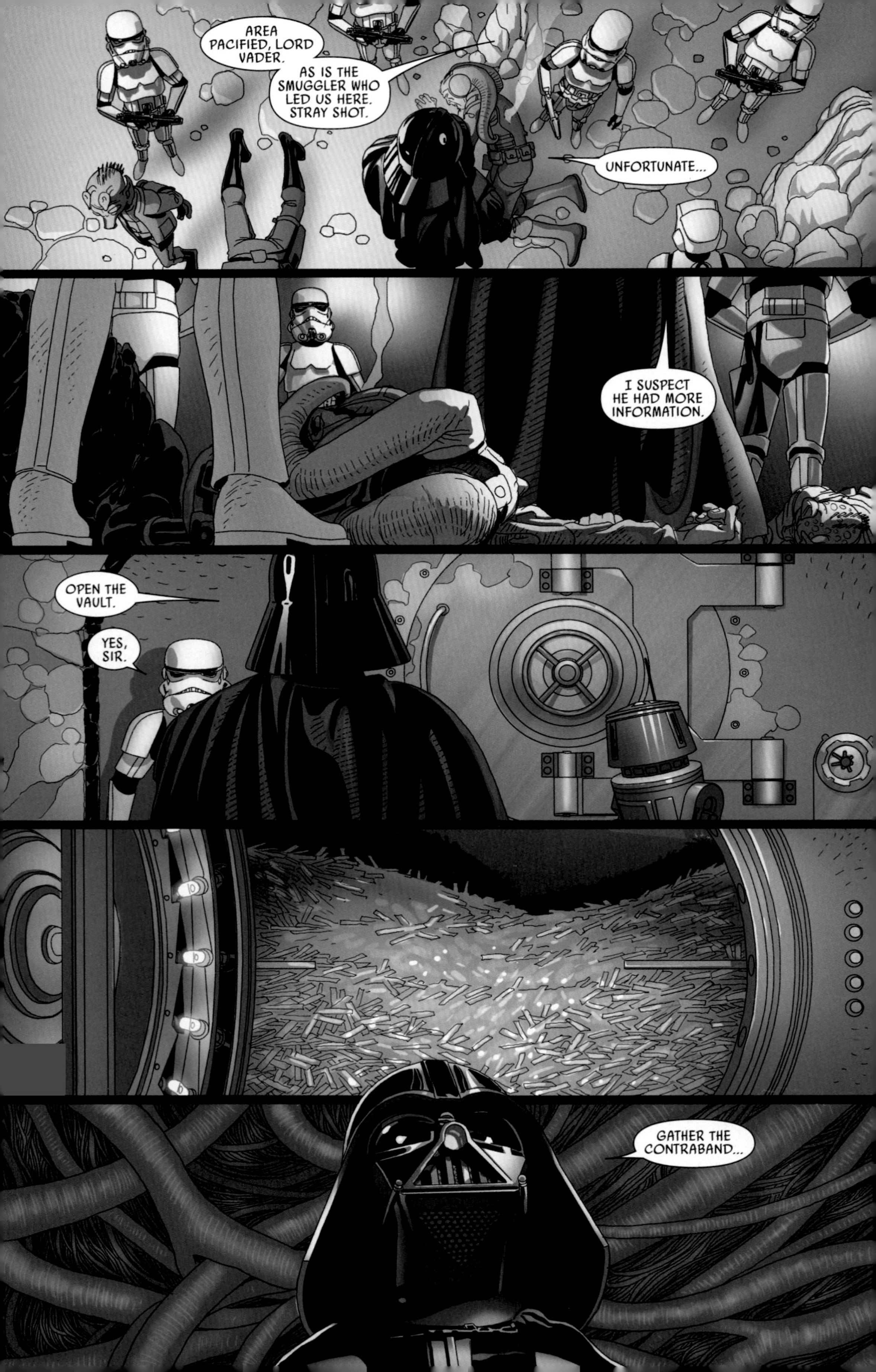
AREA PACIFIED, LORD VADER.
AS IS THE SMUGGLER WHO LED US HERE. STRAY SHOT.
UNFORTUNATE...
I SUSPECT HE HAD MORE INFORMATION.
OPEN THE VAULT.
YES, SIR.
GATHER THE CONTRABAND...

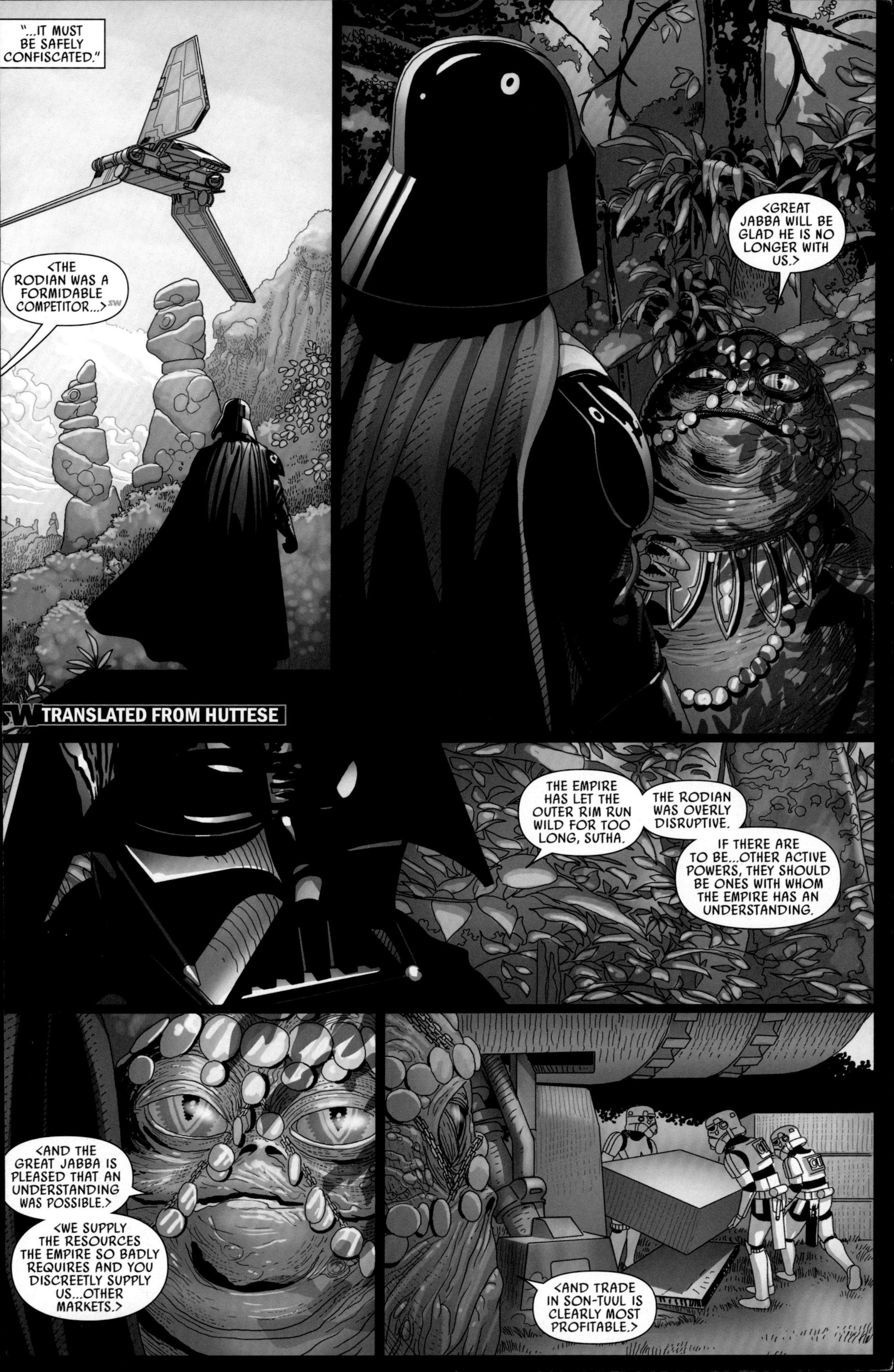
"...IT MUST BE SAFELY CONFISCATED."
<THE RODIAN WAS A FORMIDABLE COMPETITOR...>SW
<GREAT JABBA WILL BE GLAD HE IS NO LONGER WITH US.>
SW TRANSLATED FROM HUTTESE
THE EMPIRE HAS LET THE OUTER RIM RUN WILD FOR TOO LONG, SUTHA.
THE RODIAN WAS OVERLY DISRUPTIVE.
IF THERE ARE TO BE...OTHER ACTIVE POWERS, THEY SHOULD BE ONES WITH WHOM THE EMPIRE HAS AN UNDERSTANDING.
<AND THE GREAT JABBA IS PLEASED THAT AN UNDERSTANDING WAS POSSIBLE.>
<WE SUPPLY THE RESOURCES THE EMPIRE SO BADLY REQUIRES AND YOU DISCREETLY SUPPLY US...OTHER MARKETS.>
<AND TRADE IN SON-TUUL IS CLEARLY MOST PROFITABLE.>

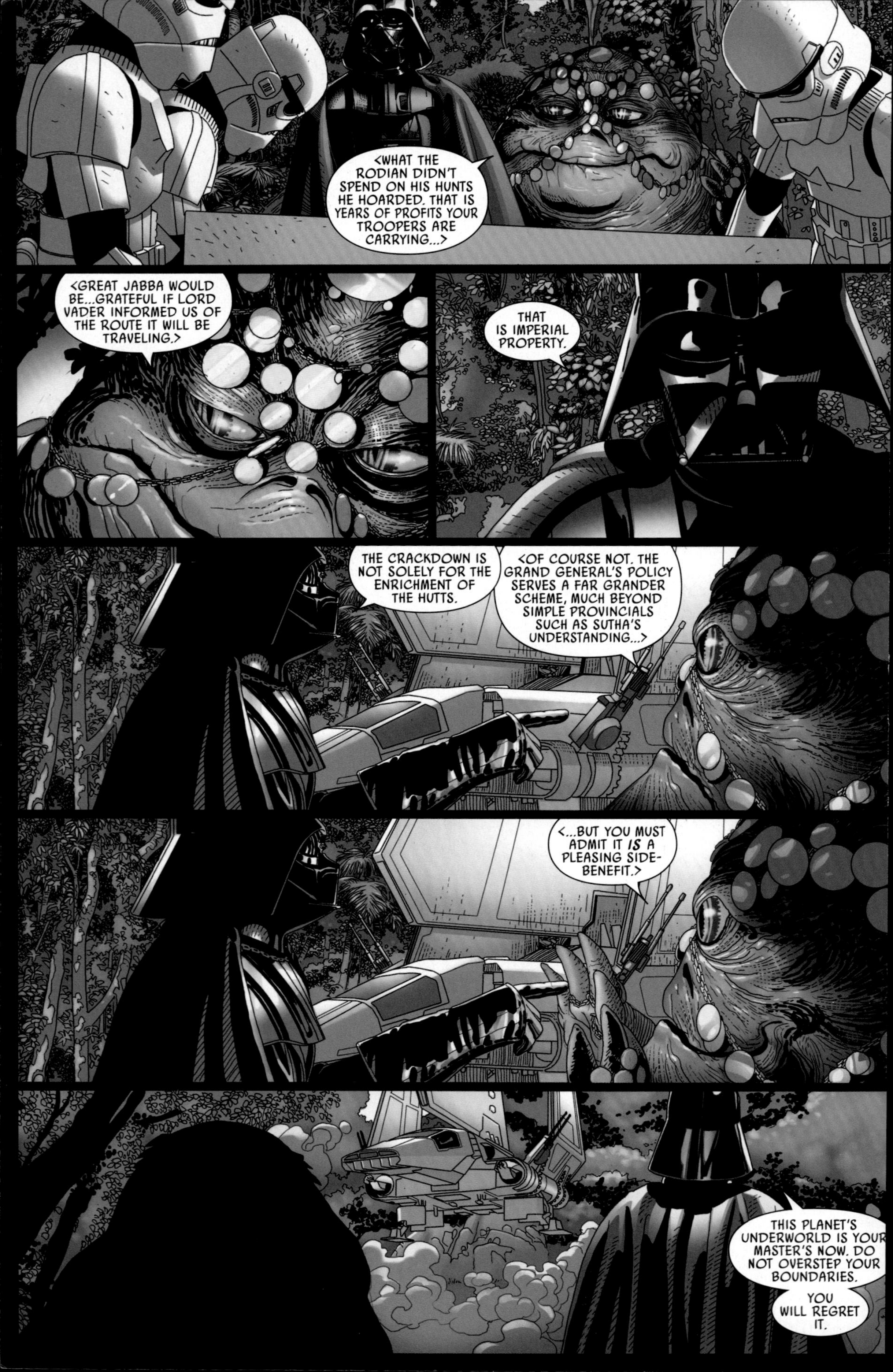
<WHAT THE RODIAN DIDN'T SPEND ON HIS HUNTS HE HOARDED. THAT IS YEARS OF PROFITS YOUR TROOPERS ARE CARRYING...>
<GREAT JABBA WOULD BE...GRATEFUL IF LORD VADER INFORMED US OF THE ROUTE IT WILL BE TRAVELING.>
THAT IS IMPERIAL PROPERTY.
THE CRACKDOWN IS NOT SOLELY FOR THE ENRICHMENT OF THE HUTTS.
<OF COURSE NOT. THE GRAND GENERAL'S POLICY SERVES A FAR GRANDER SCHEME, MUCH BEYOND SIMPLE PROVINCIALS SUCH AS SUTHA'S UNDERSTANDING...>
<...BUT YOU MUST ADMIT IT *IS* A PLEASING SIDE-BENEFIT.>
THIS PLANET'S UNDERWORLD IS YOUR MASTER'S NOW. DO NOT OVERSTEP YOUR BOUNDARIES.
YOU WILL REGRET IT.

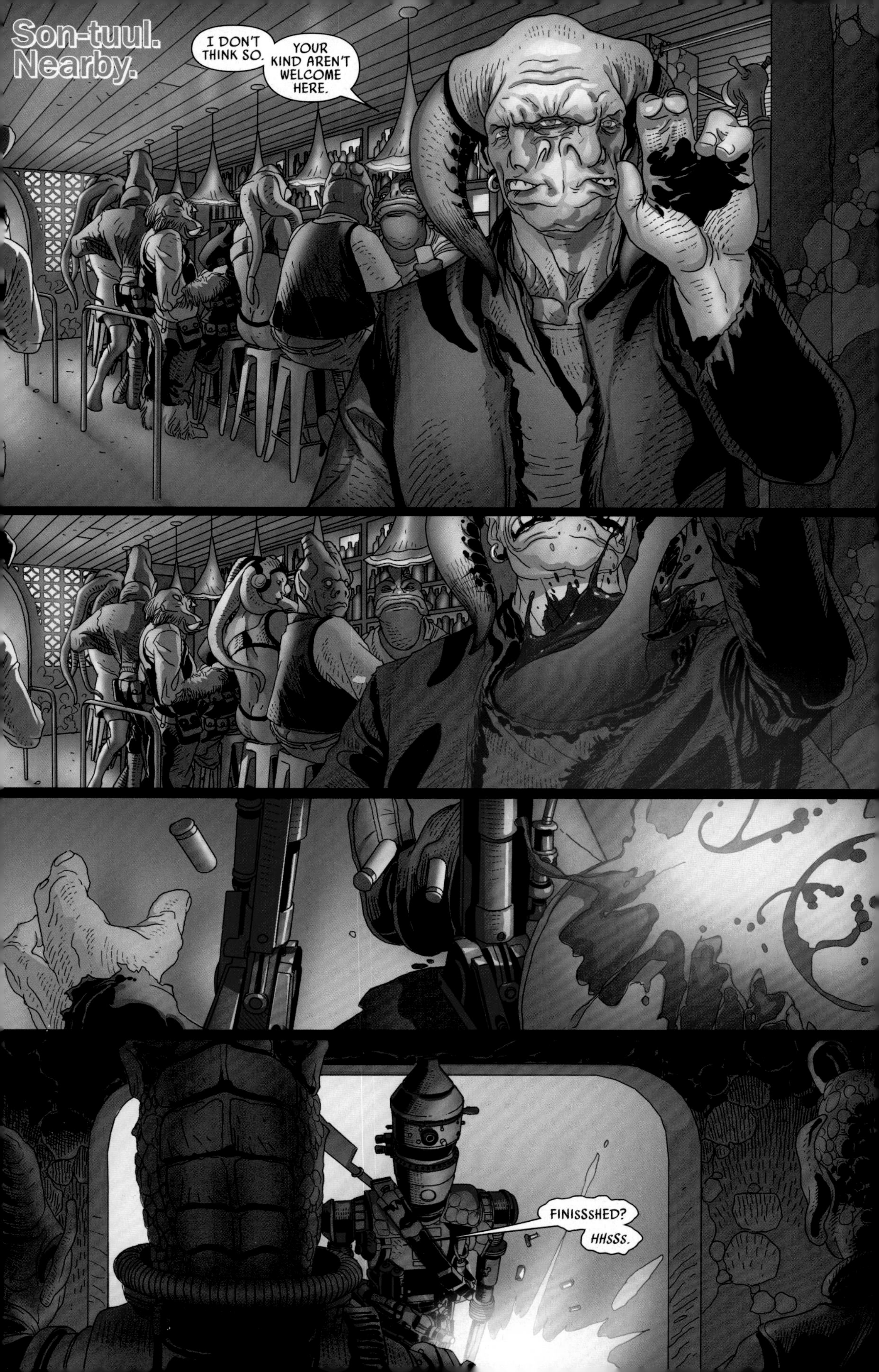
Son-tuul.
Nearby.
I DON'T THINK SO.
YOUR KIND AREN'T WELCOME HERE.
FINISSSHED?
HHSSs.

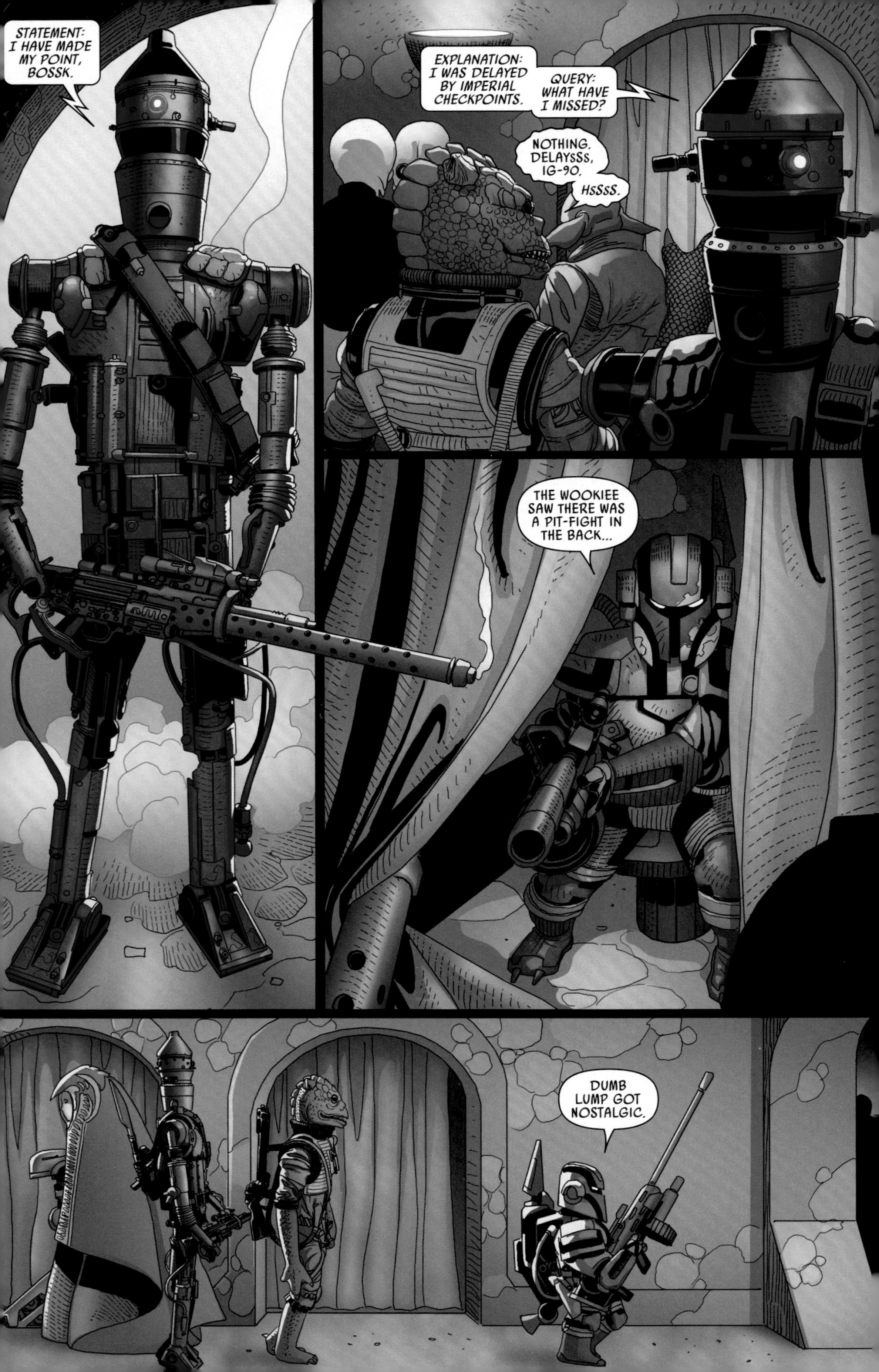
STATEMENT: I HAVE MADE MY POINT, BOSSK.
EXPLANATION: I WAS DELAYED BY IMPERIAL CHECKPOINTS.
QUERY: WHAT HAVE I MISSED?
NOTHING. DELAYSSS, IG-90.
HSSSS.
THE WOOKIEE SAW THERE WAS A PIT-FIGHT IN THE BACK...
DUMB LUMP GOT NOSTALGIC.

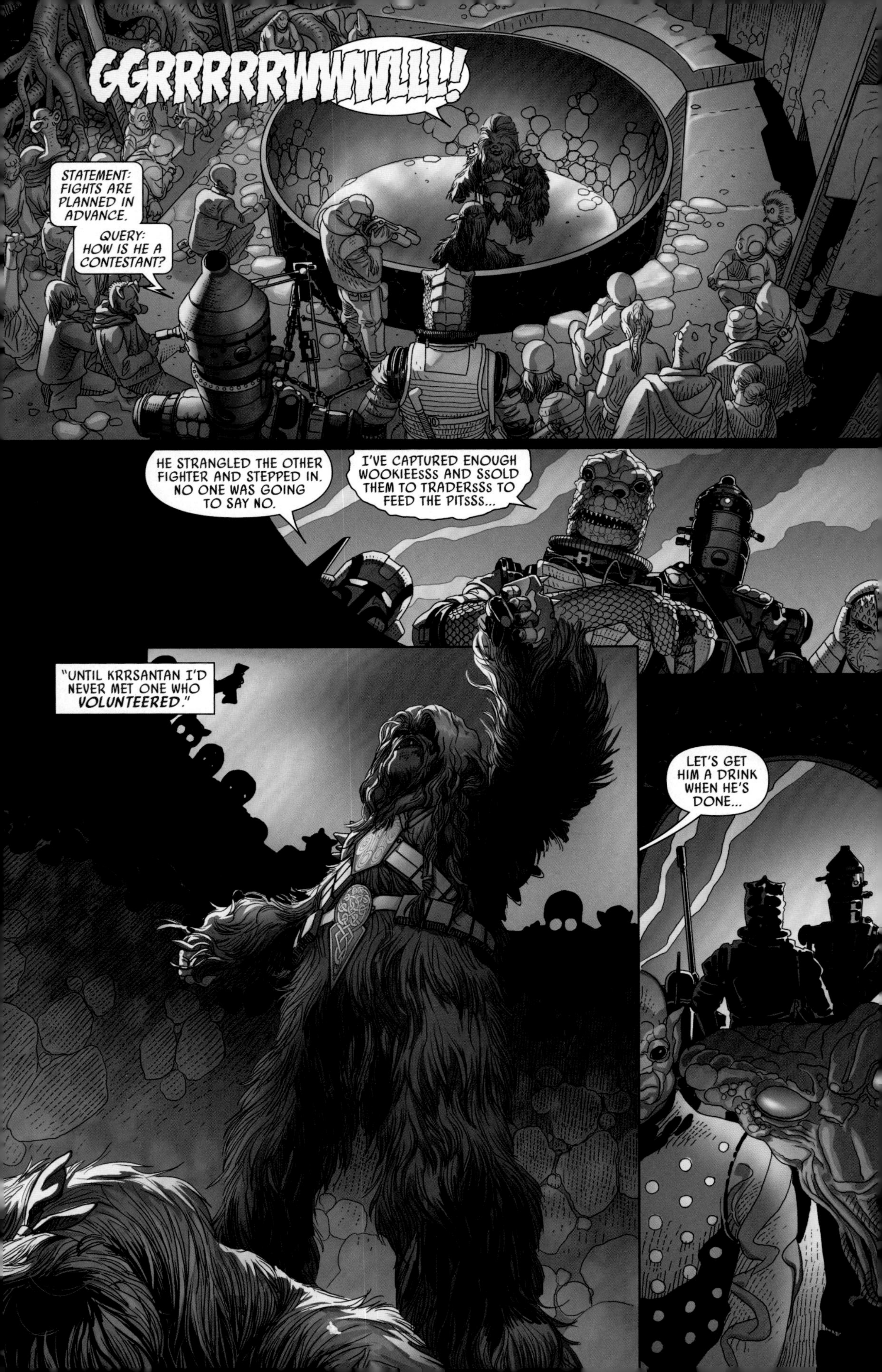
GGRRRRRRWWWLLL!
STATEMENT: FIGHTS ARE PLANNED IN ADVANCE.
QUERY: HOW IS HE A CONTESTANT?
HE STRANGLED THE OTHER FIGHTER AND STEPPED IN. NO ONE WAS GOING TO SAY NO.
I'VE CAPTURED ENOUGH WOOKIEESSS AND SSOLD THEM TO TRADERSSS TO FEED THE PITSSS...
"UNTIL KRRSANTAN I'D NEVER MET ONE WHO VOLUNTEERED."
LET'S GET HIM A DRINK WHEN HE'S DONE...

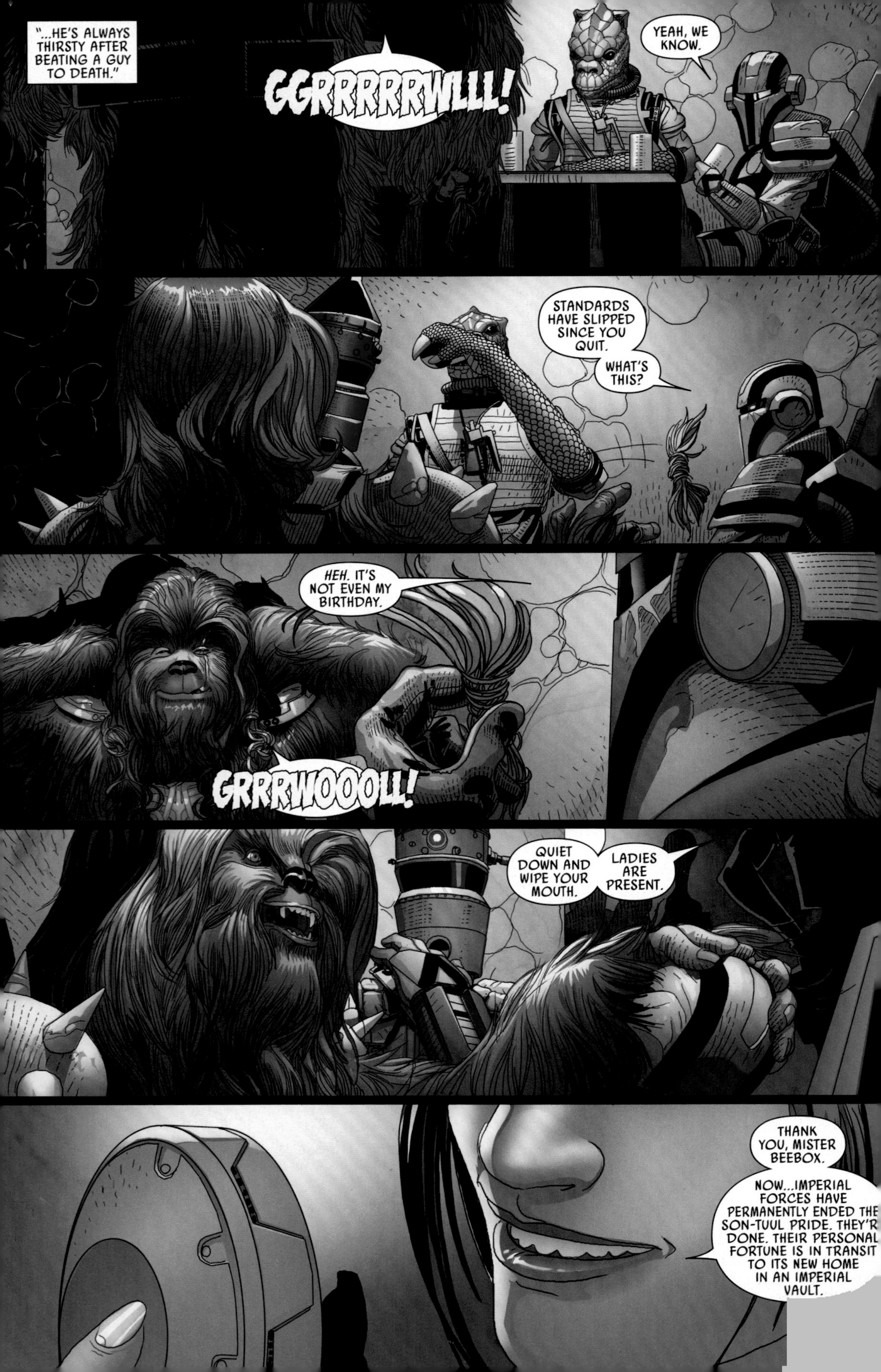
"...HE'S ALWAYS THIRSTY AFTER BEATING A GUY TO DEATH."
GGRRRRRRWLLL!
YEAH, WE KNOW.
STANDARDS HAVE SLIPPED SINCE YOU QUIT.
WHAT'S THIS?
HEH. IT'S NOT EVEN MY BIRTHDAY.
GRRRWOOOLL!
QUIET DOWN AND WIPE YOUR MOUTH.
LADIES ARE PRESENT.
THANK YOU, MISTER BEEBOX.
NOW...IMPERIAL FORCES HAVE PERMANENTLY ENDED THE SON-TUUL PRIDE. THEY'R DONE. THEIR PERSONAL FORTUNE IS IN TRANSIT TO ITS NEW HOME IN AN IMPERIAL VAULT.

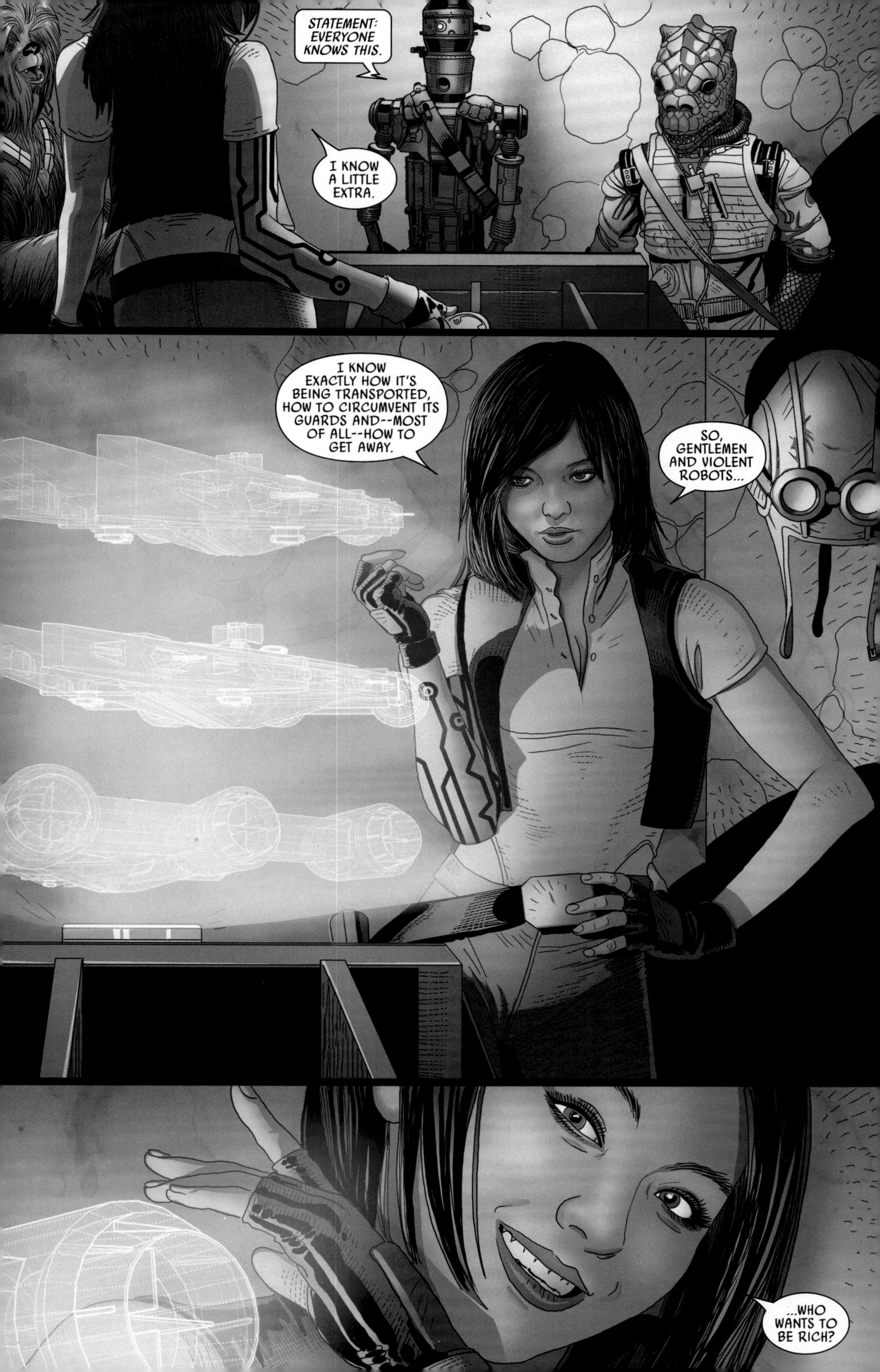
STATEMENT: EVERYONE KNOWS THIS.
I KNOW A LITTLE EXTRA.
I KNOW EXACTLY HOW IT'S BEING TRANSPORTED, HOW TO CIRCUMVENT ITS GUARDS AND--MOST OF ALL--HOW TO GET AWAY.
SO, GENTLEMEN AND VIOLENT ROBOTS...
...WHO WANTS TO BE RICH?

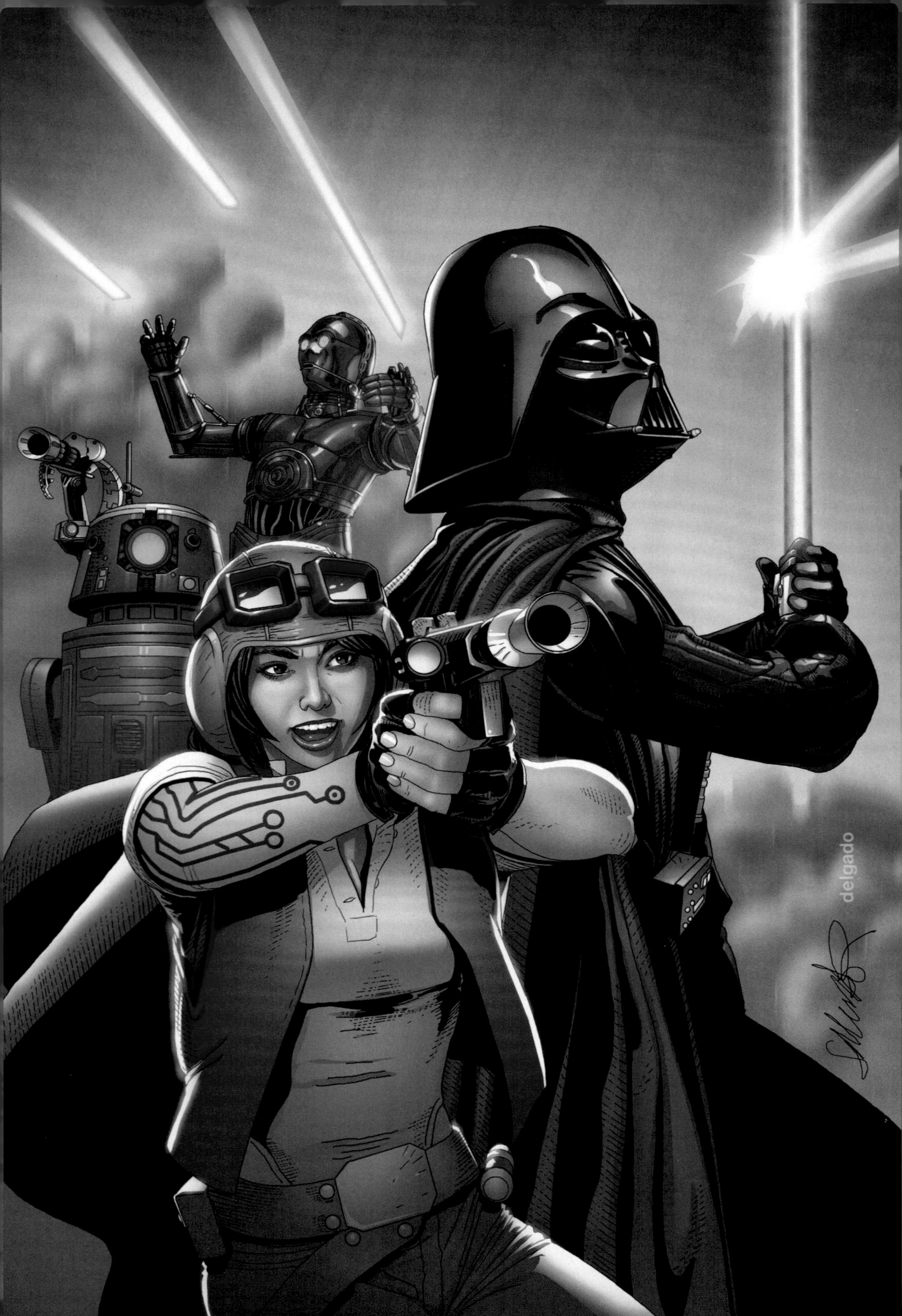
delgado

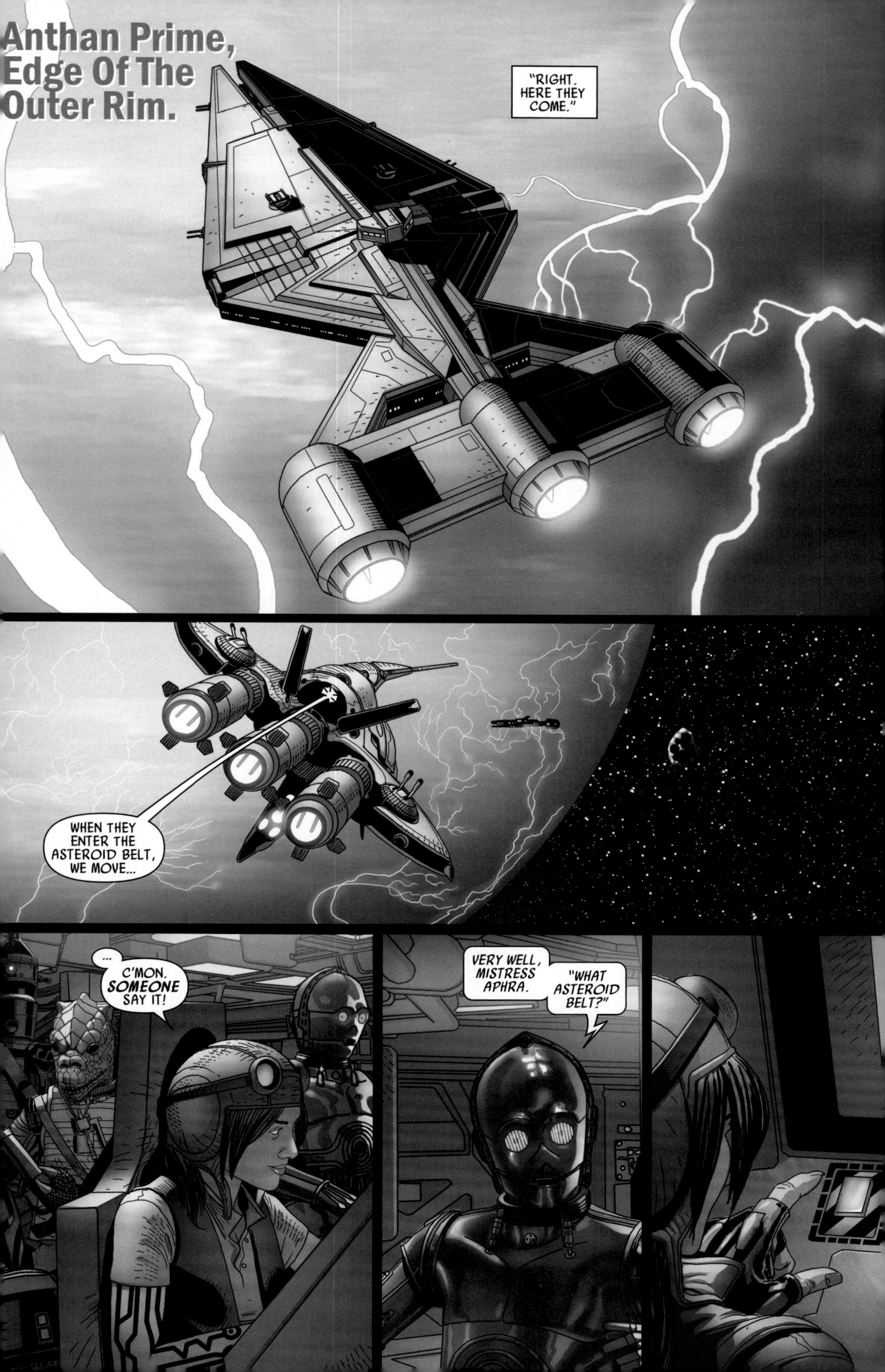
Anthan Prime, Edge Of The Outer Rim.
"RIGHT. HERE THEY COME."
WHEN THEY ENTER THE ASTEROID BELT, WE MOVE...
... C'MON. SOMEONE SAY IT!
VERY WELL, MISTRESS APHRA.
"WHAT ASTEROID BELT?"

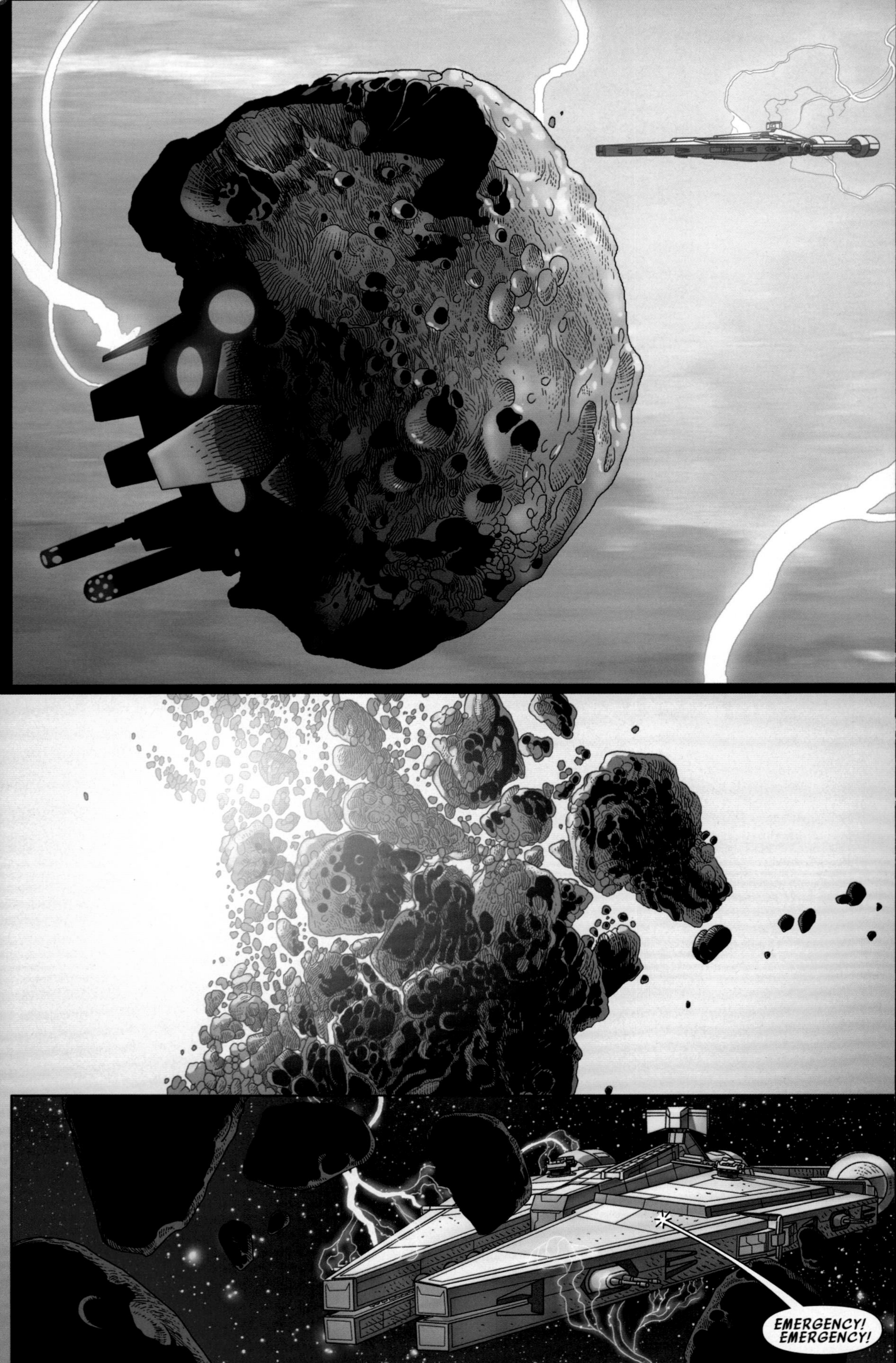
EMERGENCY! EMERGENCY!

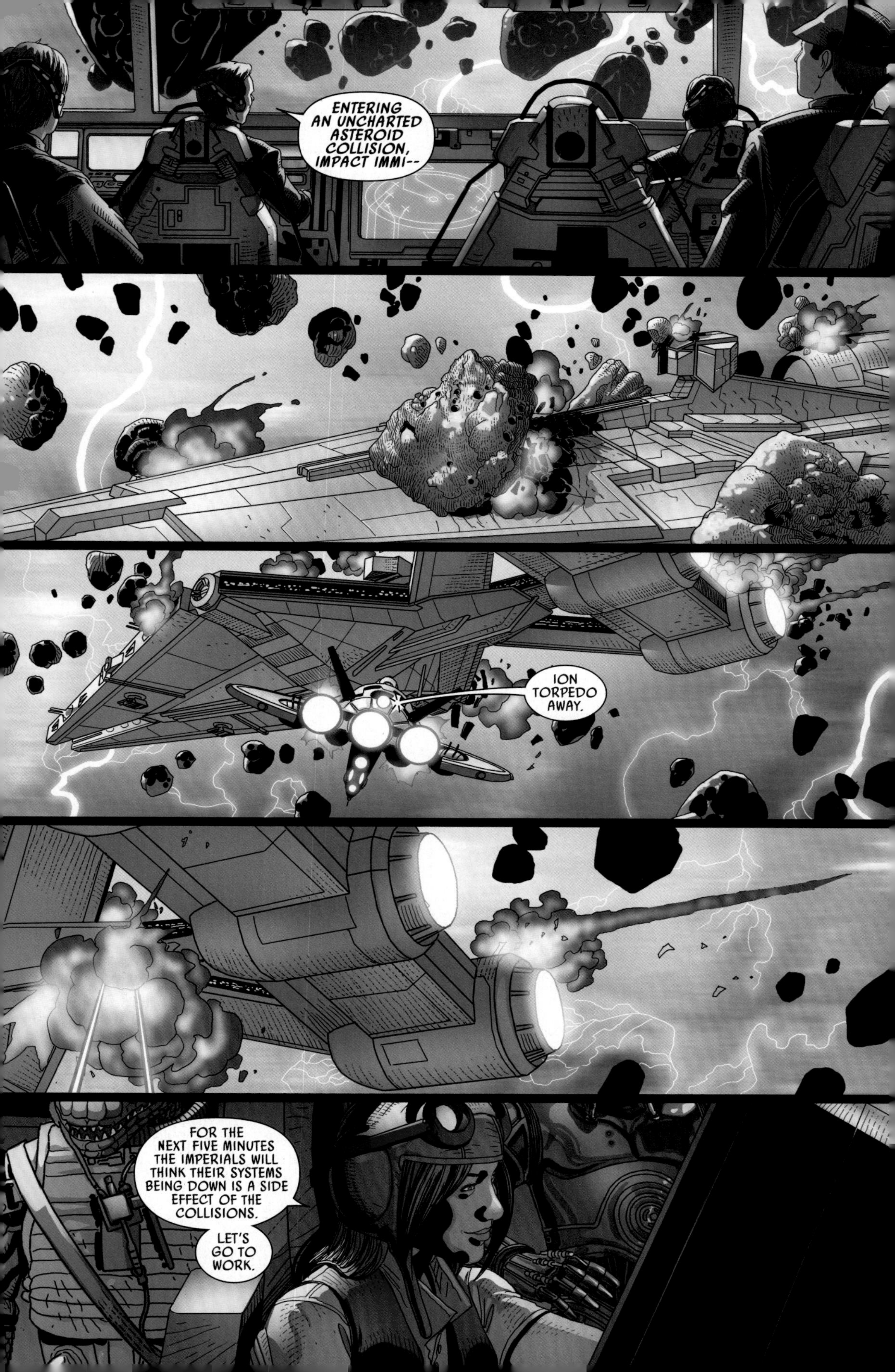
ENTERING AN UNCHARTED ASTEROID COLLISION, IMPACT IMMI--
ION TORPEDO AWAY.
FOR THE NEXT FIVE MINUTES THE IMPERIALS WILL THINK THEIR SYSTEMS BEING DOWN IS A SIDE EFFECT OF THE COLLISIONS.
LET'S GO TO WORK.

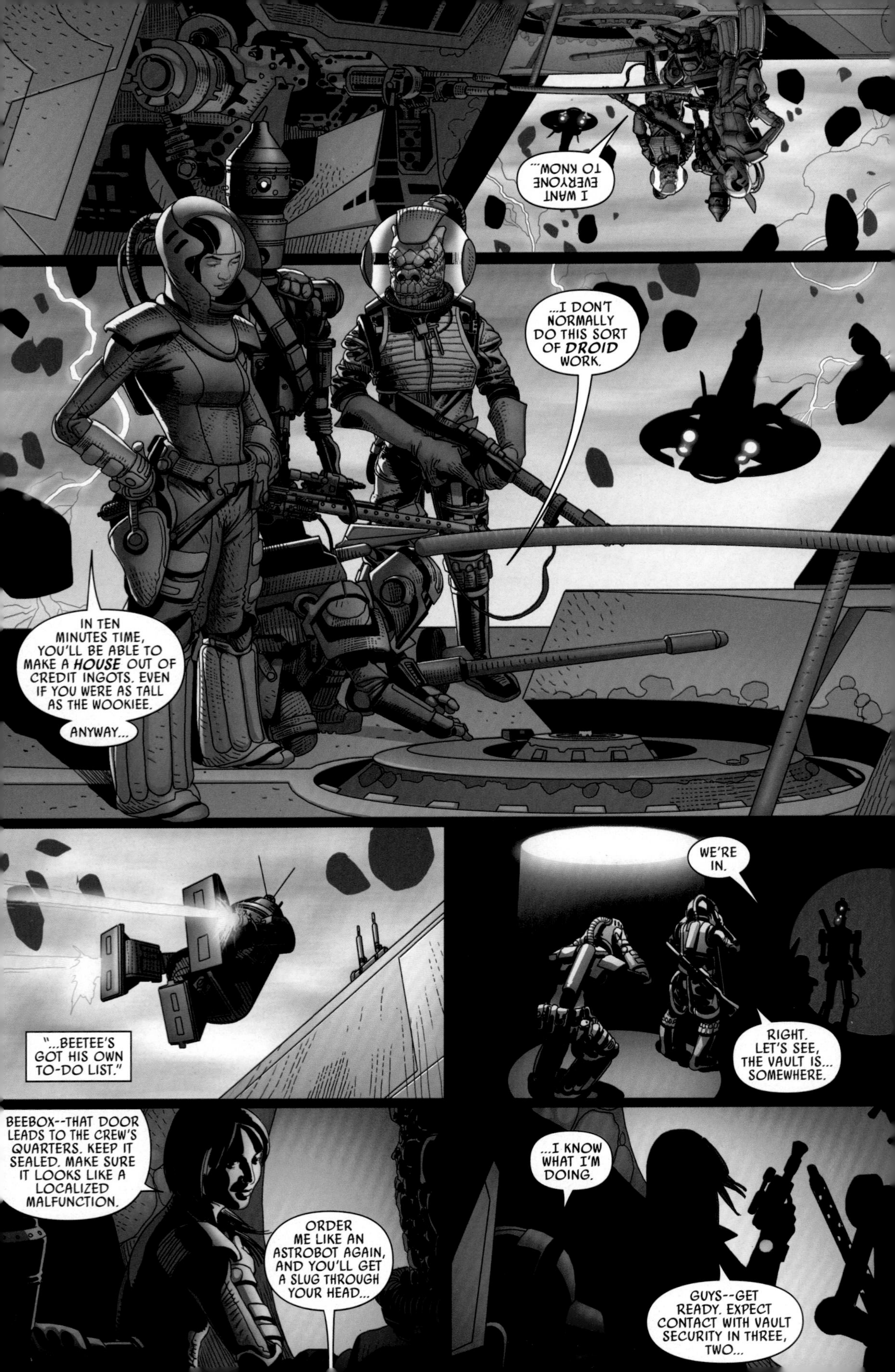
I WANT EVERYONE TO KNOW...
...I DON'T NORMALLY DO THIS SORT OF DROID WORK.
IN TEN MINUTES TIME, YOU'LL BE ABLE TO MAKE A HOUSE OUT OF CREDIT INGOTS. EVEN IF YOU WERE AS TALL AS THE WOOKIEE.
ANYWAY...
"...BEETEE'S GOT HIS OWN TO-DO LIST."
WE'RE IN.
RIGHT. LET'S SEE, THE VAULT IS... SOMEWHERE.
BEEBOX--THAT DOOR LEADS TO THE CREW'S QUARTERS. KEEP IT SEALED. MAKE SURE IT LOOKS LIKE A LOCALIZED MALFUNCTION.
ORDER ME LIKE AN ASTROBOT AGAIN, AND YOU'LL GET A SLUG THROUGH YOUR HEAD...
...I KNOW WHAT I'M DOING.
GUYS--GET READY. EXPECT CONTACT WITH VAULT SECURITY IN THREE, TWO...

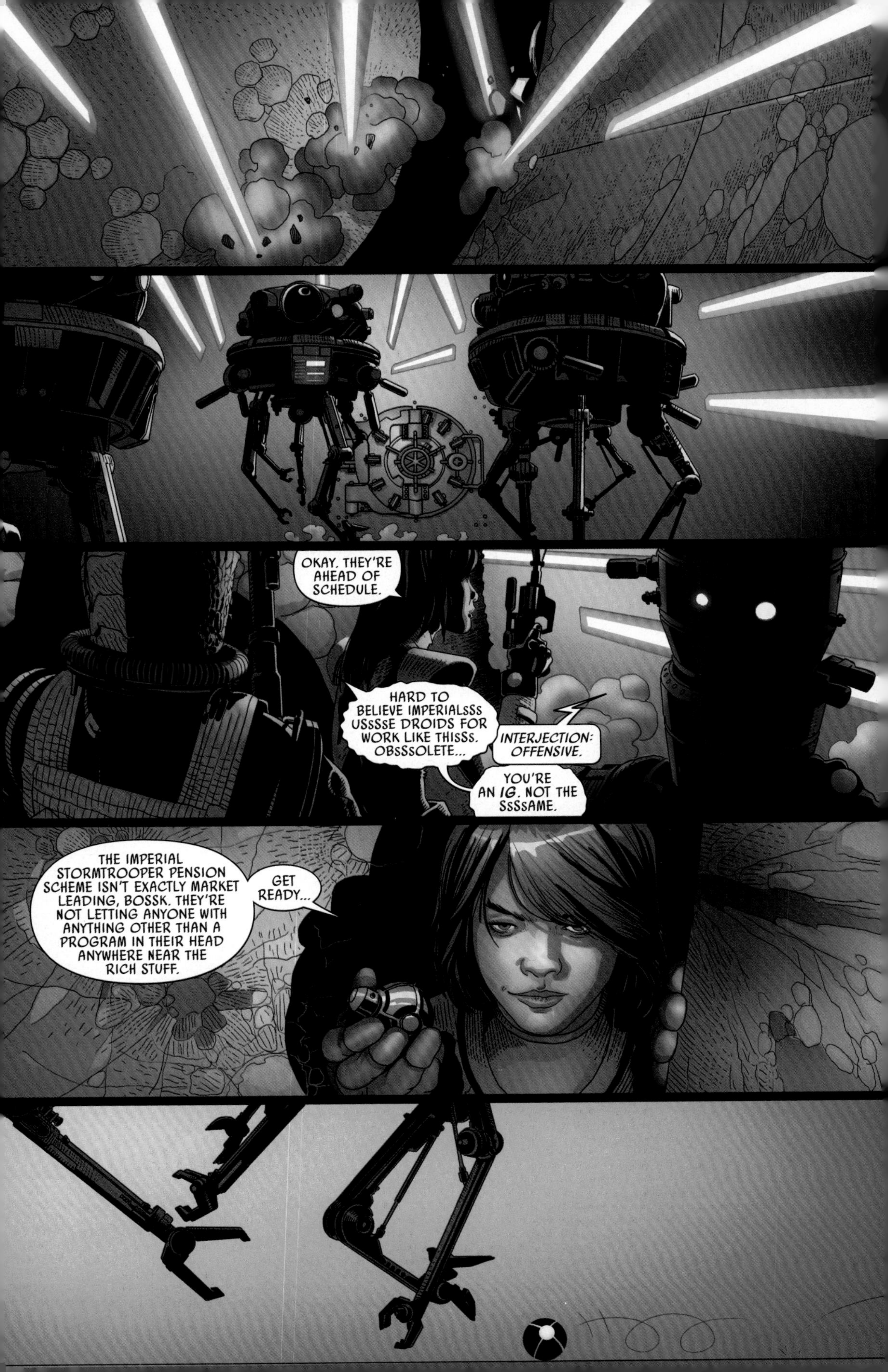

OKAY. THEY'RE AHEAD OF SCHEDULE.
HARD TO BELIEVE IMPERIALSSS USSSSE DROIDS FOR WORK LIKE THISSS. OBSSSOLETE...
INTERJECTION: OFFENSIVE.
YOU'RE AN IG. NOT THE SSSSAME.
THE IMPERIAL STORMTROOPER PENSION SCHEME ISN'T EXACTLY MARKET LEADING, BOSSK. THEY'RE NOT LETTING ANYONE WITH ANYTHING OTHER THAN A PROGRAM IN THEIR HEAD ANYWHERE NEAR THE RICH STUFF.
GET READY...

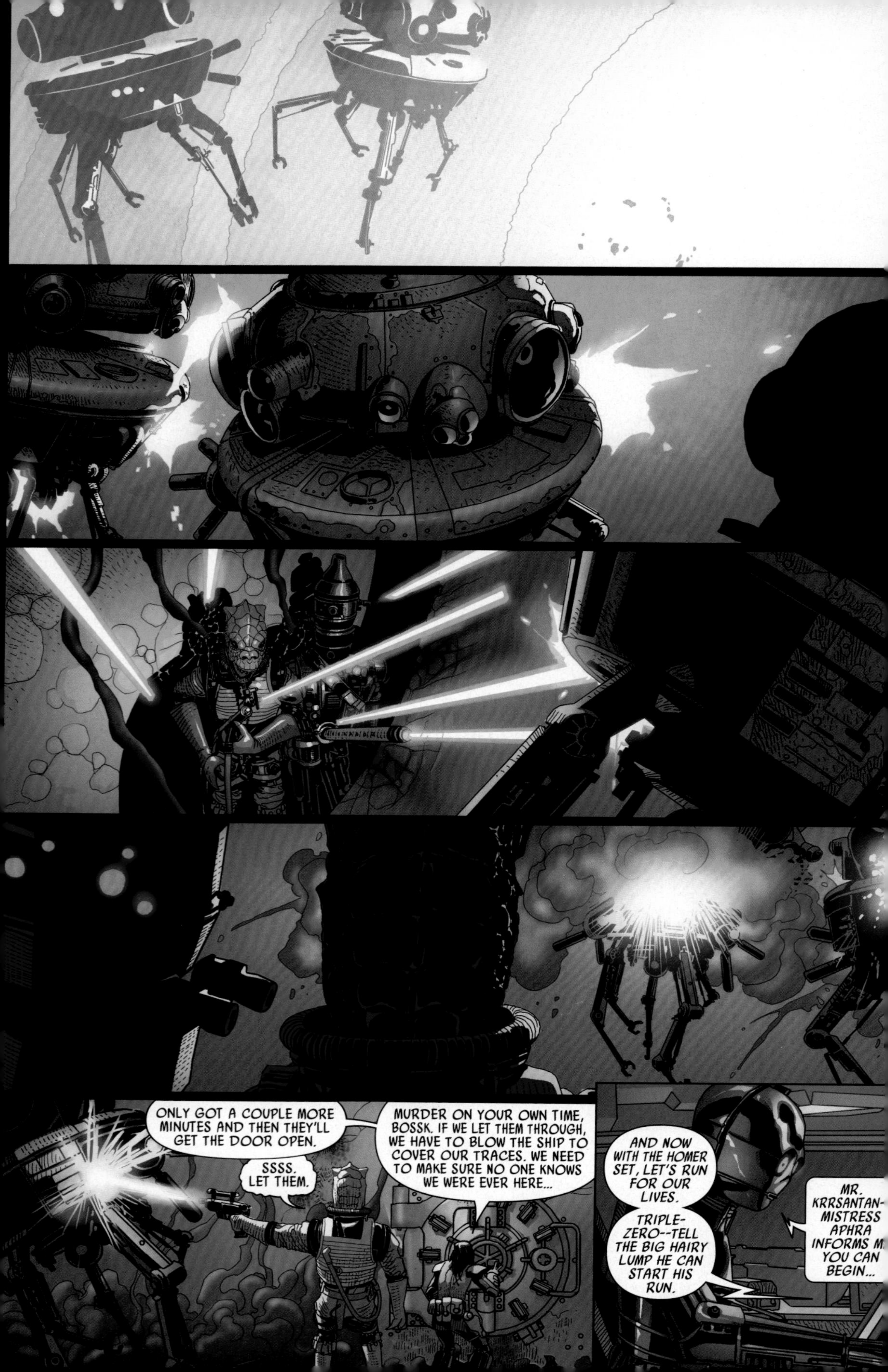
ONLY GOT A COUPLE MORE MINUTES AND THEN THEY'LL GET THE DOOR OPEN.
SSSS. LET THEM.
MURDER ON YOUR OWN TIME, BOSSK. IF WE LET THEM THROUGH, WE HAVE TO BLOW THE SHIP TO COVER OUR TRACES. WE NEED TO MAKE SURE NO ONE KNOWS WE WERE EVER HERE...
AND NOW WITH THE HOMER SET, LET'S RUN FOR OUR LIVES.
TRIPLE-ZERO--TELL THE BIG HAIRY LUMP HE CAN START HIS RUN.
MR. KRRSANTAN-MISTRESS APHRA INFORMS M YOU CAN BEGIN...

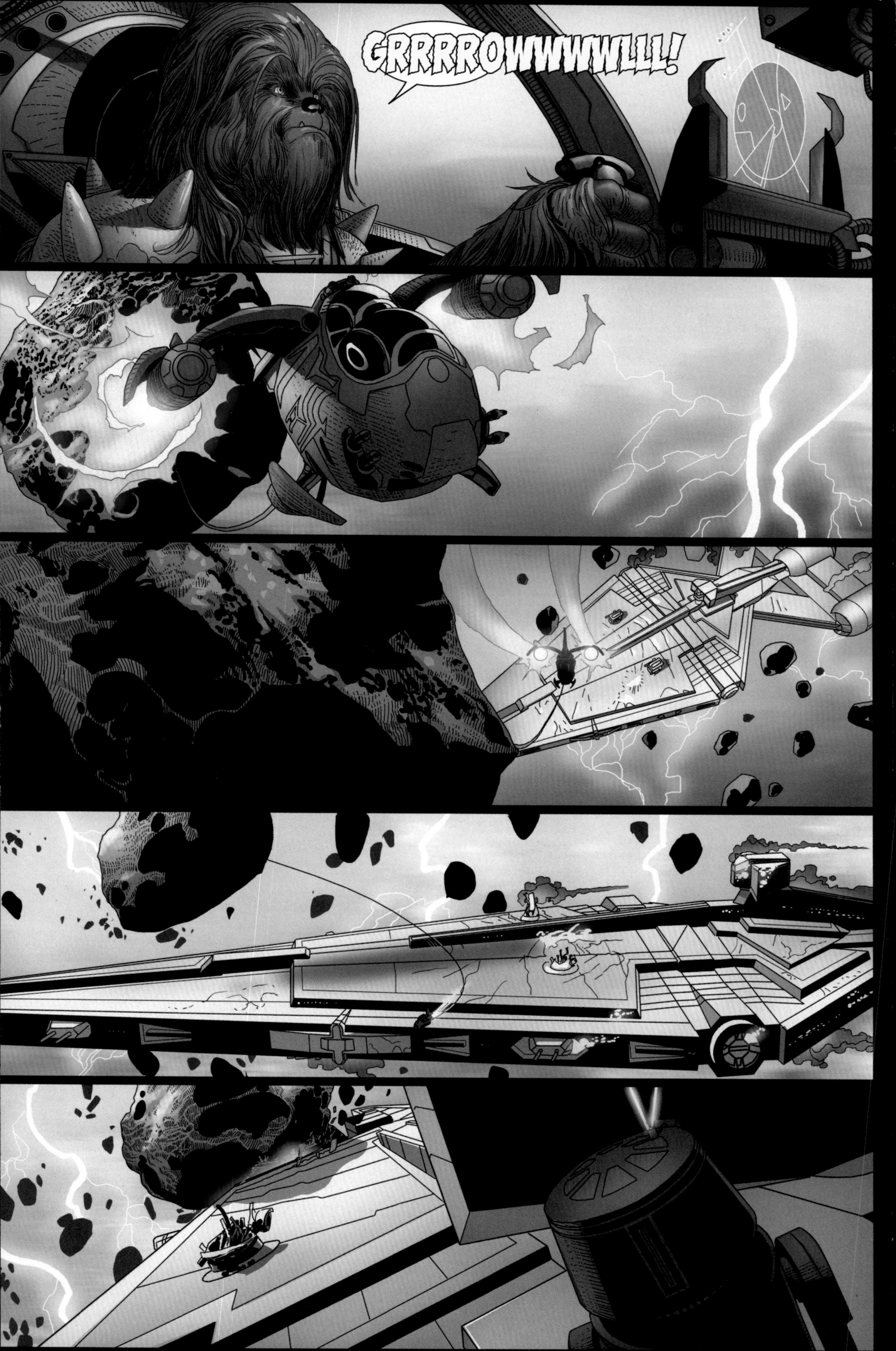
GRRRROWWWWLLL!

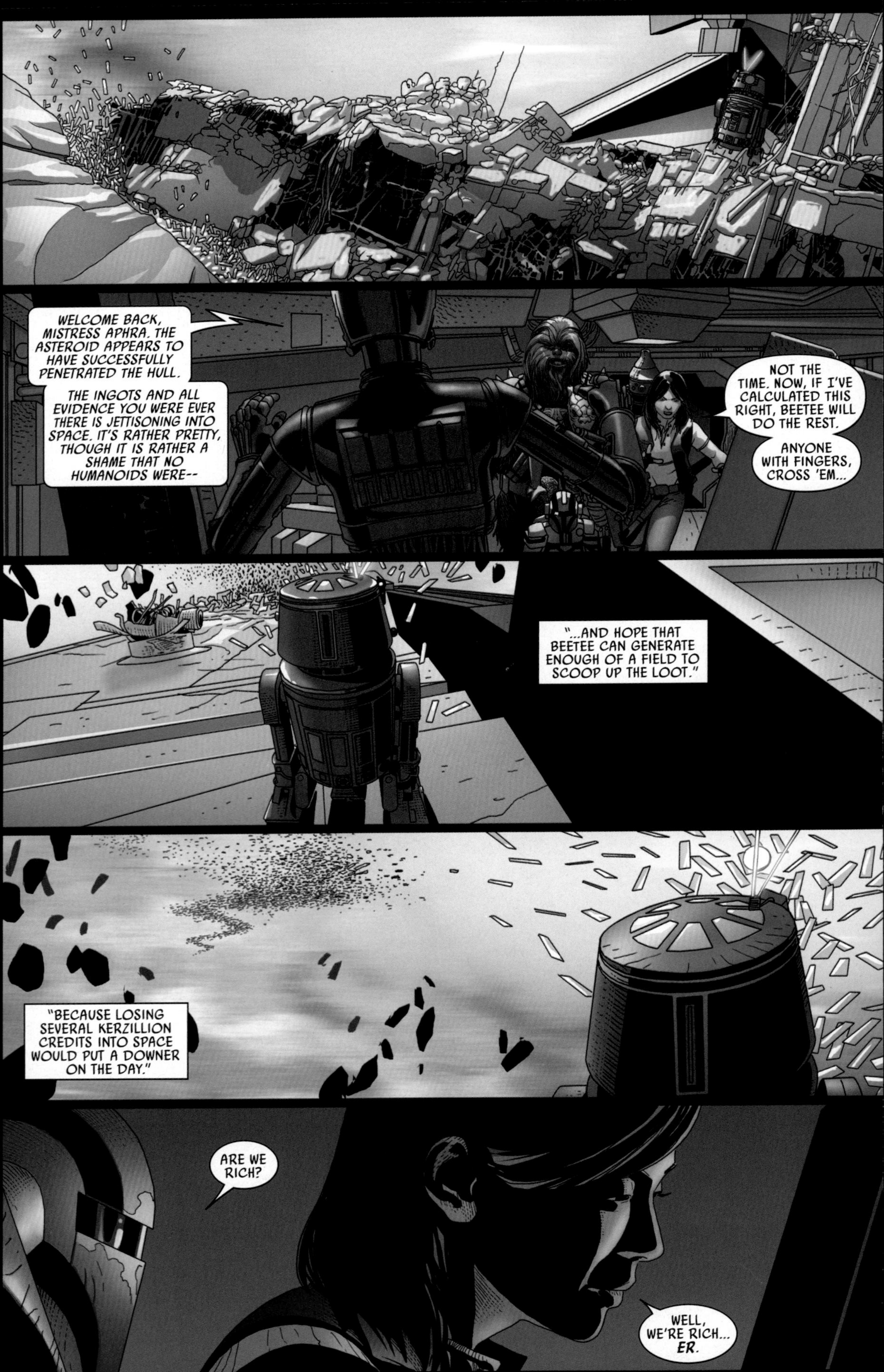
WELCOME BACK, MISTRESS APHRA. THE ASTEROID APPEARS TO HAVE SUCCESSFULLY PENETRATED THE HULL.
THE INGOTS AND ALL EVIDENCE YOU WERE EVER THERE IS JETTISONING INTO SPACE. IT'S RATHER PRETTY, THOUGH IT IS RATHER A SHAME THAT NO HUMANOIDS WERE--
NOT THE TIME. NOW, IF I'VE CALCULATED THIS RIGHT, BEETEE WILL DO THE REST.
ANYONE WITH FINGERS, CROSS 'EM...
"...AND HOPE THAT BEETEE CAN GENERATE ENOUGH OF A FIELD TO SCOOP UP THE LOOT."
"BECAUSE LOSING SEVERAL KERZILLION CREDITS INTO SPACE WOULD PUT A DOWNER ON THE DAY."
ARE WE RICH?
WELL, WE'RE RICH... *ER*.

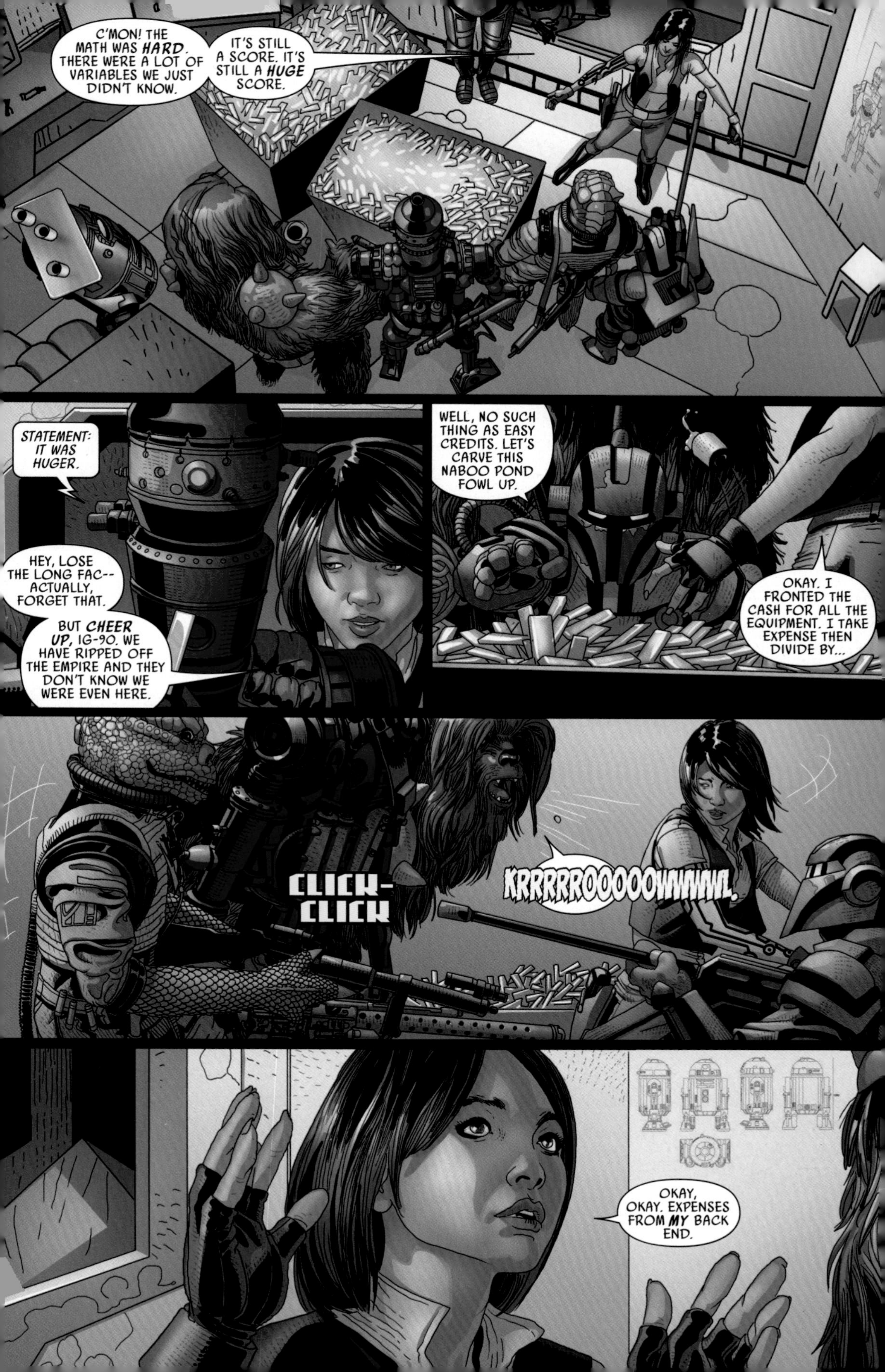
C'MON! THE MATH WAS HARD. THERE WERE A LOT OF VARIABLES WE JUST DIDN'T KNOW.
IT'S STILL A SCORE. IT'S STILL A HUGE SCORE.
STATEMENT: IT WAS HUGER.
HEY, LOSE THE LONG FAC-- ACTUALLY, FORGET THAT.
BUT CHEER UP, IG-90. WE HAVE RIPPED OFF THE EMPIRE AND THEY DON'T KNOW WE WERE EVEN HERE.
WELL, NO SUCH THING AS EASY CREDITS. LET'S CARVE THIS NABOO POND FOWL UP.
OKAY. I FRONTED THE CASH FOR ALL THE EQUIPMENT. I TAKE EXPENSE THEN DIVIDE BY...
CLICK-CLICK
KRRRRROOOOOWWWWL.
OKAY, OKAY. EXPENSES FROM MY BACK END.

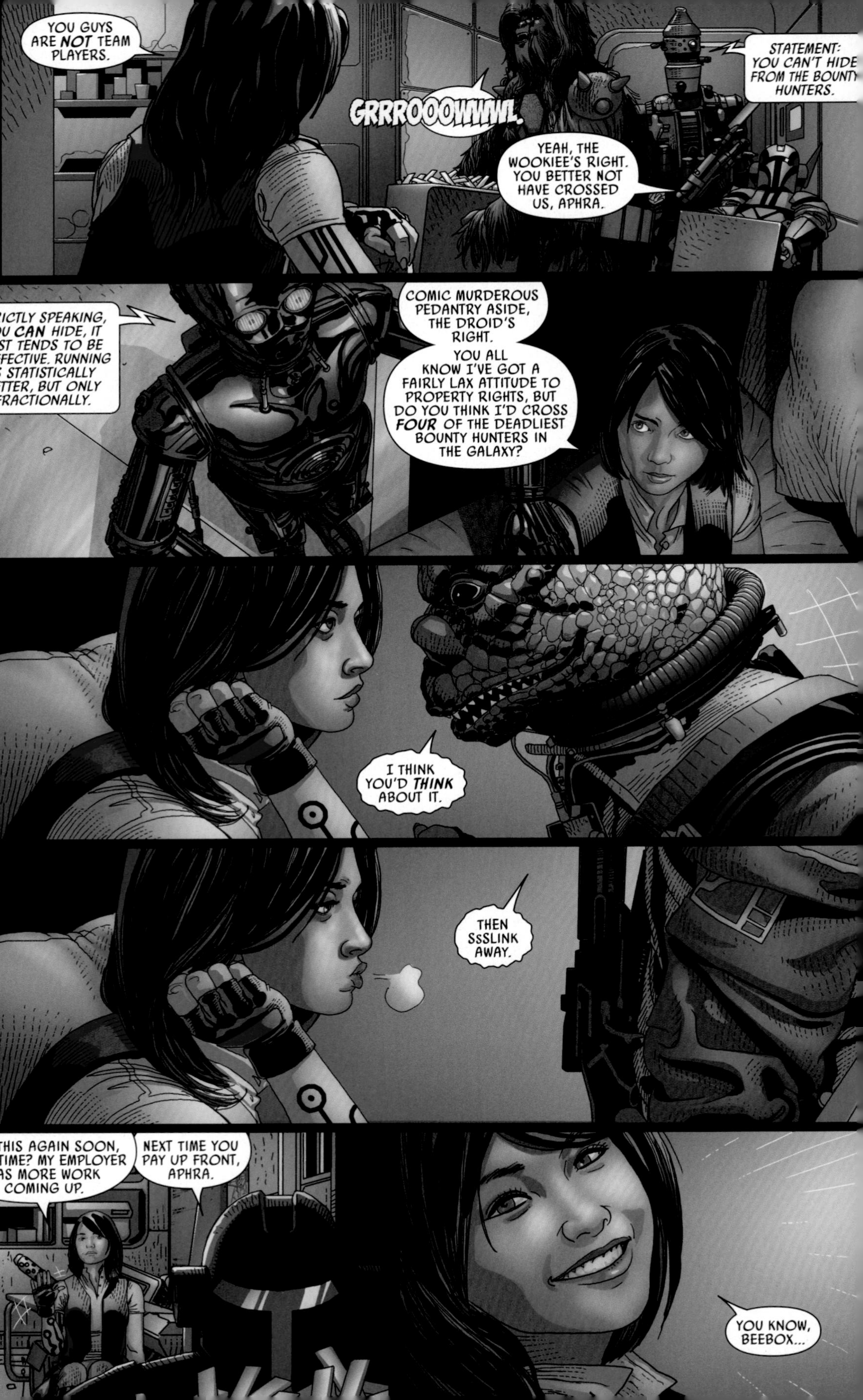
YOU GUYS ARE NOT TEAM PLAYERS.
GRRROOOWWWL.
STATEMENT: YOU CAN'T HIDE FROM THE BOUNTY HUNTERS.
YEAH, THE WOOKIEE'S RIGHT. YOU BETTER NOT HAVE CROSSED US, APHRA.
STRICTLY SPEAKING, YOU CAN HIDE, IT JUST TENDS TO BE INEFFECTIVE. RUNNING IS STATISTICALLY BETTER, BUT ONLY FRACTIONALLY.
COMIC MURDEROUS PEDANTRY ASIDE, THE DROID'S RIGHT.
YOU ALL KNOW I'VE GOT A FAIRLY LAX ATTITUDE TO PROPERTY RIGHTS, BUT DO YOU THINK I'D CROSS FOUR OF THE DEADLIEST BOUNTY HUNTERS IN THE GALAXY?
I THINK YOU'D THINK ABOUT IT.
THEN SSSLINK AWAY.
OMETIME? MY EMPLOYER HAS MORE WORK COMING UP.
NEXT TIME YOU PAY UP FRONT, APHRA.
YOU KNOW, BEEBOX...

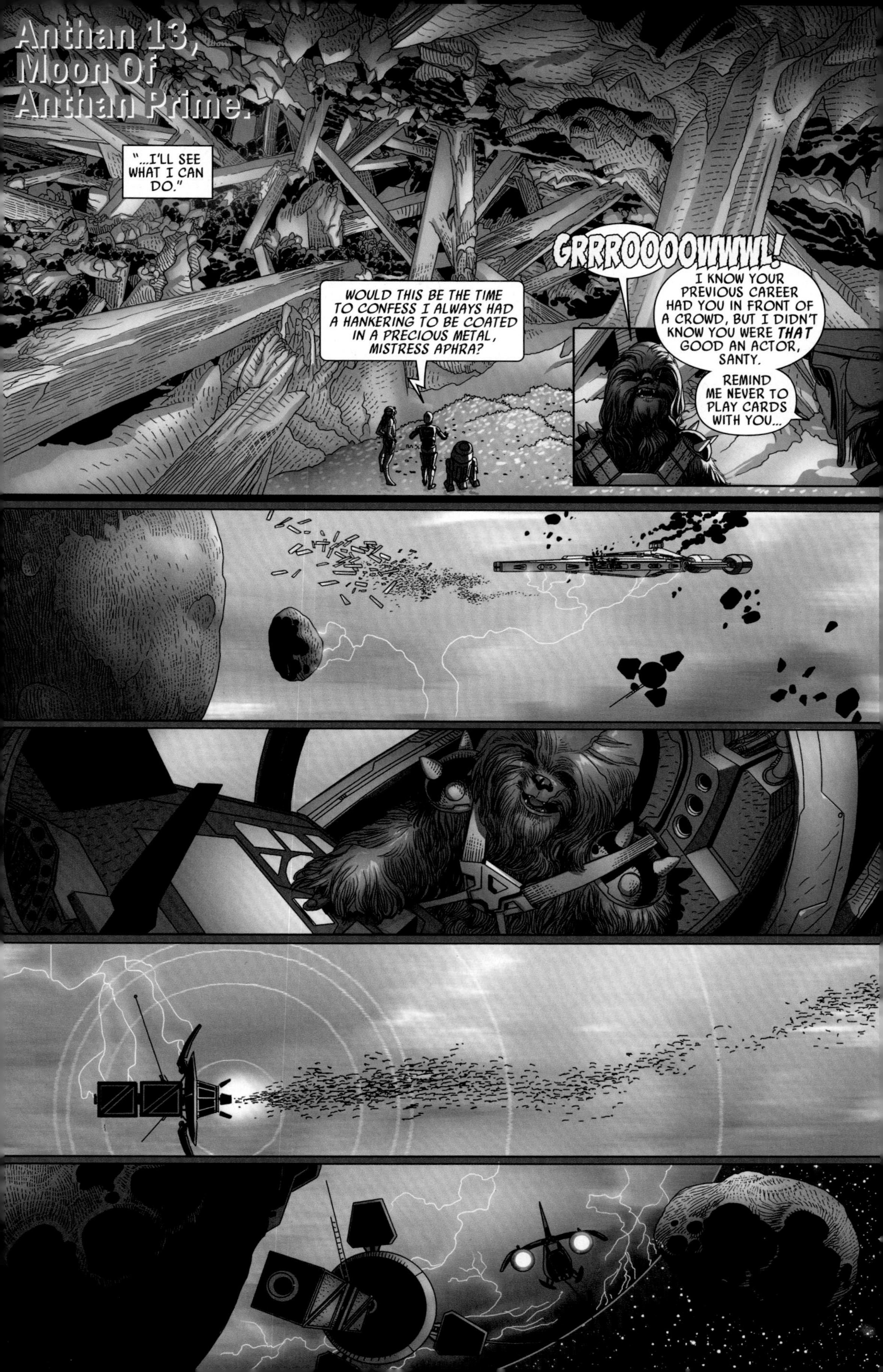
Anthan 13, Moon Of Anthan Prime.
"...I'LL SEE WHAT I CAN DO."
WOULD THIS BE THE TIME TO CONFESS I ALWAYS HAD A HANKERING TO BE COATED IN A PRECIOUS METAL, MISTRESS APHRA?
GRRROOOOWWWL!
I KNOW YOUR PREVIOUS CAREER HAD YOU IN FRONT OF A CROWD, BUT I DIDN'T KNOW YOU WERE THAT GOOD AN ACTOR, SANTY.
REMIND ME NEVER TO PLAY CARDS WITH YOU...

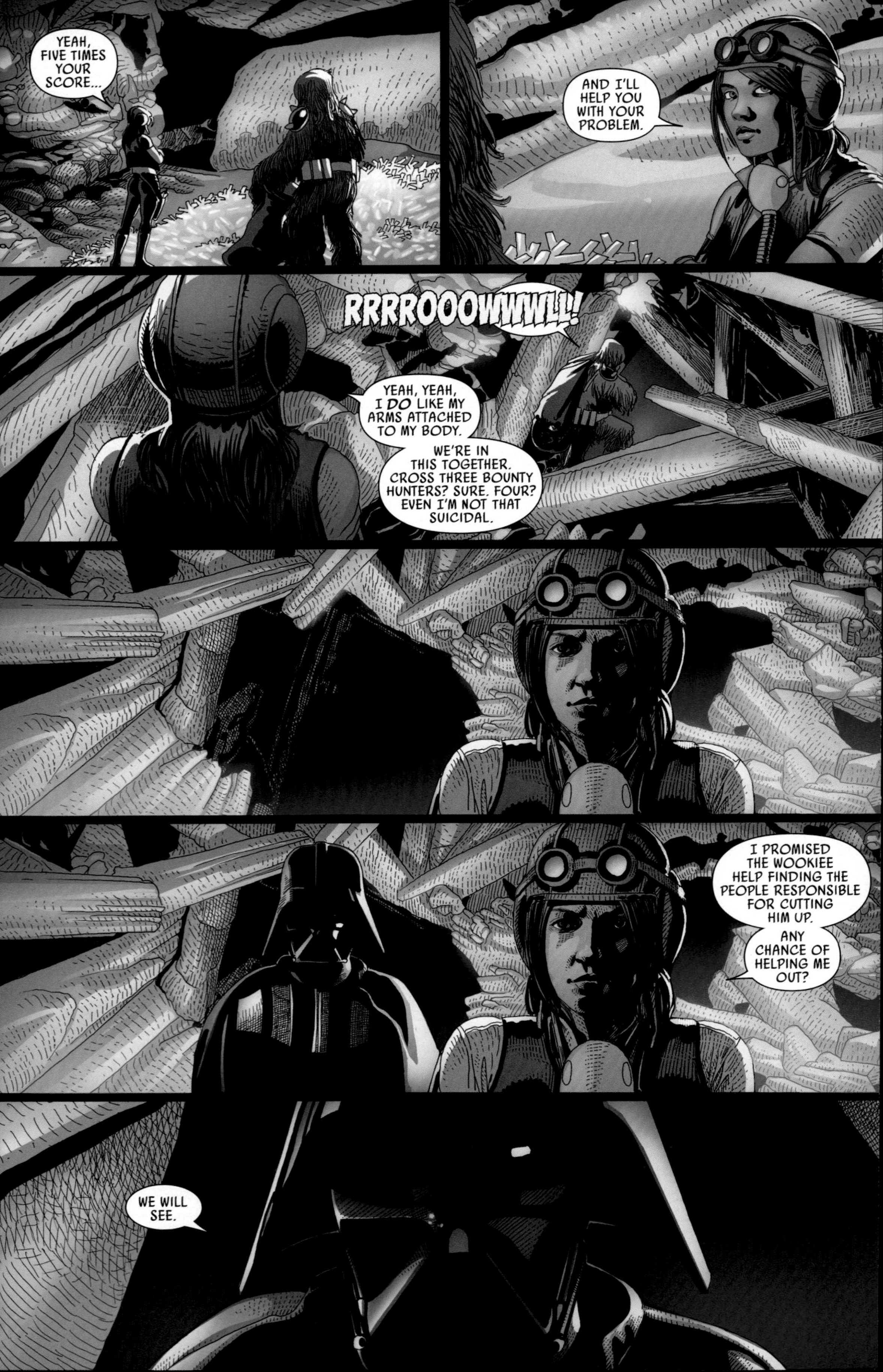
YEAH, FIVE TIMES YOUR SCORE...
AND I'LL HELP YOU WITH YOUR PROBLEM.
RRRROOOWWWLL!
YEAH, YEAH, I *DO* LIKE MY ARMS ATTACHED TO MY BODY.
WE'RE IN THIS TOGETHER. CROSS THREE BOUNTY HUNTERS? SURE. FOUR? EVEN I'M NOT THAT SUICIDAL.
I PROMISED THE WOOKIEE HELP FINDING THE PEOPLE RESPONSIBLE FOR CUTTING HIM UP.
ANY CHANCE OF HELPING ME OUT?
WE WILL SEE.

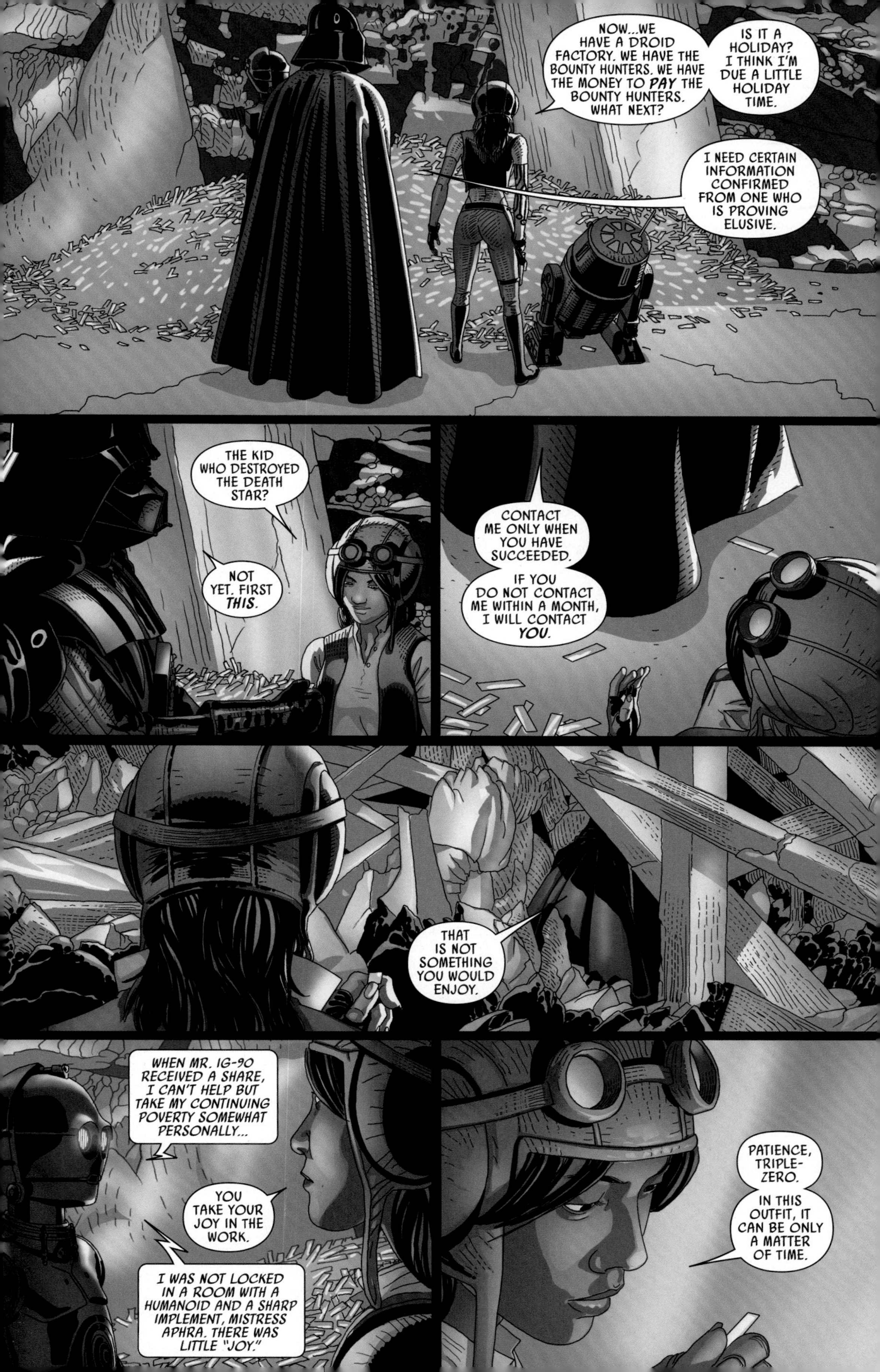
NOW...WE HAVE A DROID FACTORY. WE HAVE THE BOUNTY HUNTERS. WE HAVE THE MONEY TO PAY THE BOUNTY HUNTERS. WHAT NEXT?
IS IT A HOLIDAY? I THINK I'M DUE A LITTLE HOLIDAY TIME.
I NEED CERTAIN INFORMATION CONFIRMED FROM ONE WHO IS PROVING ELUSIVE.
THE KID WHO DESTROYED THE DEATH STAR?
NOT YET. FIRST THIS.
CONTACT ME ONLY WHEN YOU HAVE SUCCEEDED.
IF YOU DO NOT CONTACT ME WITHIN A MONTH, I WILL CONTACT YOU.
THAT IS NOT SOMETHING YOU WOULD ENJOY.
WHEN MR. IG-90 RECEIVED A SHARE, I CAN'T HELP BUT TAKE MY CONTINUING POVERTY SOMEWHAT PERSONALLY...
YOU TAKE YOUR JOY IN THE WORK.
I WAS NOT LOCKED IN A ROOM WITH A HUMANOID AND A SHARP IMPLEMENT, MISTRESS APHRA. THERE WAS LITTLE "JOY."
PATIENCE, TRIPLE-ZERO.
IN THIS OUTFIT, IT CAN BE ONLY A MATTER OF TIME.

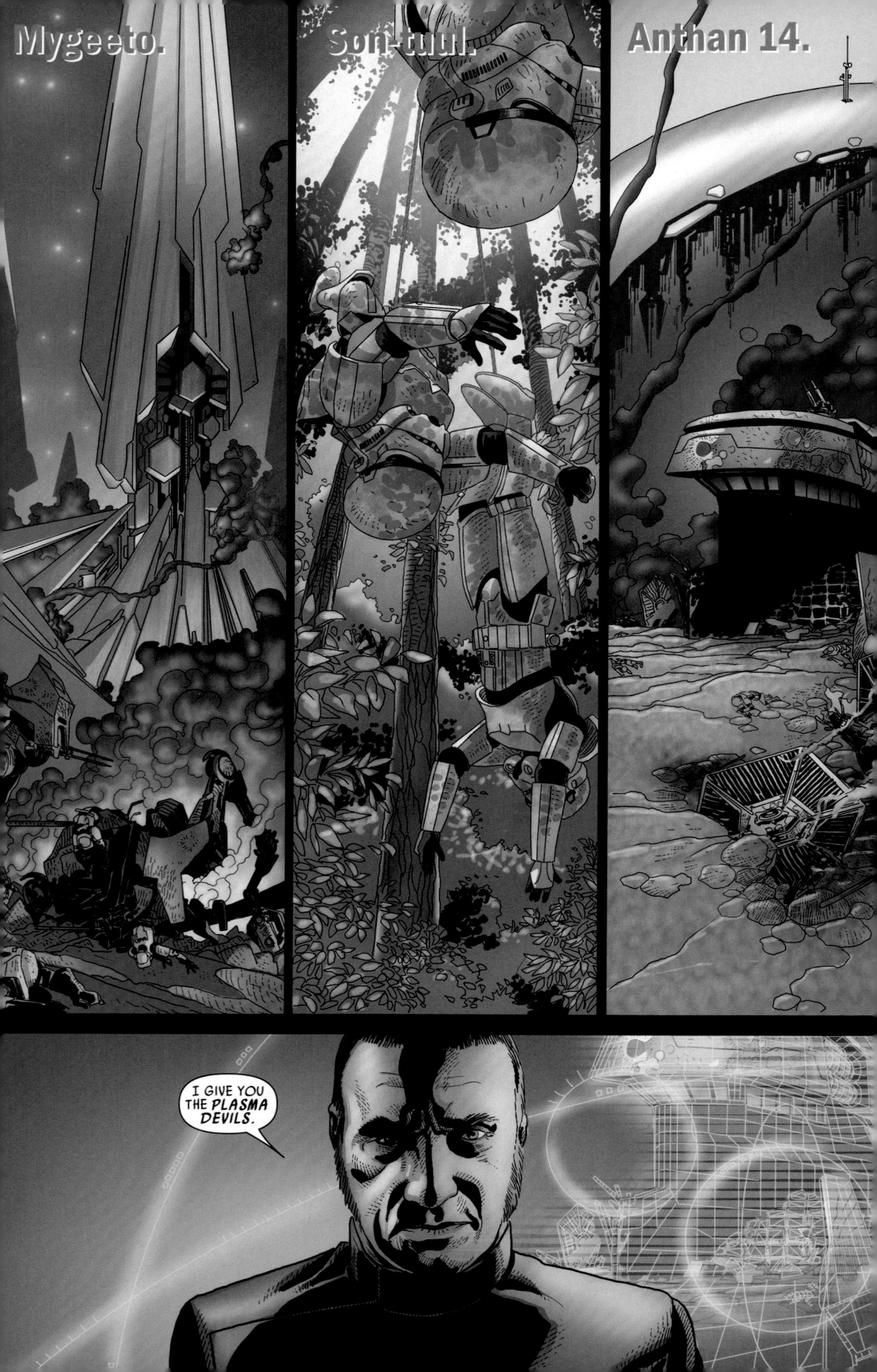
Mygeeto.
Son-tuul.
Anthan 14.
I GIVE YOU THE PLASMA DEVILS.

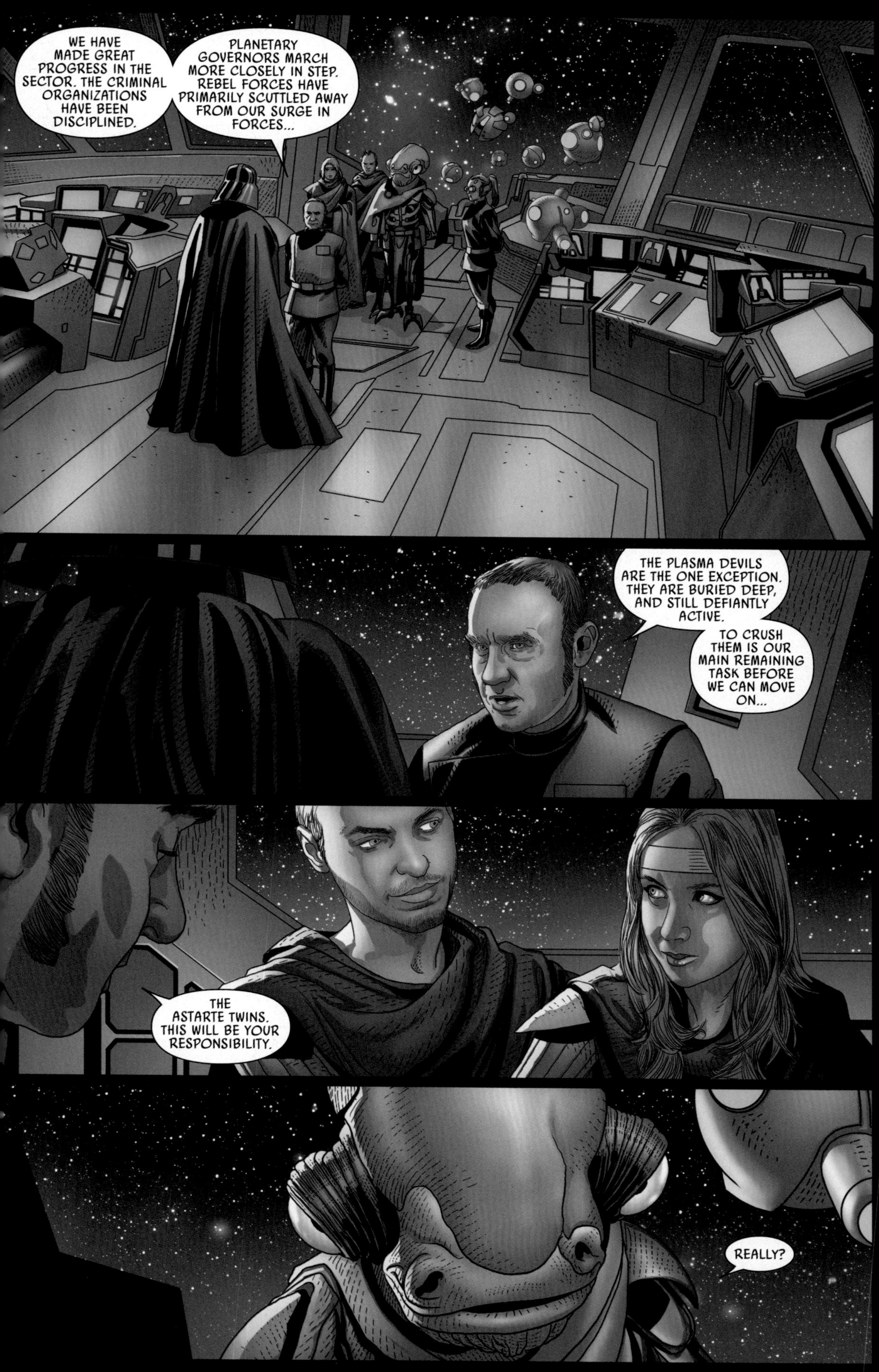
WE HAVE MADE GREAT PROGRESS IN THE SECTOR. THE CRIMINAL ORGANIZATIONS HAVE BEEN DISCIPLINED.
PLANETARY GOVERNORS MARCH MORE CLOSELY IN STEP. REBEL FORCES HAVE PRIMARILY SCUTTLED AWAY FROM OUR SURGE IN FORCES...
THE PLASMA DEVILS ARE THE ONE EXCEPTION. THEY ARE BURIED DEEP, AND STILL DEFIANTLY ACTIVE.
TO CRUSH THEM IS OUR MAIN REMAINING TASK BEFORE WE CAN MOVE ON...
THE ASTARTE TWINS. THIS WILL BE YOUR RESPONSIBILITY.
REALLY?

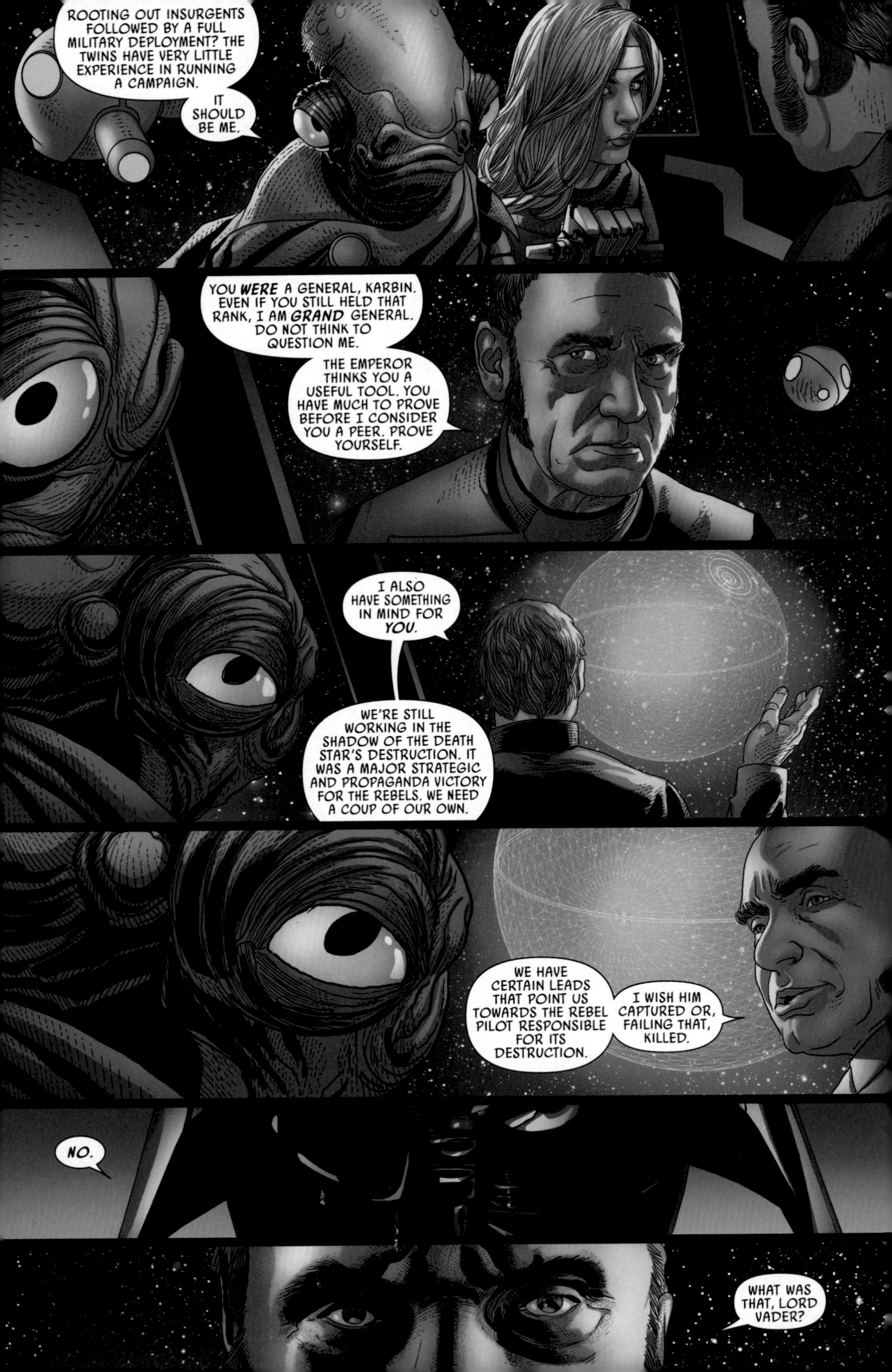
ROOTING OUT INSURGENTS FOLLOWED BY A FULL MILITARY DEPLOYMENT? THE TWINS HAVE VERY LITTLE EXPERIENCE IN RUNNING A CAMPAIGN.
IT SHOULD BE ME.
YOU *WERE* A GENERAL, KARBIN. EVEN IF YOU STILL HELD THAT RANK, I AM *GRAND* GENERAL. DO NOT THINK TO QUESTION ME.
THE EMPEROR THINKS YOU A USEFUL TOOL. YOU HAVE MUCH TO PROVE BEFORE I CONSIDER YOU A PEER. PROVE YOURSELF.
I ALSO HAVE SOMETHING IN MIND FOR *YOU*.
WE'RE STILL WORKING IN THE SHADOW OF THE DEATH STAR'S DESTRUCTION. IT WAS A MAJOR STRATEGIC AND PROPAGANDA VICTORY FOR THE REBELS. WE NEED A COUP OF OUR OWN.
WE HAVE CERTAIN LEADS THAT POINT US TOWARDS THE REBEL PILOT RESPONSIBLE FOR ITS DESTRUCTION.
I WISH HIM CAPTURED OR, FAILING THAT, KILLED.
NO.
WHAT WAS THAT, LORD VADER?

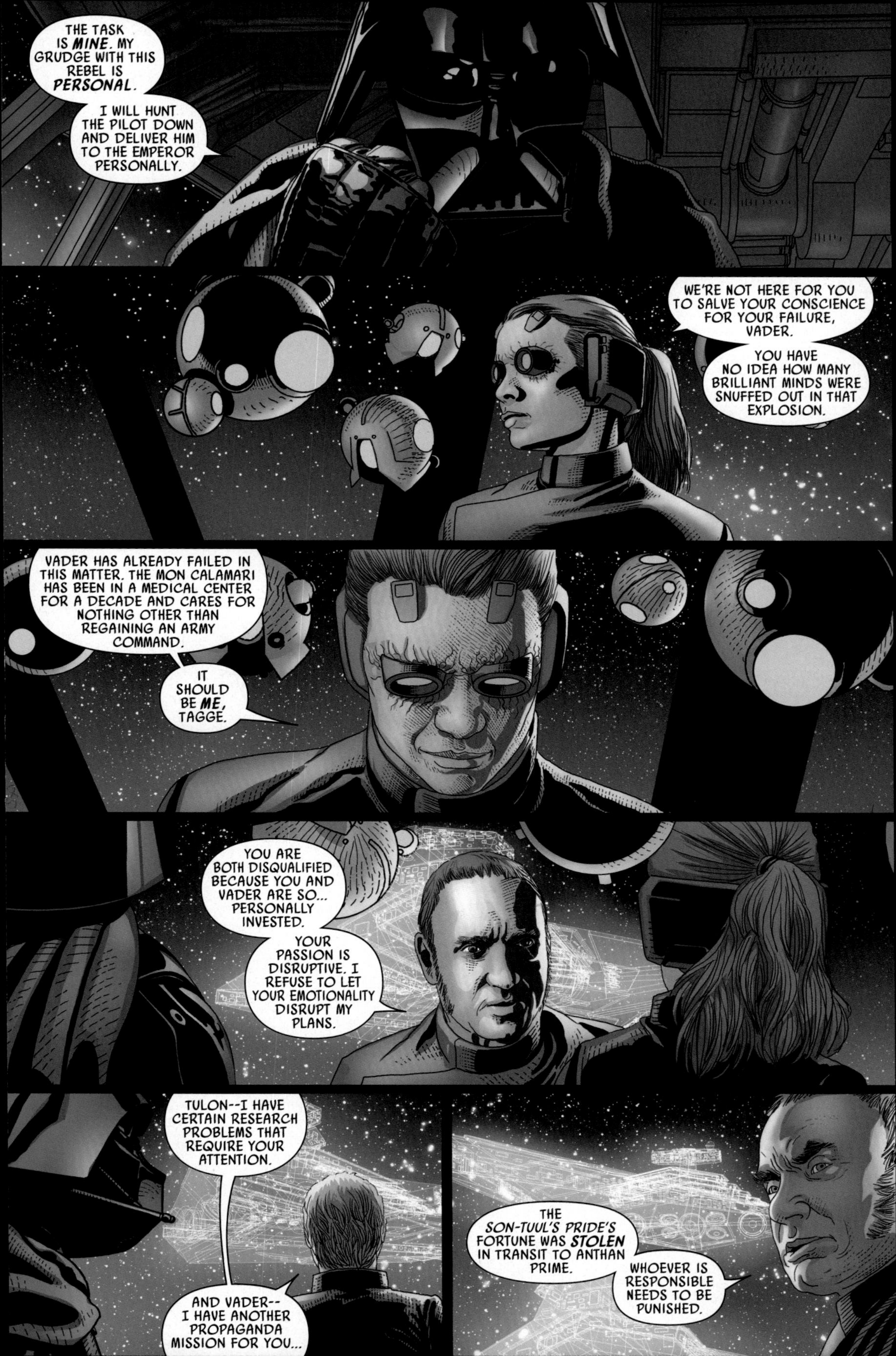
THE TASK IS **MINE**. MY GRUDGE WITH THIS REBEL IS **PERSONAL**.
I WILL HUNT THE PILOT DOWN AND DELIVER HIM TO THE EMPEROR PERSONALLY.
WE'RE NOT HERE FOR YOU TO SALVE YOUR CONSCIENCE FOR YOUR FAILURE, VADER.
YOU HAVE NO IDEA HOW MANY BRILLIANT MINDS WERE SNUFFED OUT IN THAT EXPLOSION.
VADER HAS ALREADY FAILED IN THIS MATTER. THE MON CALAMARI HAS BEEN IN A MEDICAL CENTER FOR A DECADE AND CARES FOR NOTHING OTHER THAN REGAINING AN ARMY COMMAND.
IT SHOULD BE **ME**, TAGGE.
YOU ARE BOTH DISQUALIFIED BECAUSE YOU AND VADER ARE SO... PERSONALLY INVESTED.
YOUR PASSION IS DISRUPTIVE. I REFUSE TO LET YOUR EMOTIONALITY DISRUPT MY PLANS.
TULON--I HAVE CERTAIN RESEARCH PROBLEMS THAT REQUIRE YOUR ATTENTION.
AND VADER-- I HAVE ANOTHER PROPAGANDA MISSION FOR YOU...
THE *SON-TUUL'S PRIDE'S* FORTUNE WAS **STOLEN** IN TRANSIT TO ANTHAN PRIME.
WHOEVER IS RESPONSIBLE NEEDS TO BE PUNISHED.

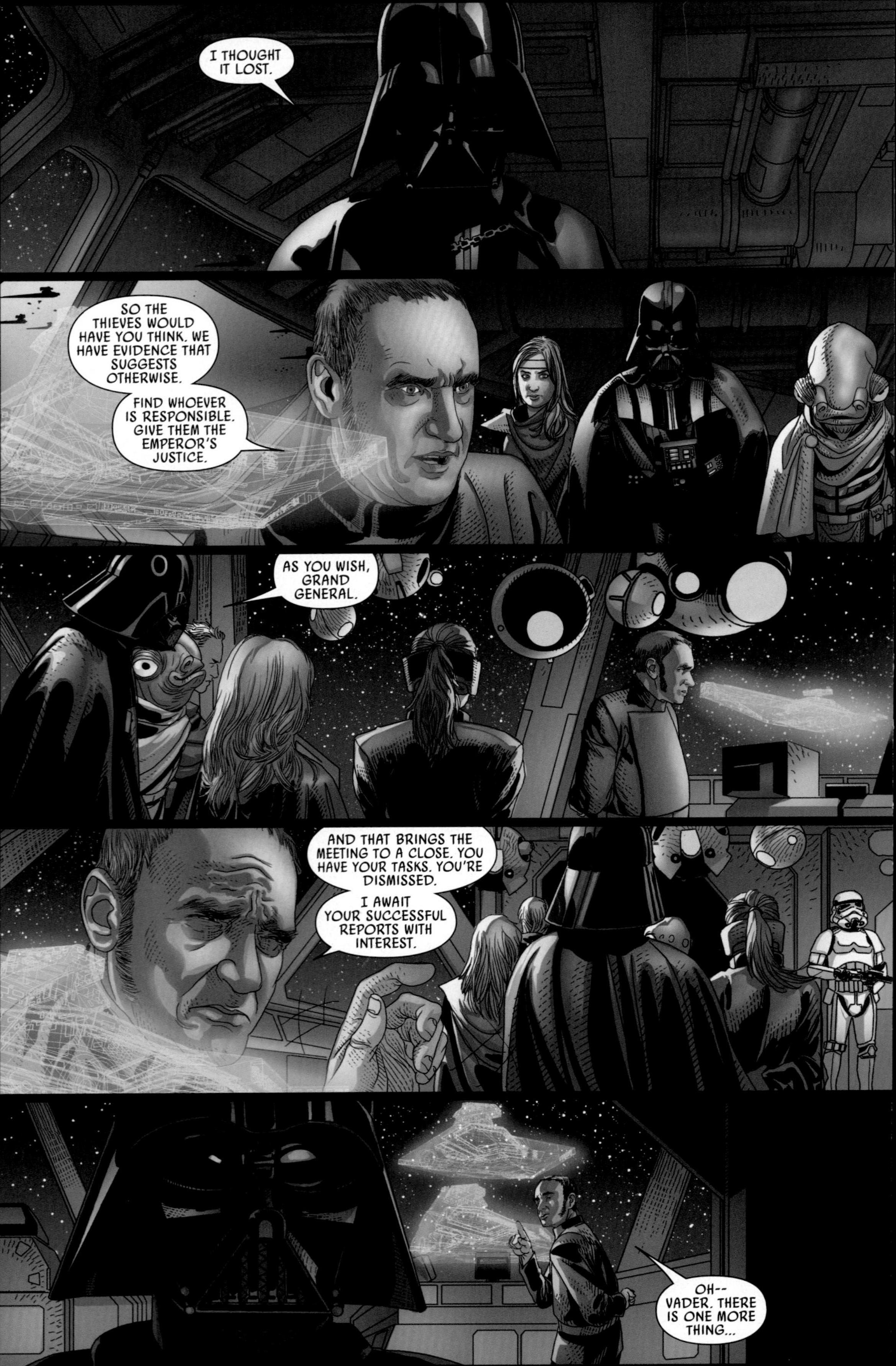
I THOUGHT IT LOST.
SO THE THIEVES WOULD HAVE YOU THINK. WE HAVE EVIDENCE THAT SUGGESTS OTHERWISE.
FIND WHOEVER IS RESPONSIBLE. GIVE THEM THE EMPEROR'S JUSTICE.
AS YOU WISH, GRAND GENERAL.
AND THAT BRINGS THE MEETING TO A CLOSE. YOU HAVE YOUR TASKS. YOU'RE DISMISSED.
I AWAIT YOUR SUCCESSFUL REPORTS WITH INTEREST.
OH-- VADER. THERE IS ONE MORE THING...

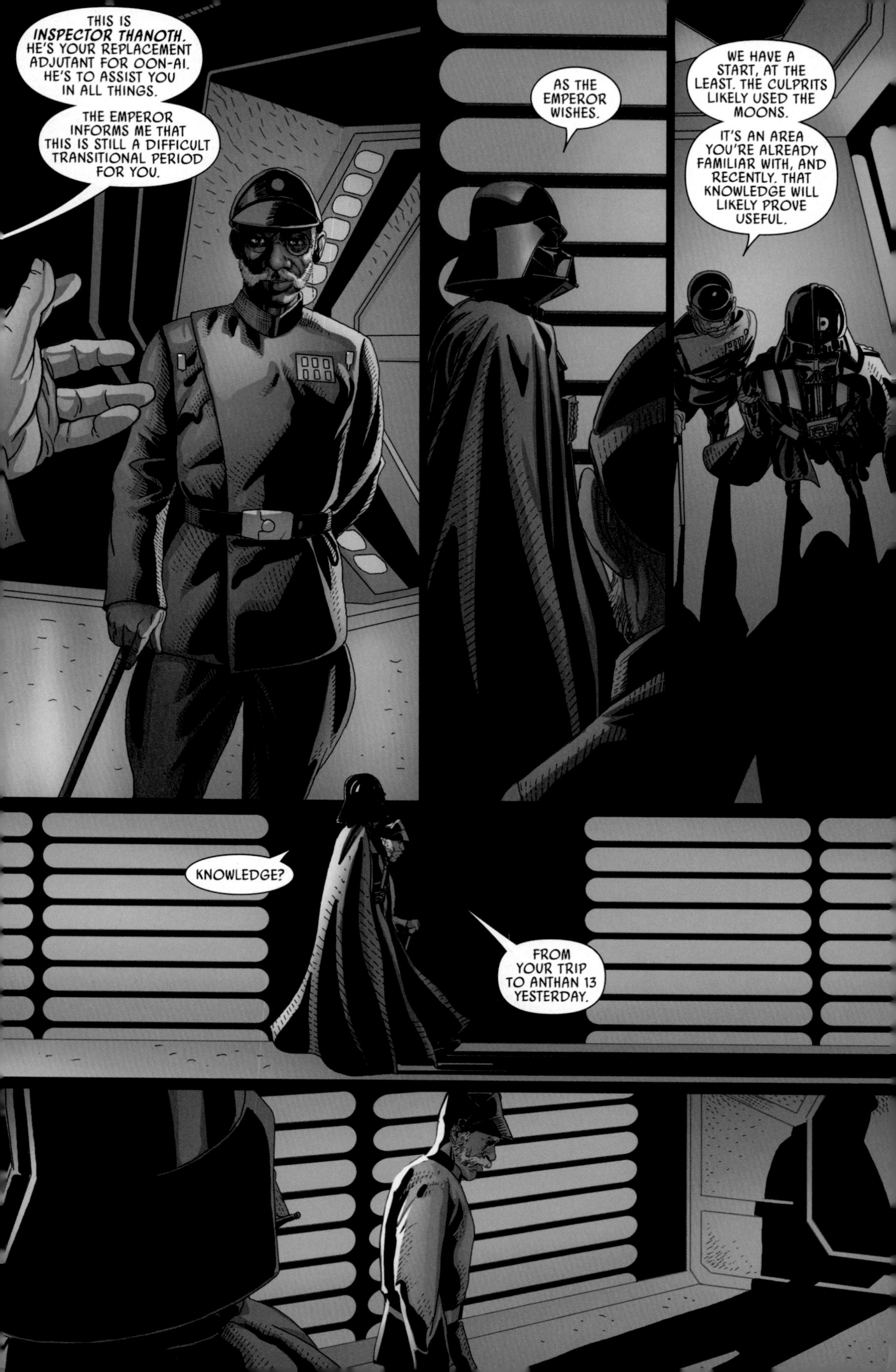

THIS IS INSPECTOR THANOTH. HE'S YOUR REPLACEMENT ADJUTANT FOR OON-AI. HE'S TO ASSIST YOU IN ALL THINGS.
THE EMPEROR INFORMS ME THAT THIS IS STILL A DIFFICULT TRANSITIONAL PERIOD FOR YOU.
AS THE EMPEROR WISHES.
WE HAVE A START, AT THE LEAST. THE CULPRITS LIKELY USED THE MOONS.
IT'S AN AREA YOU'RE ALREADY FAMILIAR WITH, AND RECENTLY. THAT KNOWLEDGE WILL LIKELY PROVE USEFUL.
KNOWLEDGE?
FROM YOUR TRIP TO ANTHAN 13 YESTERDAY.

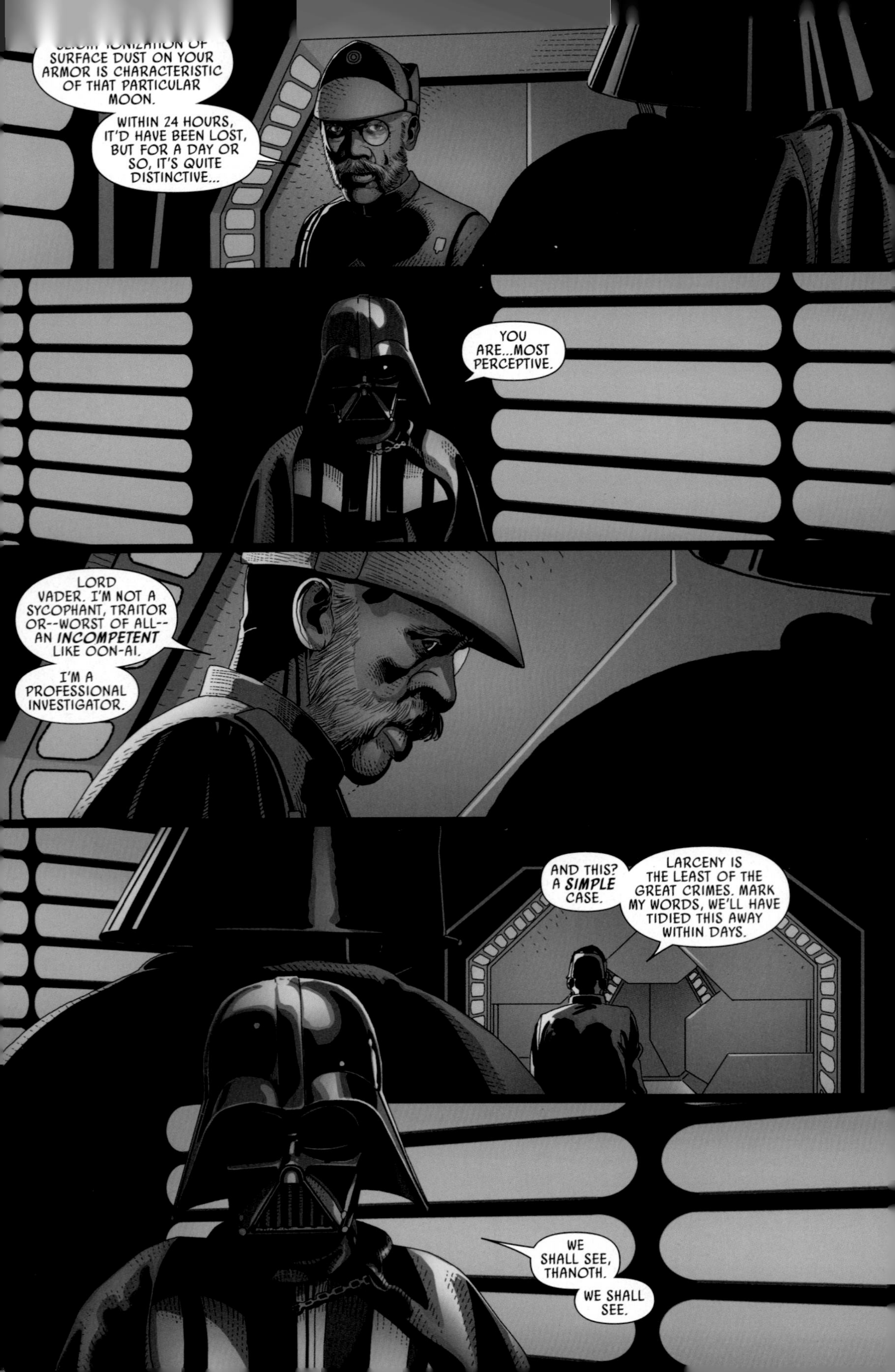
SURFACE DUST ON YOUR ARMOR IS CHARACTERISTIC OF THAT PARTICULAR MOON.
WITHIN 24 HOURS, IT'D HAVE BEEN LOST, BUT FOR A DAY OR SO, IT'S QUITE DISTINCTIVE...
YOU ARE...MOST PERCEPTIVE.
LORD VADER. I'M NOT A SYCOPHANT, TRAITOR OR--WORST OF ALL--AN **INCOMPETENT** LIKE OON-AI.
I'M A PROFESSIONAL INVESTIGATOR.
AND THIS? A **SIMPLE** CASE.
LARCENY IS THE LEAST OF THE GREAT CRIMES. MARK MY WORDS, WE'LL HAVE TIDIED THIS AWAY WITHIN DAYS.
WE SHALL SEE, THANOTH.
WE SHALL SEE.

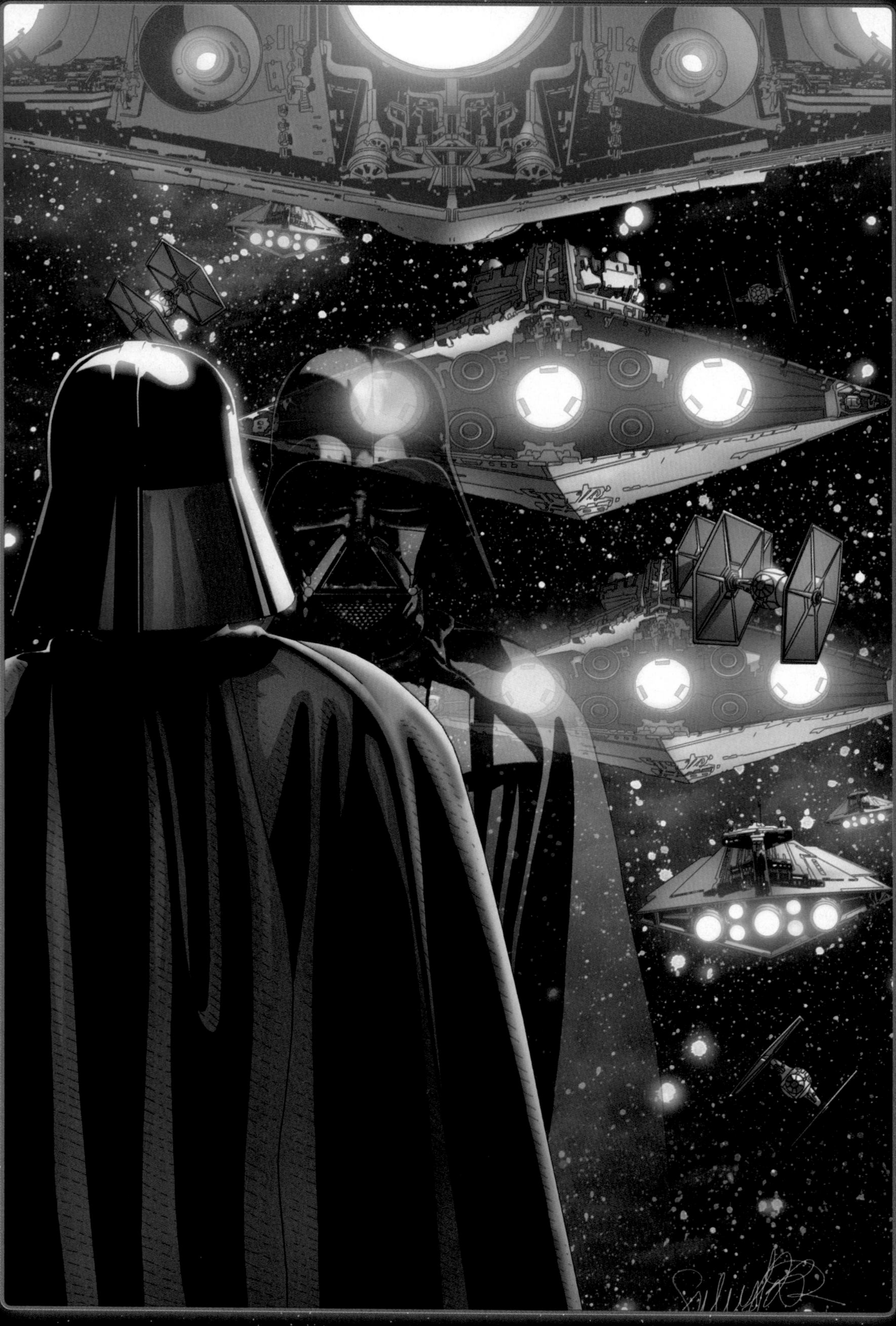

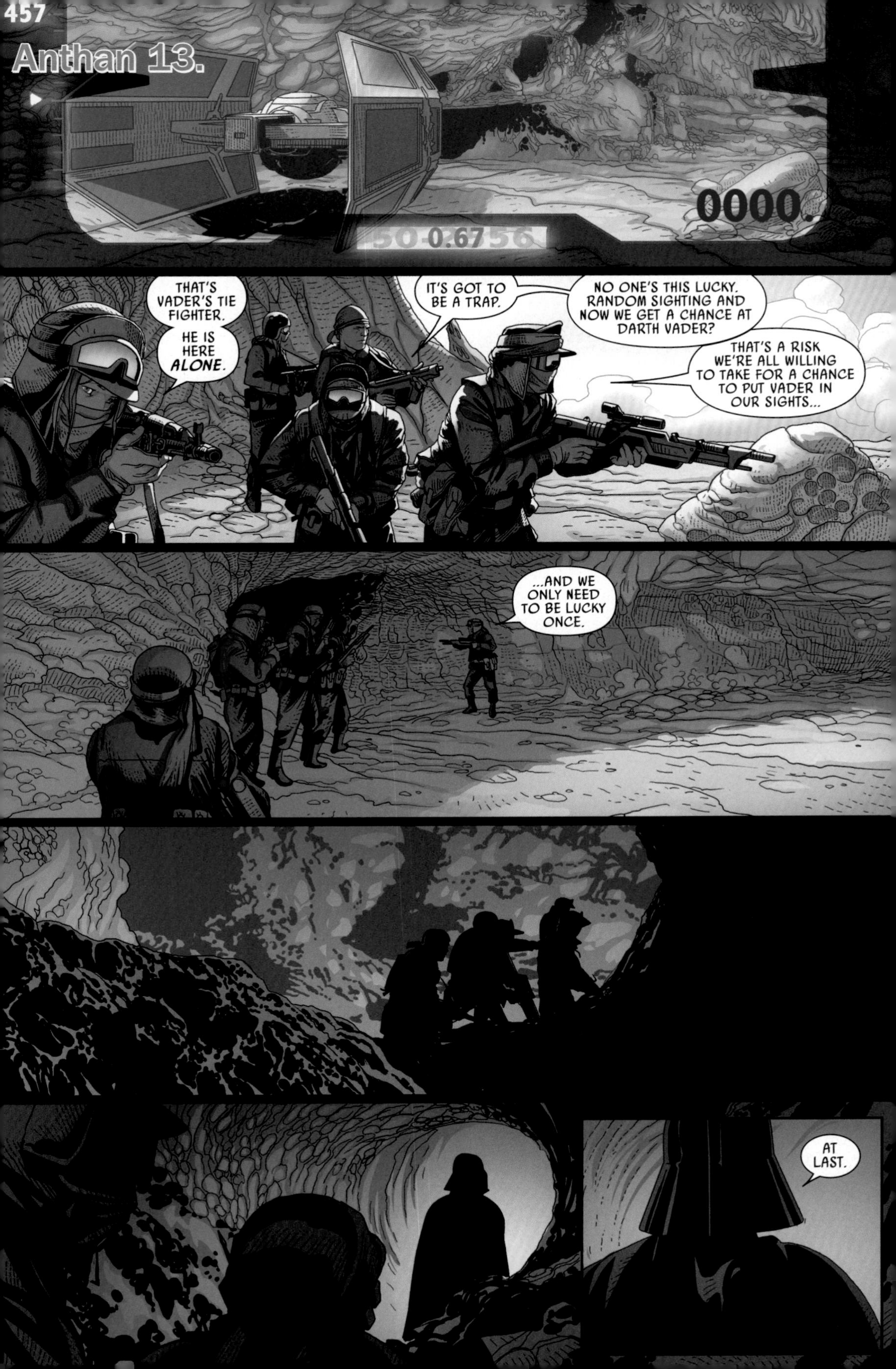
Anthan 13.
0000.
50 0.67 56
THAT'S VADER'S TIE FIGHTER.
HE IS HERE ALONE.
IT'S GOT TO BE A TRAP.
NO ONE'S THIS LUCKY. RANDOM SIGHTING AND NOW WE GET A CHANCE AT DARTH VADER?
THAT'S A RISK WE'RE ALL WILLING TO TAKE FOR A CHANCE TO PUT VADER IN OUR SIGHTS...
...AND WE ONLY NEED TO BE LUCKY ONCE.
AT LAST.

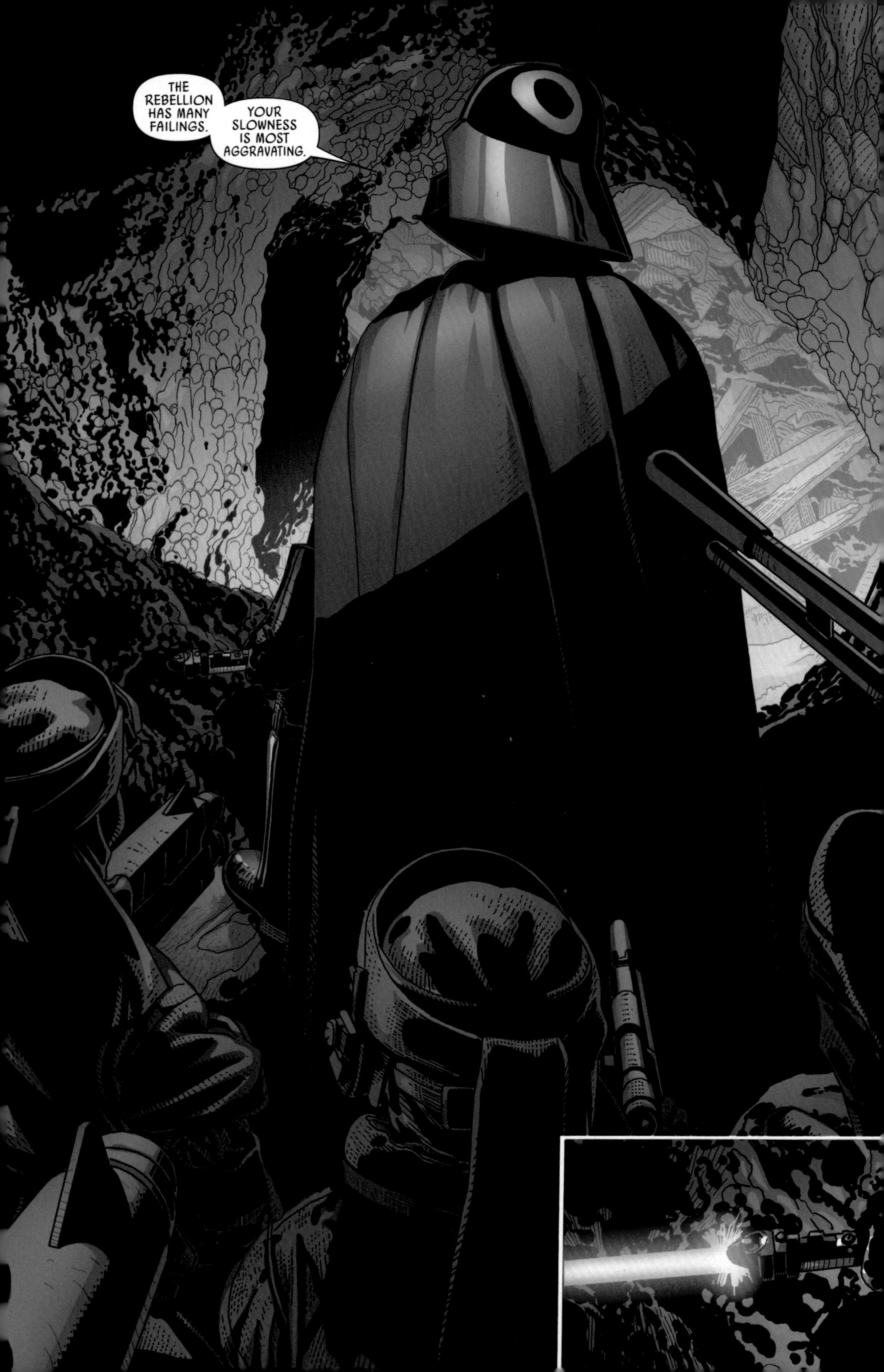
THE REBELLION HAS MANY FAILINGS.
YOUR SLOWNESS IS MOST AGGRAVATING.

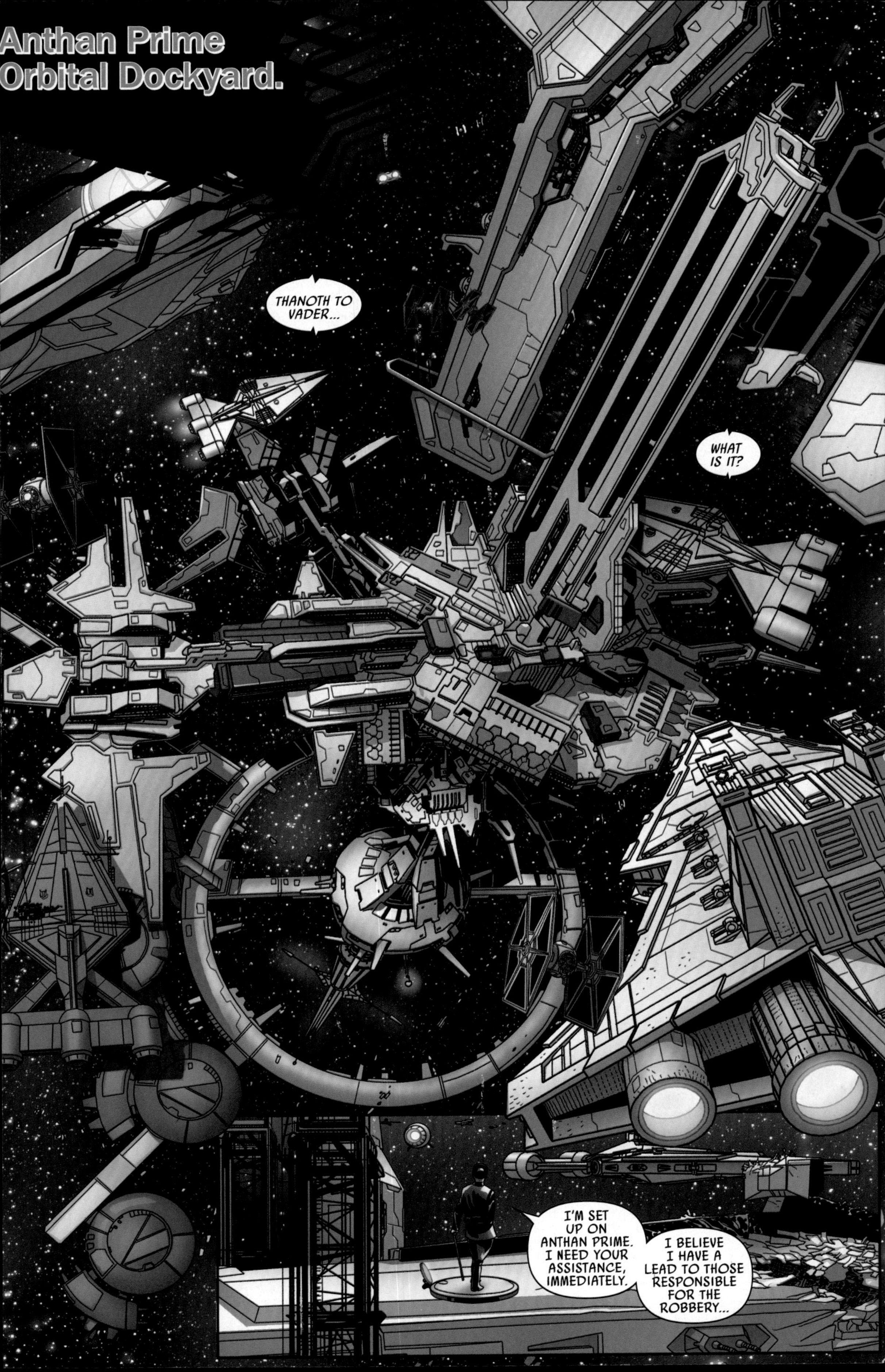
Anthan Prime
Orbital Dockyard.
THANOTH TO VADER...
WHAT IS IT?
I'M SET UP ON ANTHAN PRIME. I NEED YOUR ASSISTANCE, IMMEDIATELY.
I BELIEVE I HAVE A LEAD TO THOSE RESPONSIBLE FOR THE ROBBERY...

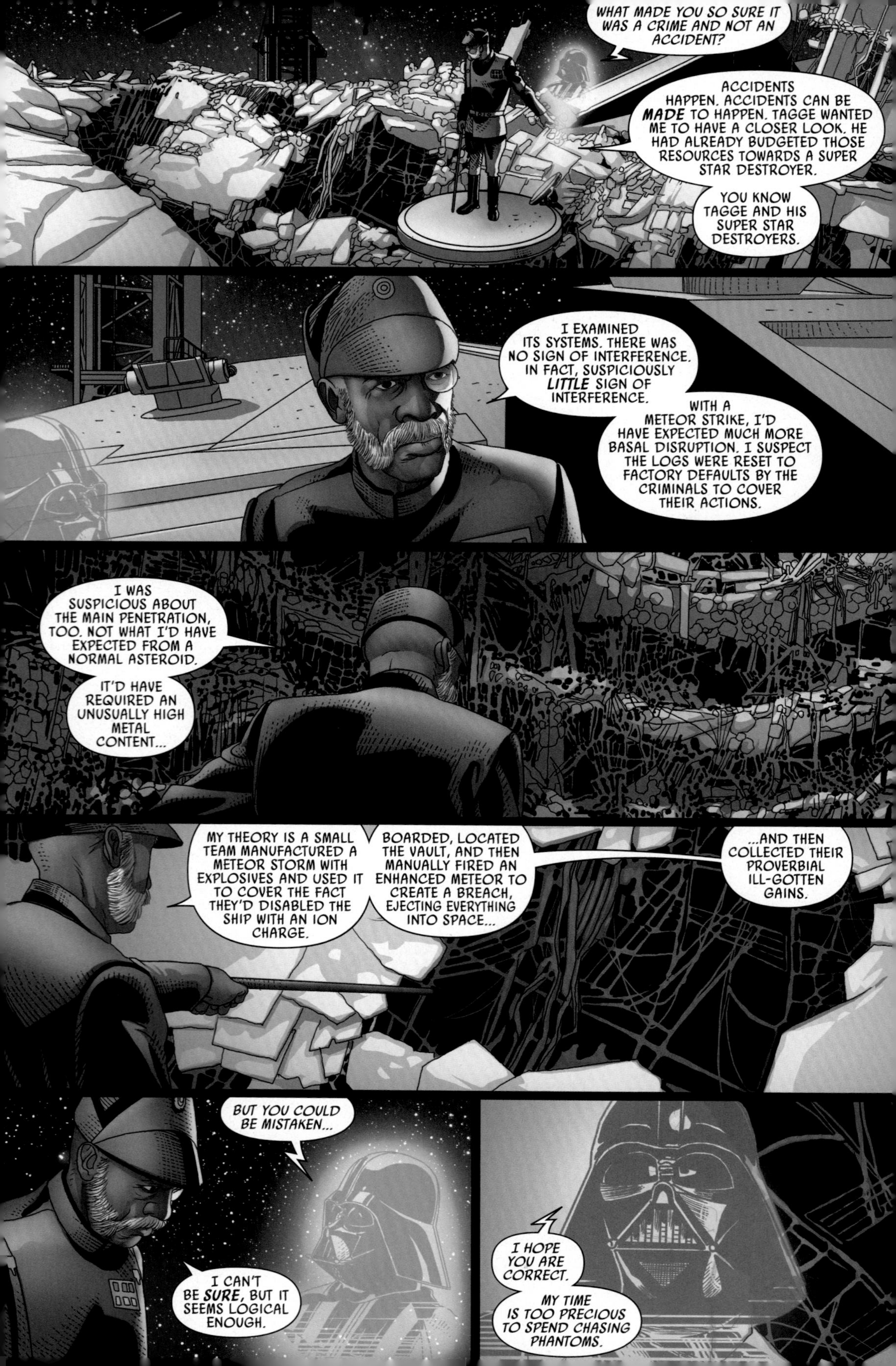
WHAT MADE YOU SO SURE IT WAS A CRIME AND NOT AN ACCIDENT?
ACCIDENTS HAPPEN. ACCIDENTS CAN BE MADE TO HAPPEN. TAGGE WANTED ME TO HAVE A CLOSER LOOK. HE HAD ALREADY BUDGETED THOSE RESOURCES TOWARDS A SUPER STAR DESTROYER.
YOU KNOW TAGGE AND HIS SUPER STAR DESTROYERS.
I EXAMINED ITS SYSTEMS. THERE WAS NO SIGN OF INTERFERENCE. IN FACT, SUSPICIOUSLY LITTLE SIGN OF INTERFERENCE.
WITH A METEOR STRIKE, I'D HAVE EXPECTED MUCH MORE BASAL DISRUPTION. I SUSPECT THE LOGS WERE RESET TO FACTORY DEFAULTS BY THE CRIMINALS TO COVER THEIR ACTIONS.
I WAS SUSPICIOUS ABOUT THE MAIN PENETRATION, TOO. NOT WHAT I'D HAVE EXPECTED FROM A NORMAL ASTEROID.
IT'D HAVE REQUIRED AN UNUSUALLY HIGH METAL CONTENT...
MY THEORY IS A SMALL TEAM MANUFACTURED A METEOR STORM WITH EXPLOSIVES AND USED IT TO COVER THE FACT THEY'D DISABLED THE SHIP WITH AN ION CHARGE.
BOARDED, LOCATED THE VAULT, AND THEN MANUALLY FIRED AN ENHANCED METEOR TO CREATE A BREACH, EJECTING EVERYTHING INTO SPACE...
...AND THEN COLLECTED THEIR PROVERBIAL ILL-GOTTEN GAINS.
BUT YOU COULD BE MISTAKEN...
I CAN'T BE SURE, BUT IT SEEMS LOGICAL ENOUGH.
I HOPE YOU ARE CORRECT.
MY TIME IS TOO PRECIOUS TO SPEND CHASING PHANTOMS.

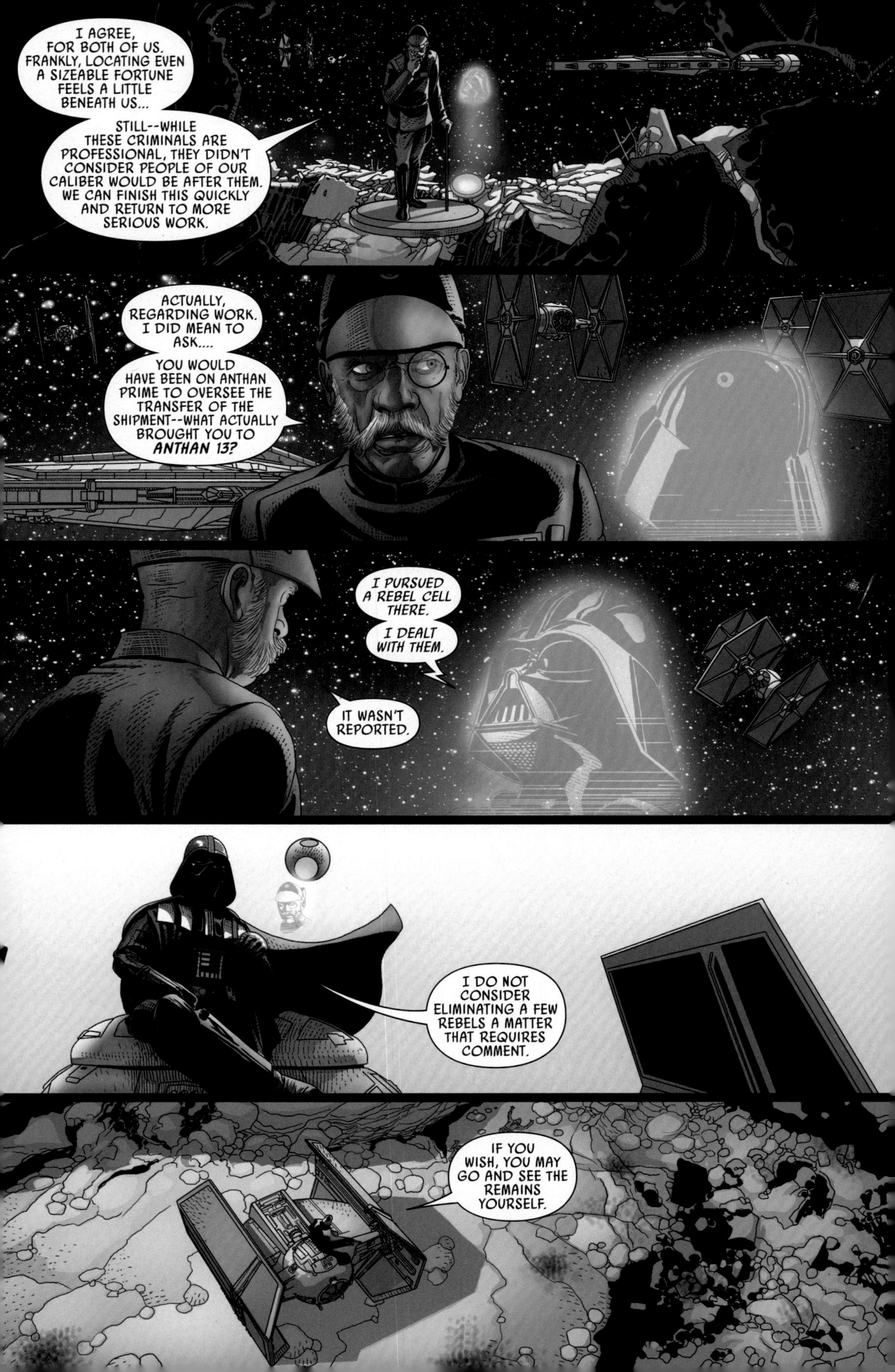
I AGREE, FOR BOTH OF US. FRANKLY, LOCATING EVEN A SIZEABLE FORTUNE FEELS A LITTLE BENEATH US...
STILL--WHILE THESE CRIMINALS ARE PROFESSIONAL, THEY DIDN'T CONSIDER PEOPLE OF OUR CALIBER WOULD BE AFTER THEM. WE CAN FINISH THIS QUICKLY AND RETURN TO MORE SERIOUS WORK.
ACTUALLY, REGARDING WORK. I DID MEAN TO ASK....
YOU WOULD HAVE BEEN ON ANTHAN PRIME TO OVERSEE THE TRANSFER OF THE SHIPMENT--WHAT ACTUALLY BROUGHT YOU TO ANTHAN 13?
I PURSUED A REBEL CELL THERE.
I DEALT WITH THEM.
IT WASN'T REPORTED.
I DO NOT CONSIDER ELIMINATING A FEW REBELS A MATTER THAT REQUIRES COMMENT.
IF YOU WISH, YOU MAY GO AND SEE THE REMAINS YOURSELF.

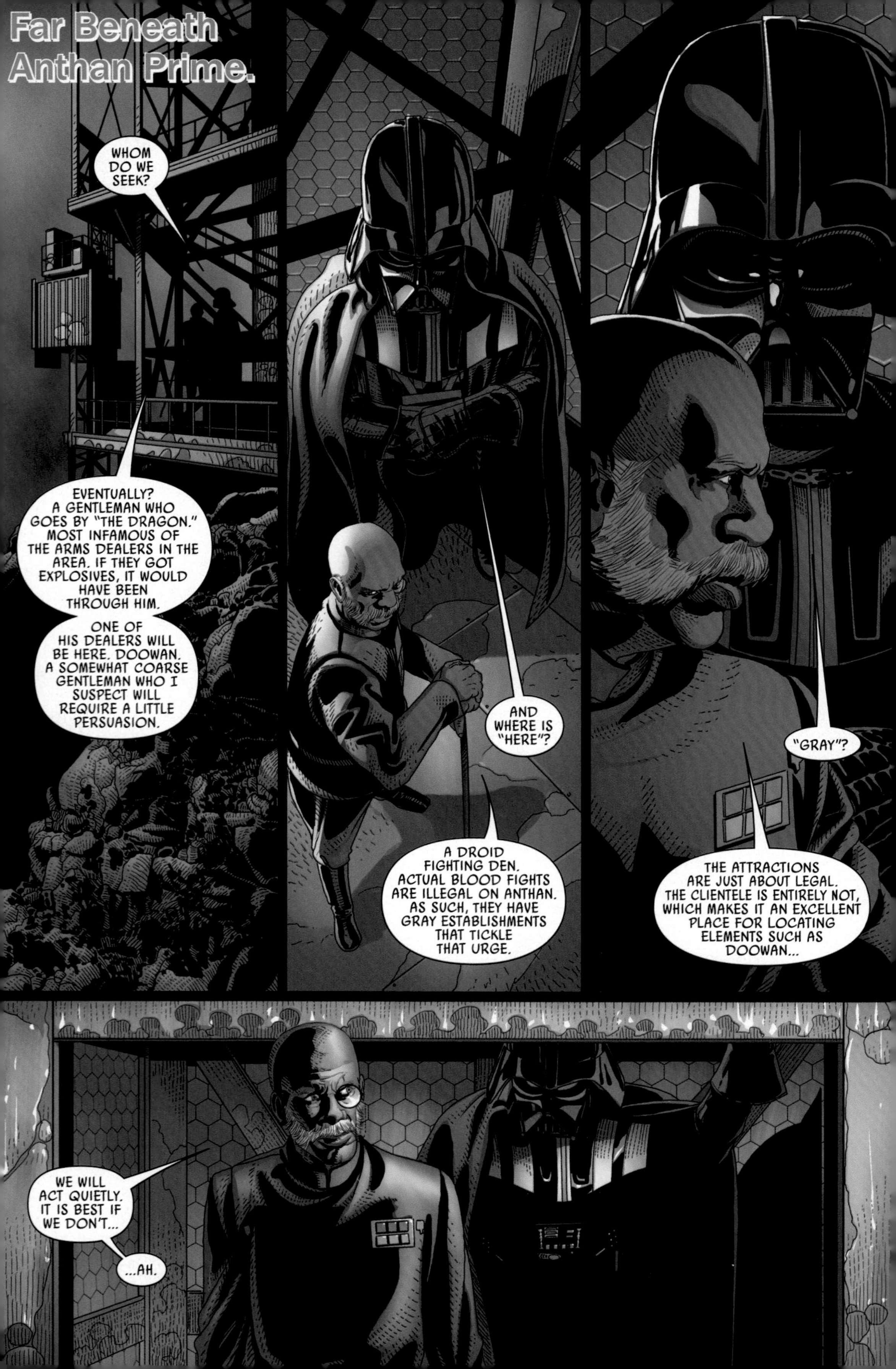
Far Beneath Anthan Prime.
WHOM DO WE SEEK?
EVENTUALLY? A GENTLEMAN WHO GOES BY "THE DRAGON." MOST INFAMOUS OF THE ARMS DEALERS IN THE AREA. IF THEY GOT EXPLOSIVES, IT WOULD HAVE BEEN THROUGH HIM.
ONE OF HIS DEALERS WILL BE HERE. DOOWAN. A SOMEWHAT COARSE GENTLEMAN WHO I SUSPECT WILL REQUIRE A LITTLE PERSUASION.
AND WHERE IS "HERE"?
A DROID FIGHTING DEN. ACTUAL BLOOD FIGHTS ARE ILLEGAL ON ANTHAN. AS SUCH, THEY HAVE GRAY ESTABLISHMENTS THAT TICKLE THAT URGE.
"GRAY"?
THE ATTRACTIONS ARE JUST ABOUT LEGAL. THE CLIENTELE IS ENTIRELY NOT, WHICH MAKES IT AN EXCELLENT PLACE FOR LOCATING ELEMENTS SUCH AS DOOWAN...
WE WILL ACT QUIETLY. IT IS BEST IF WE DON'T...
...AH.

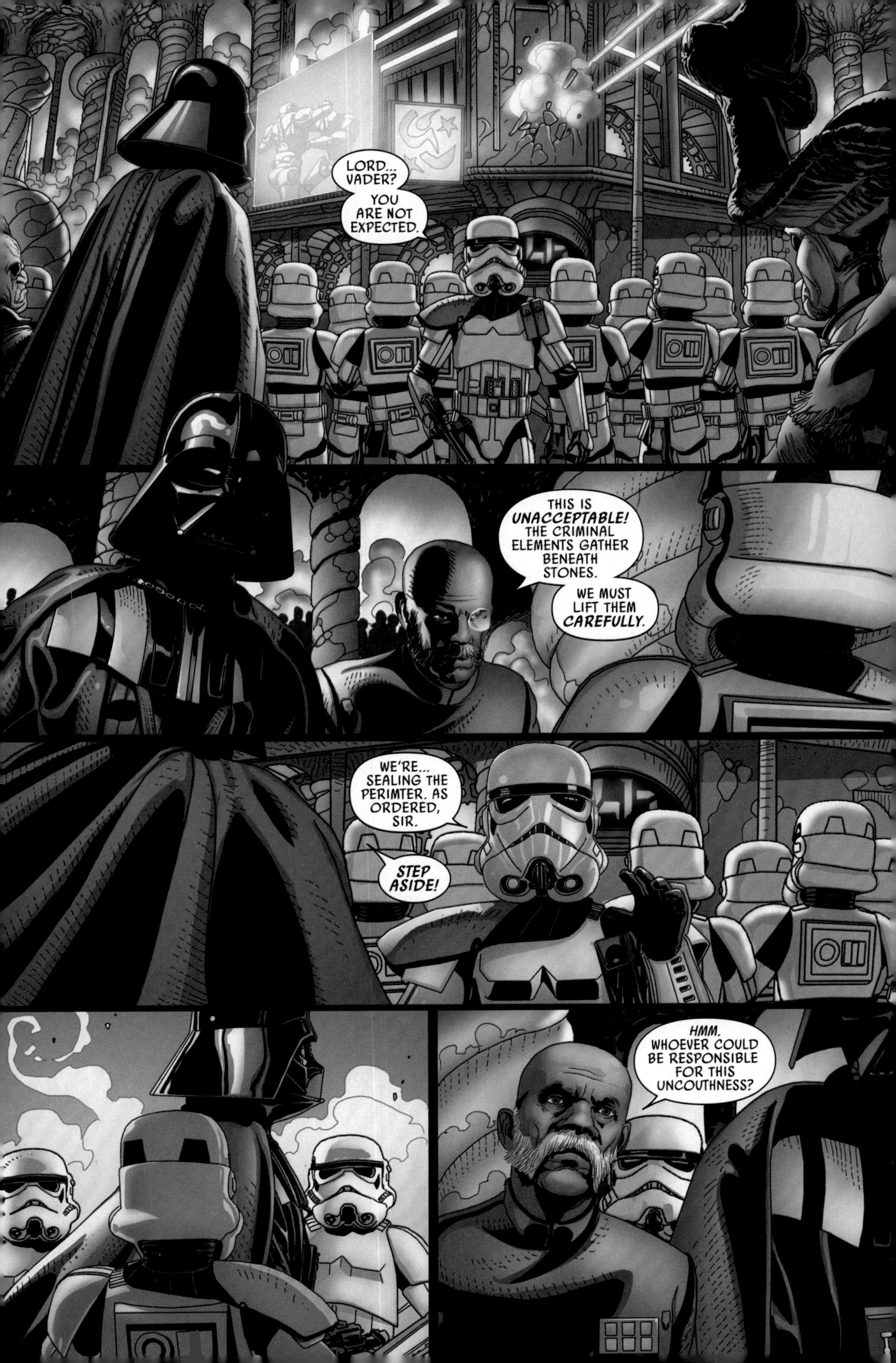
LORD... VADER?
YOU ARE NOT EXPECTED.
THIS IS UNACCEPTABLE! THE CRIMINAL ELEMENTS GATHER BENEATH STONES.
WE MUST LIFT THEM CAREFULLY.
WE'RE... SEALING THE PERIMTER. AS ORDERED, SIR.
STEP ASIDE!
HMM. WHOEVER COULD BE RESPONSIBLE FOR THIS UNCOUTHNESS?

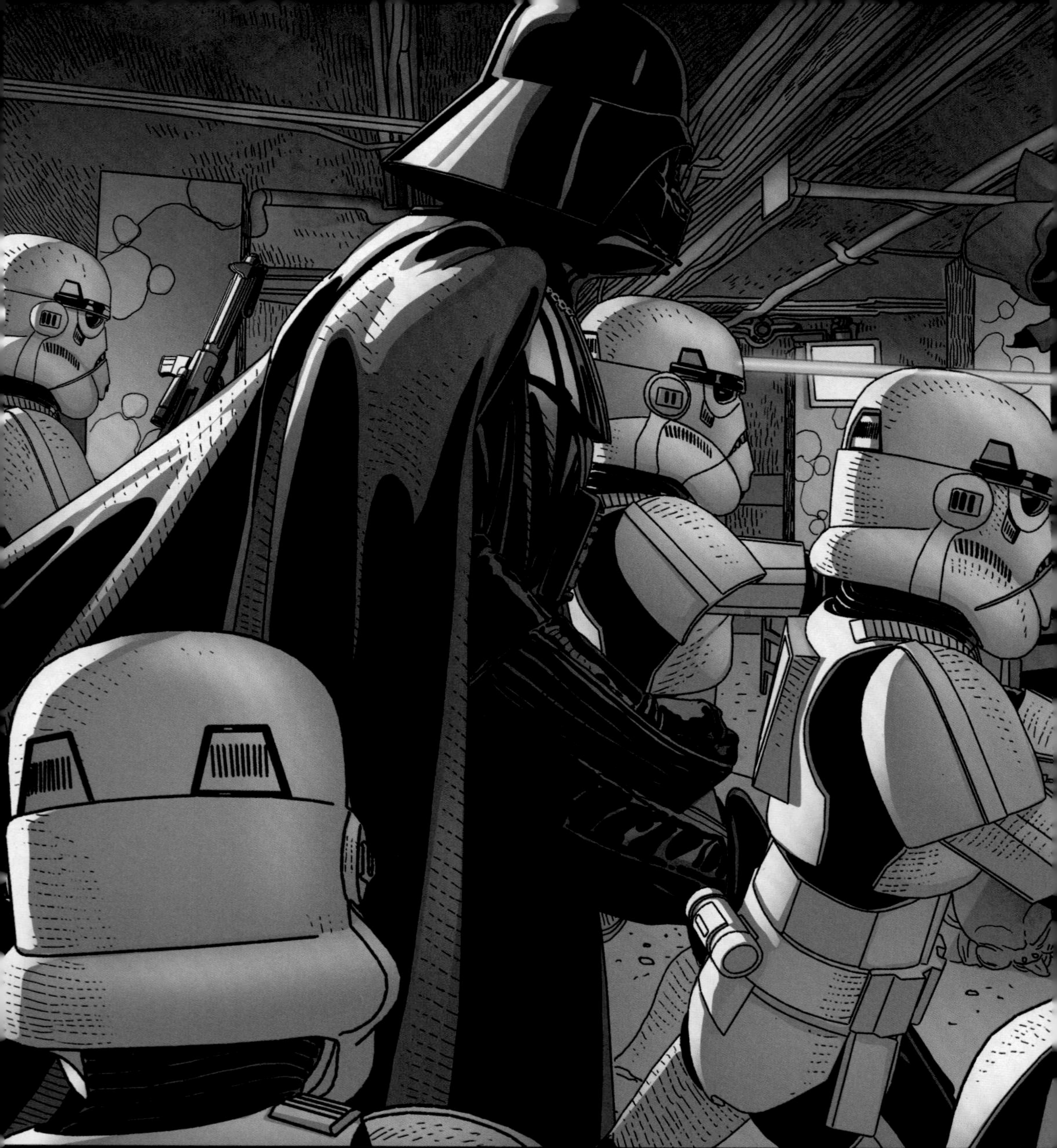

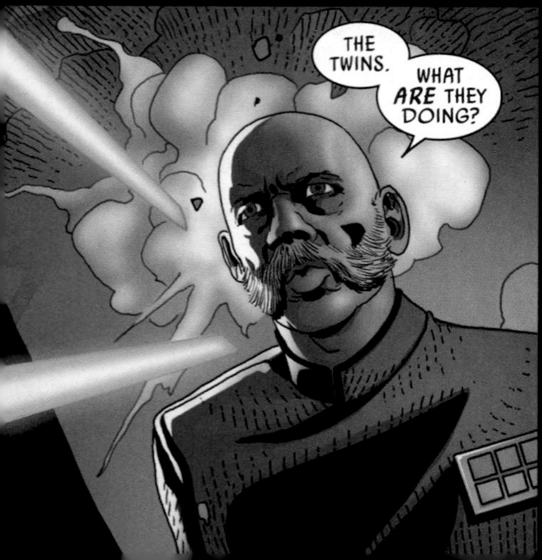
THE TWINS.
WHAT ARE THEY DOING?

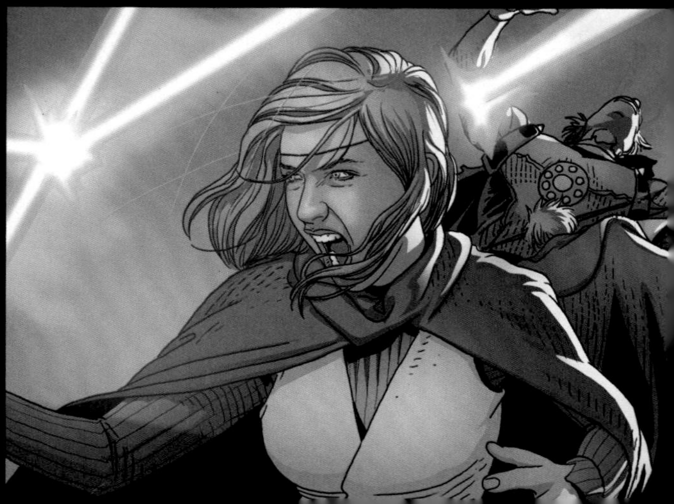

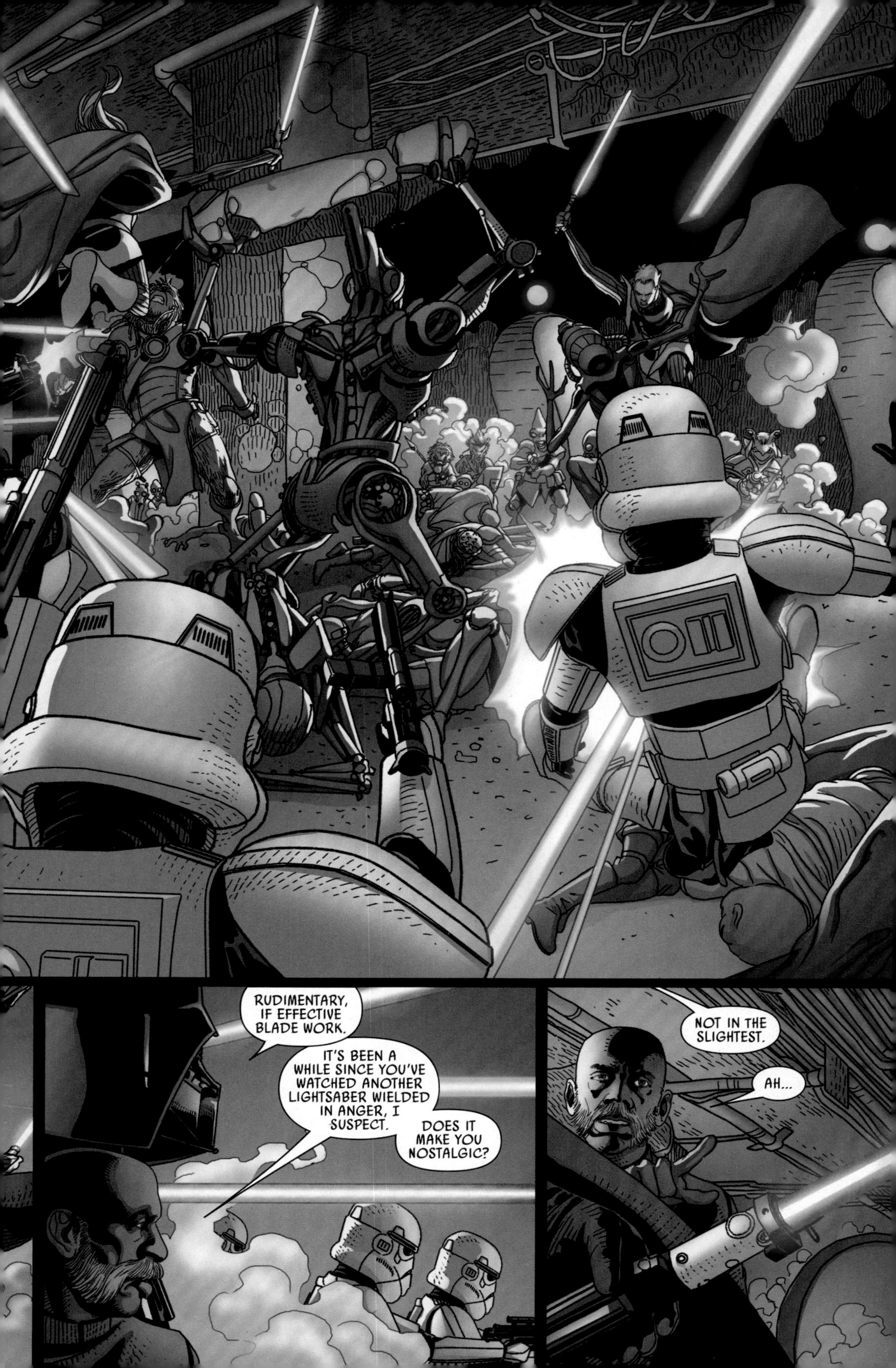
RUDIMENTARY, IF EFFECTIVE BLADE WORK.
IT'S BEEN A WHILE SINCE YOU'VE WATCHED ANOTHER LIGHTSABER WIELDED IN ANGER, I SUSPECT.
DOES IT MAKE YOU NOSTALGIC?
NOT IN THE SLIGHTEST.
AH...

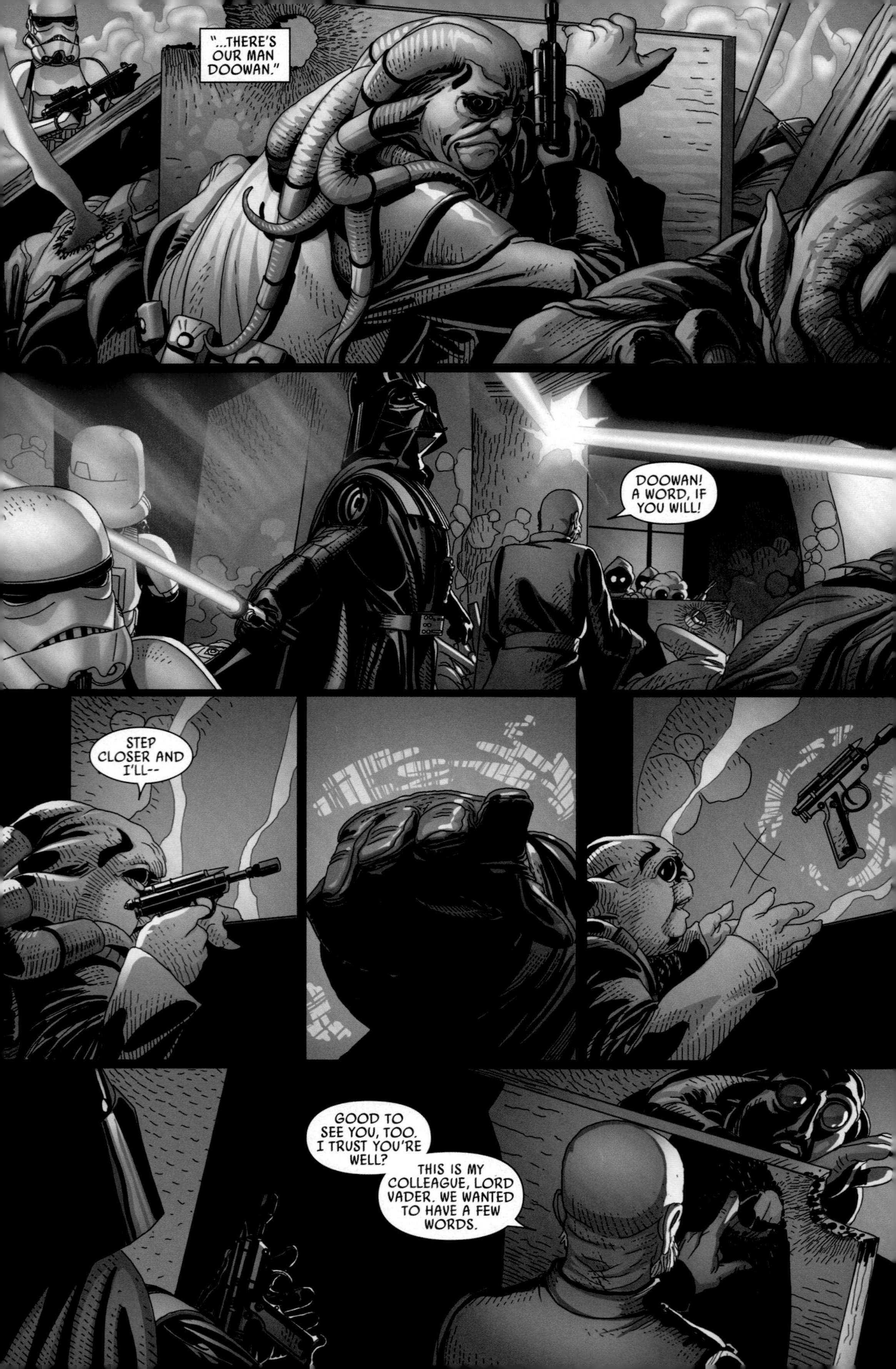
"...THERE'S OUR MAN DOOWAN."
DOOWAN! A WORD, IF YOU WILL!
STEP CLOSER AND I'LL--
GOOD TO SEE YOU, TOO. I TRUST YOU'RE WELL?
THIS IS MY COLLEAGUE, LORD VADER. WE WANTED TO HAVE A FEW WORDS.

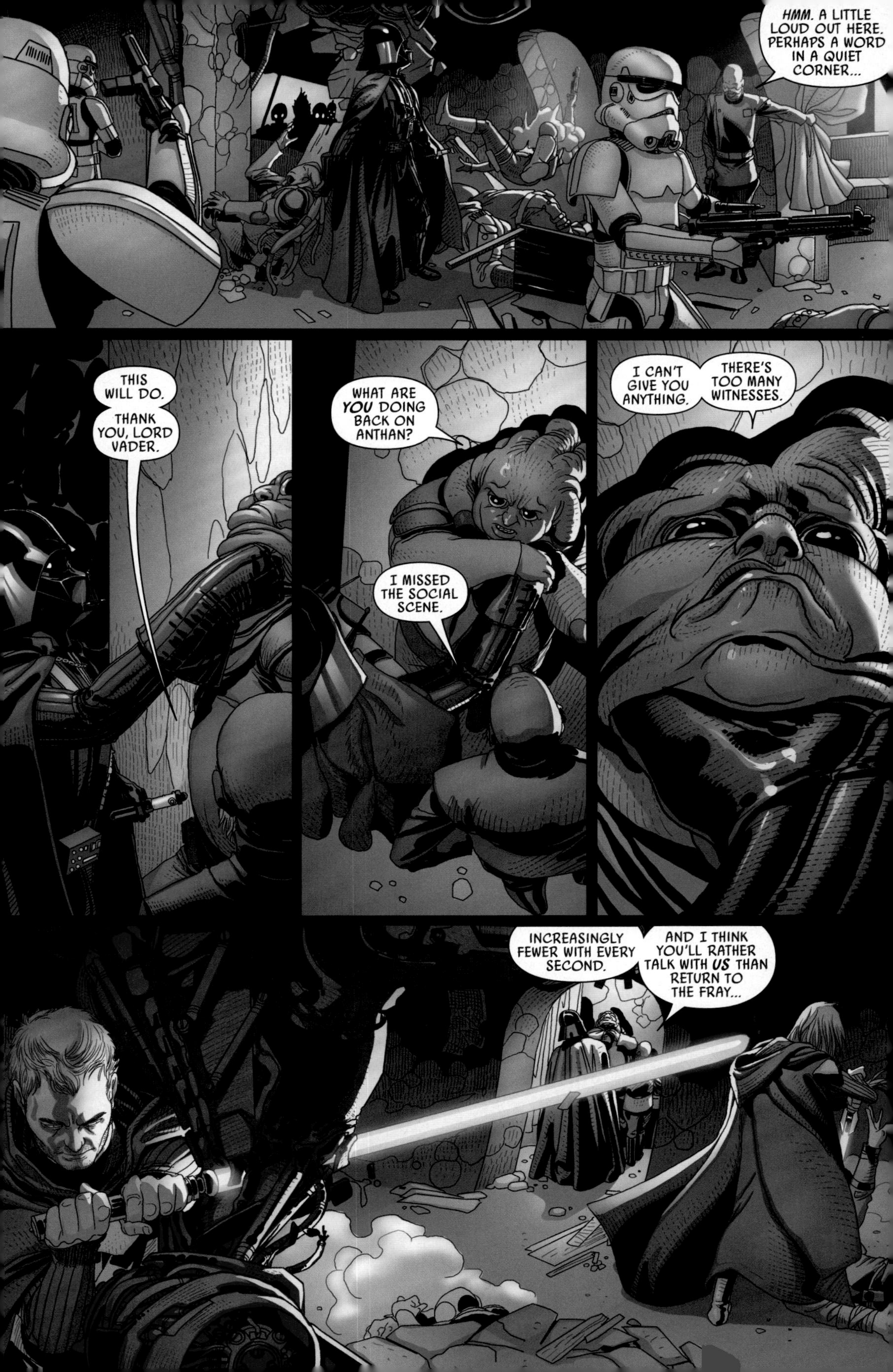
HMM. A LITTLE LOUD OUT HERE. PERHAPS A WORD IN A QUIET CORNER...
THIS WILL DO.
THANK YOU, LORD VADER.
WHAT ARE YOU DOING BACK ON ANTHAN?
I MISSED THE SOCIAL SCENE.
I CAN'T GIVE YOU ANYTHING.
THERE'S TOO MANY WITNESSES.
INCREASINGLY FEWER WITH EVERY SECOND.
AND I THINK YOU'LL RATHER TALK WITH US THAN RETURN TO THE FRAY...

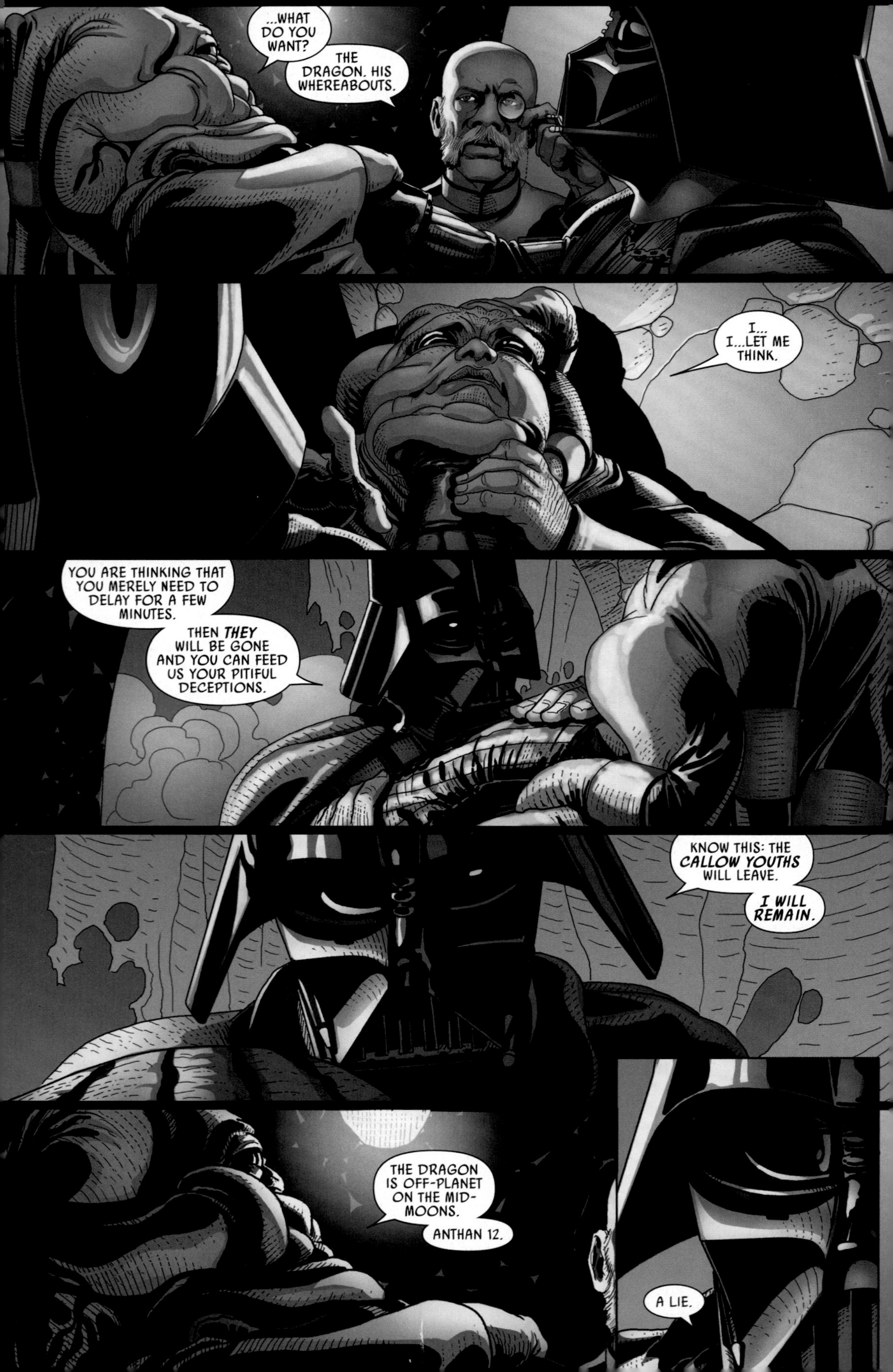
...WHAT DO YOU WANT?
THE DRAGON. HIS WHEREABOUTS.
I... I...LET ME THINK.
YOU ARE THINKING THAT YOU MERELY NEED TO DELAY FOR A FEW MINUTES.
THEN THEY WILL BE GONE AND YOU CAN FEED US YOUR PITIFUL DECEPTIONS.
KNOW THIS: THE CALLOW YOUTHS WILL LEAVE.
I WILL REMAIN.
THE DRAGON IS OFF-PLANET ON THE MID-MOONS.
ANTHAN 12.
A LIE.

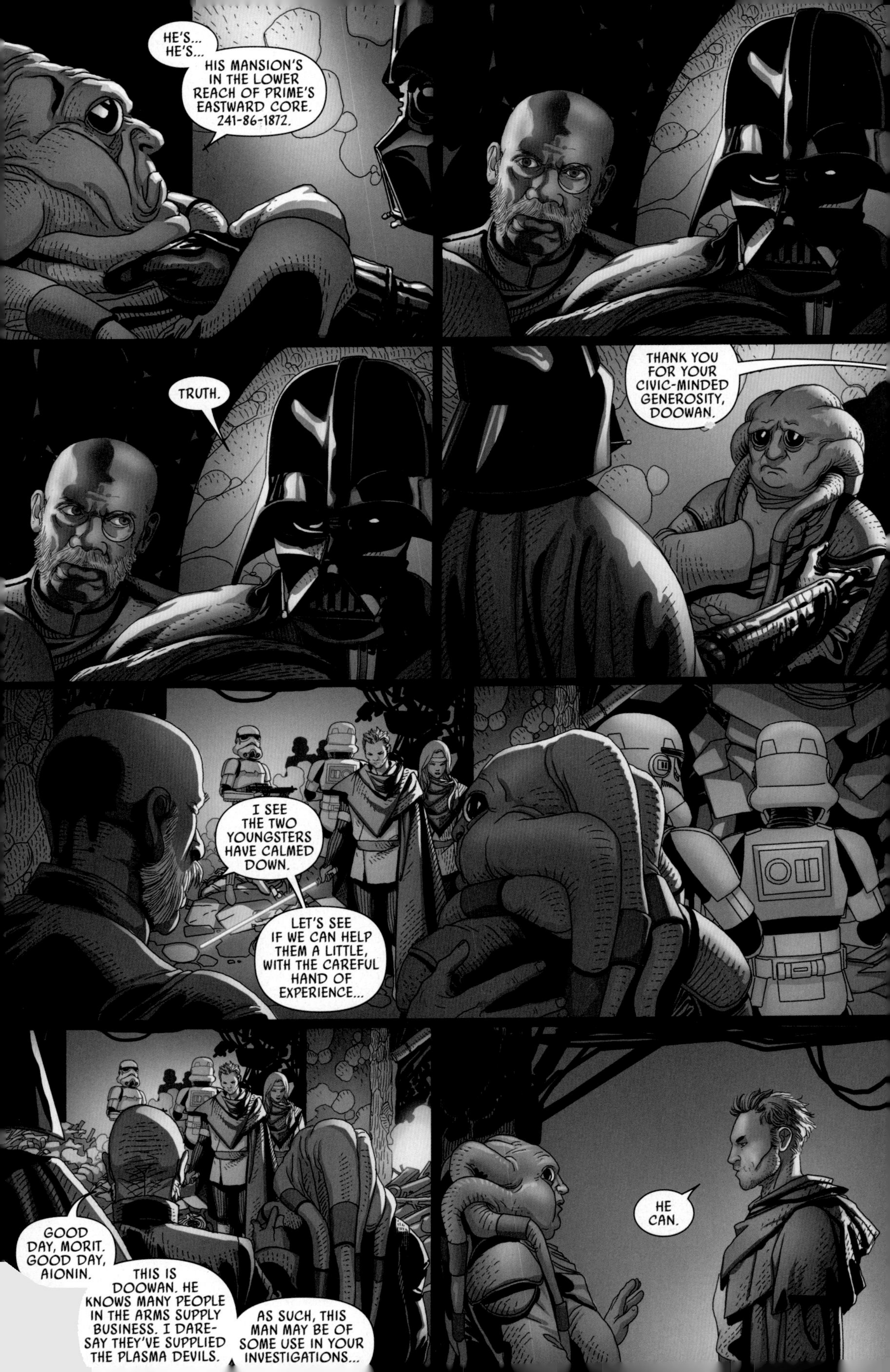
HE'S... HE'S...
HIS MANSION'S IN THE LOWER REACH OF PRIME'S EASTWARD CORE. 241-86-1872.
TRUTH.
THANK YOU FOR YOUR CIVIC-MINDED GENEROSITY, DOOWAN.
I SEE THE TWO YOUNGSTERS HAVE CALMED DOWN.
LET'S SEE IF WE CAN HELP THEM A LITTLE, WITH THE CAREFUL HAND OF EXPERIENCE...
GOOD DAY, MORIT. GOOD DAY, AIONIN.
THIS IS DOOWAN. HE KNOWS MANY PEOPLE IN THE ARMS SUPPLY BUSINESS. I DARE-SAY THEY'VE SUPPLIED THE PLASMA DEVILS.
AS SUCH, THIS MAN MAY BE OF SOME USE IN YOUR INVESTIGATIONS...
HE CAN.

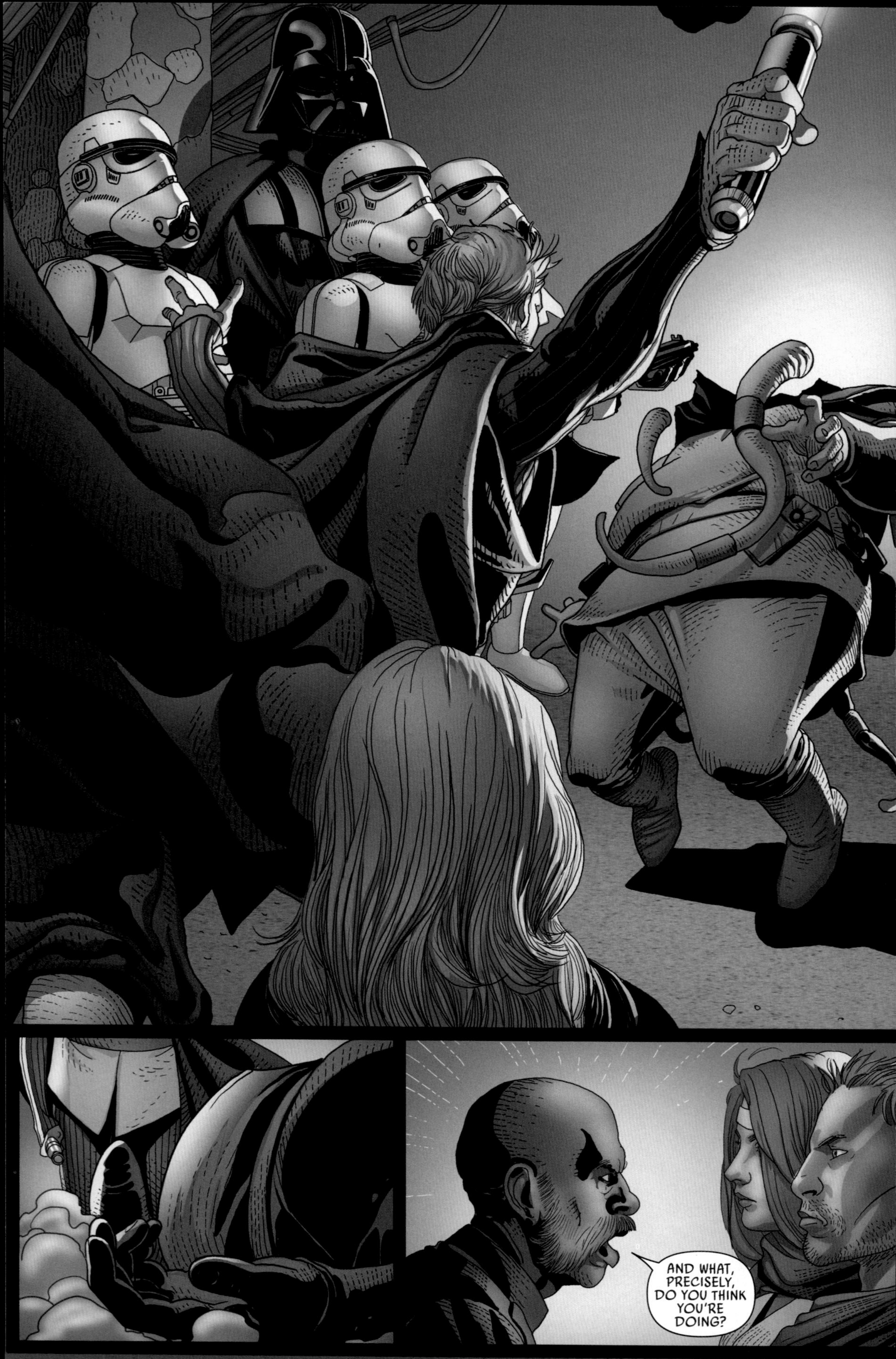
AND WHAT, PRECISELY, DO YOU THINK YOU'RE DOING?

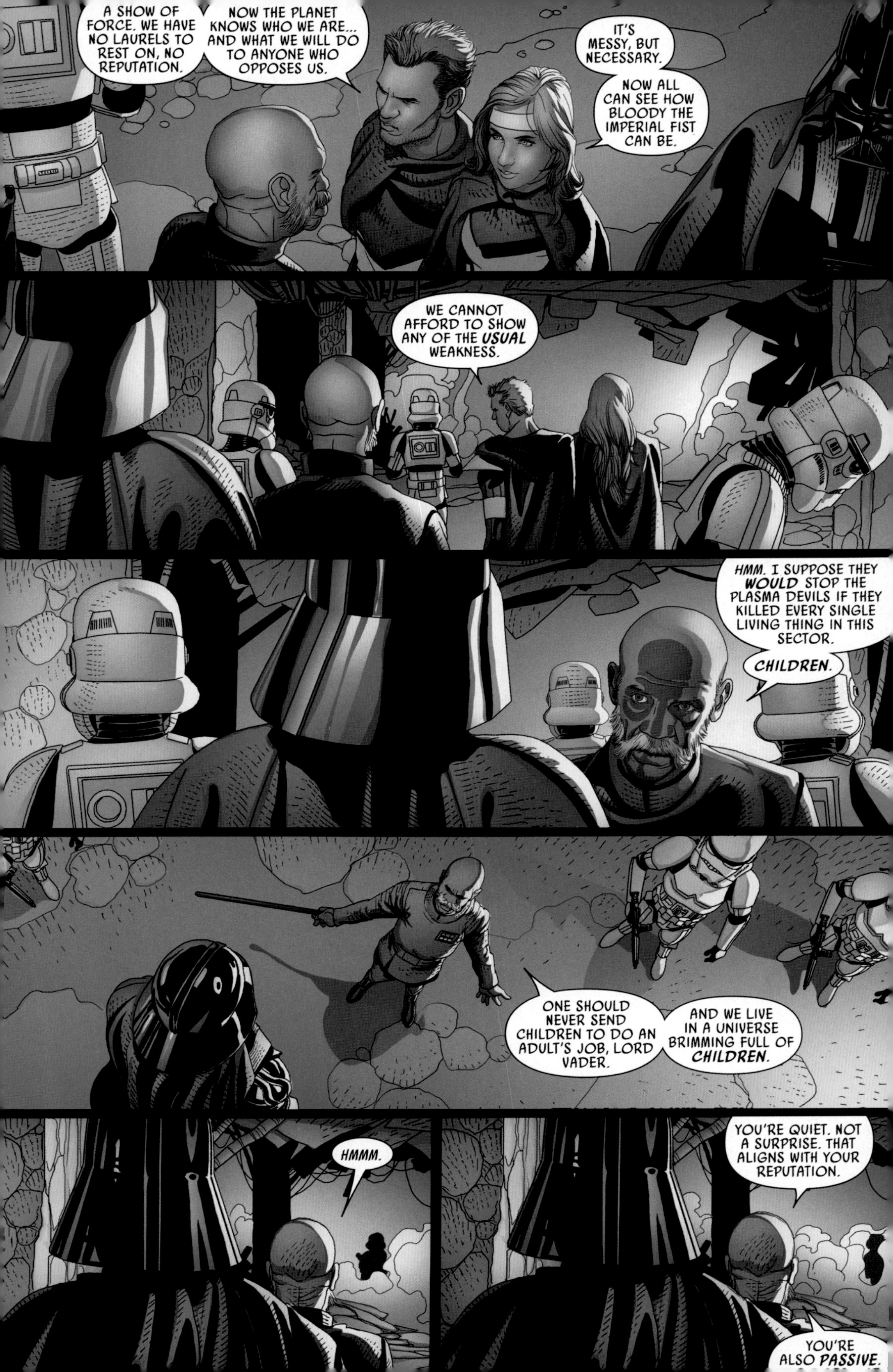
A SHOW OF FORCE. WE HAVE NO LAURELS TO REST ON, NO REPUTATION.
NOW THE PLANET KNOWS WHO WE ARE... AND WHAT WE WILL DO TO ANYONE WHO OPPOSES US.
IT'S MESSY, BUT NECESSARY.
NOW ALL CAN SEE HOW BLOODY THE IMPERIAL FIST CAN BE.
WE CANNOT AFFORD TO SHOW ANY OF THE *USUAL* WEAKNESS.
HMM. I SUPPOSE THEY **WOULD** STOP THE PLASMA DEVILS IF THEY KILLED EVERY SINGLE LIVING THING IN THIS SECTOR.
CHILDREN.
ONE SHOULD NEVER SEND CHILDREN TO DO AN ADULT'S JOB, LORD VADER.
AND WE LIVE IN A UNIVERSE BRIMMING FULL OF ***CHILDREN***.
HMMM.
YOU'RE QUIET. NOT A SURPRISE. THAT ALIGNS WITH YOUR REPUTATION.
YOU'RE ALSO ***PASSIVE***.

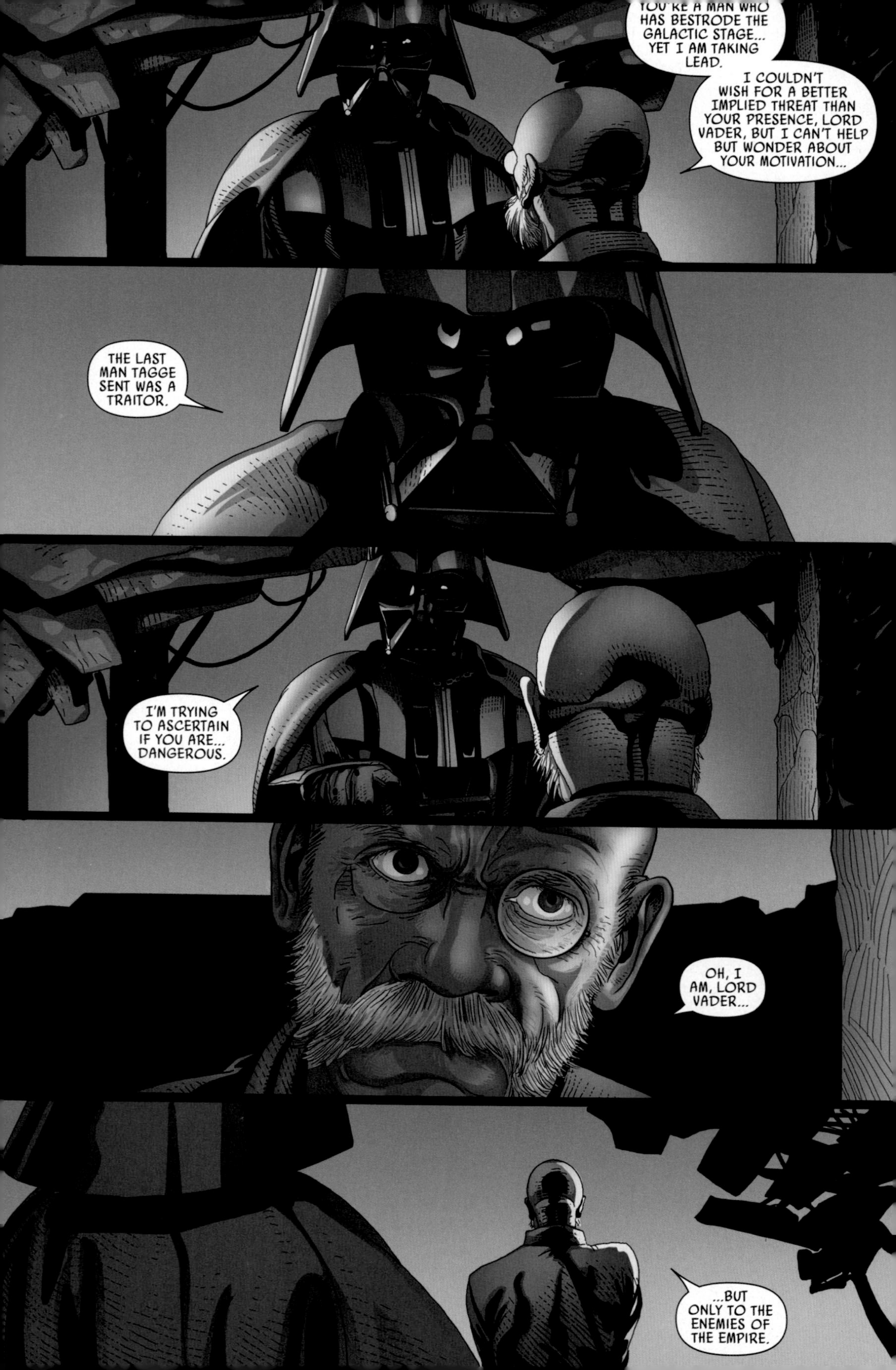
YOU'RE A MAN WHO HAS BESTRODE THE GALACTIC STAGE... YET I AM TAKING LEAD.
I COULDN'T WISH FOR A BETTER IMPLIED THREAT THAN YOUR PRESENCE, LORD VADER, BUT I CAN'T HELP BUT WONDER ABOUT YOUR MOTIVATION...
THE LAST MAN TAGGE SENT WAS A TRAITOR.
I'M TRYING TO ASCERTAIN IF YOU ARE... DANGEROUS.
OH, I AM, LORD VADER...
...BUT ONLY TO THE ENEMIES OF THE EMPIRE.

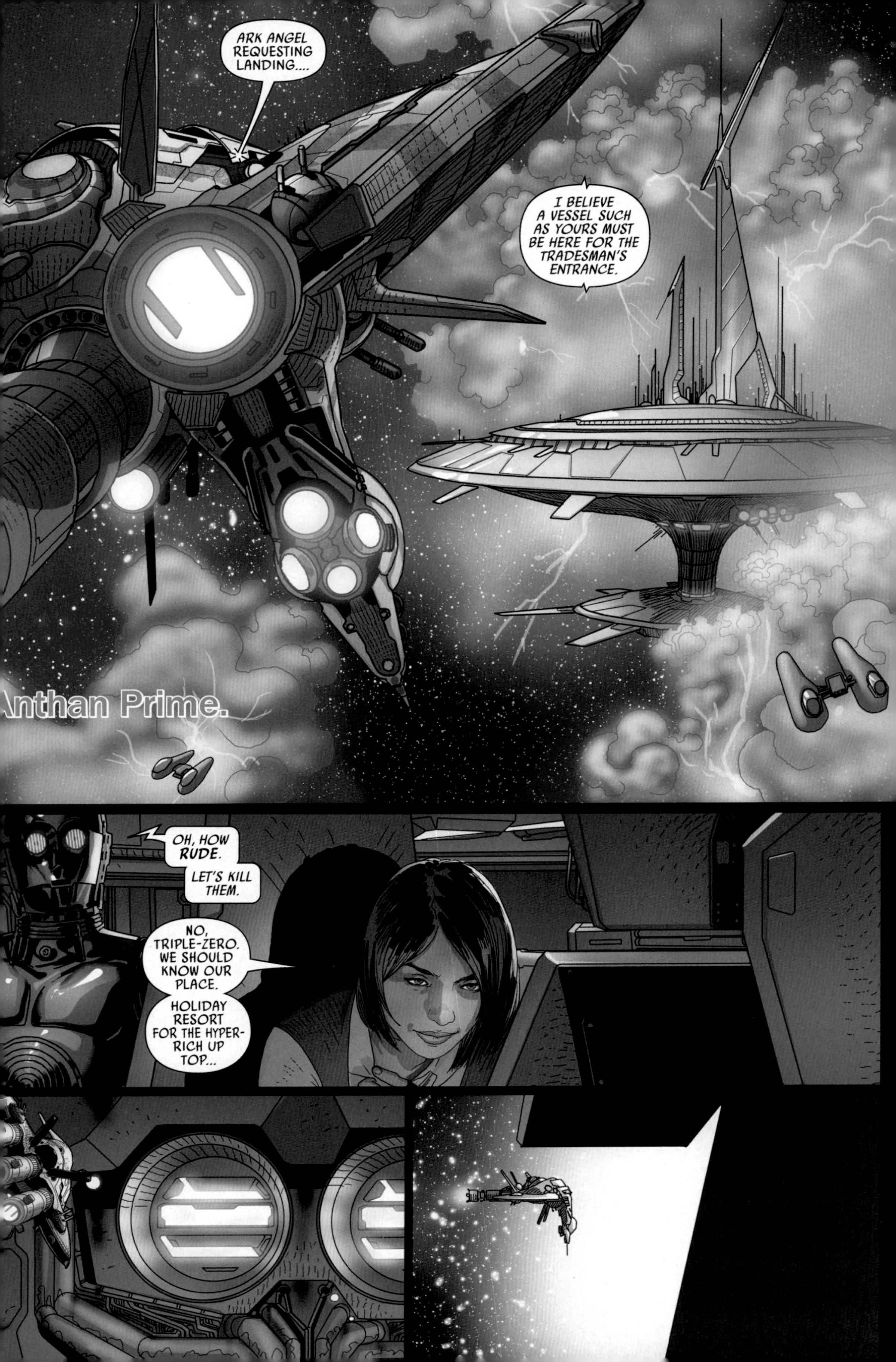
ARK ANGEL REQUESTING LANDING....
I BELIEVE A VESSEL SUCH AS YOURS MUST BE HERE FOR THE TRADESMAN'S ENTRANCE.
Anthan Prime.
OH, HOW RUDE.
LET'S KILL THEM.
NO, TRIPLE-ZERO. WE SHOULD KNOW OUR PLACE.
HOLIDAY RESORT FOR THE HYPER-RICH UP TOP...

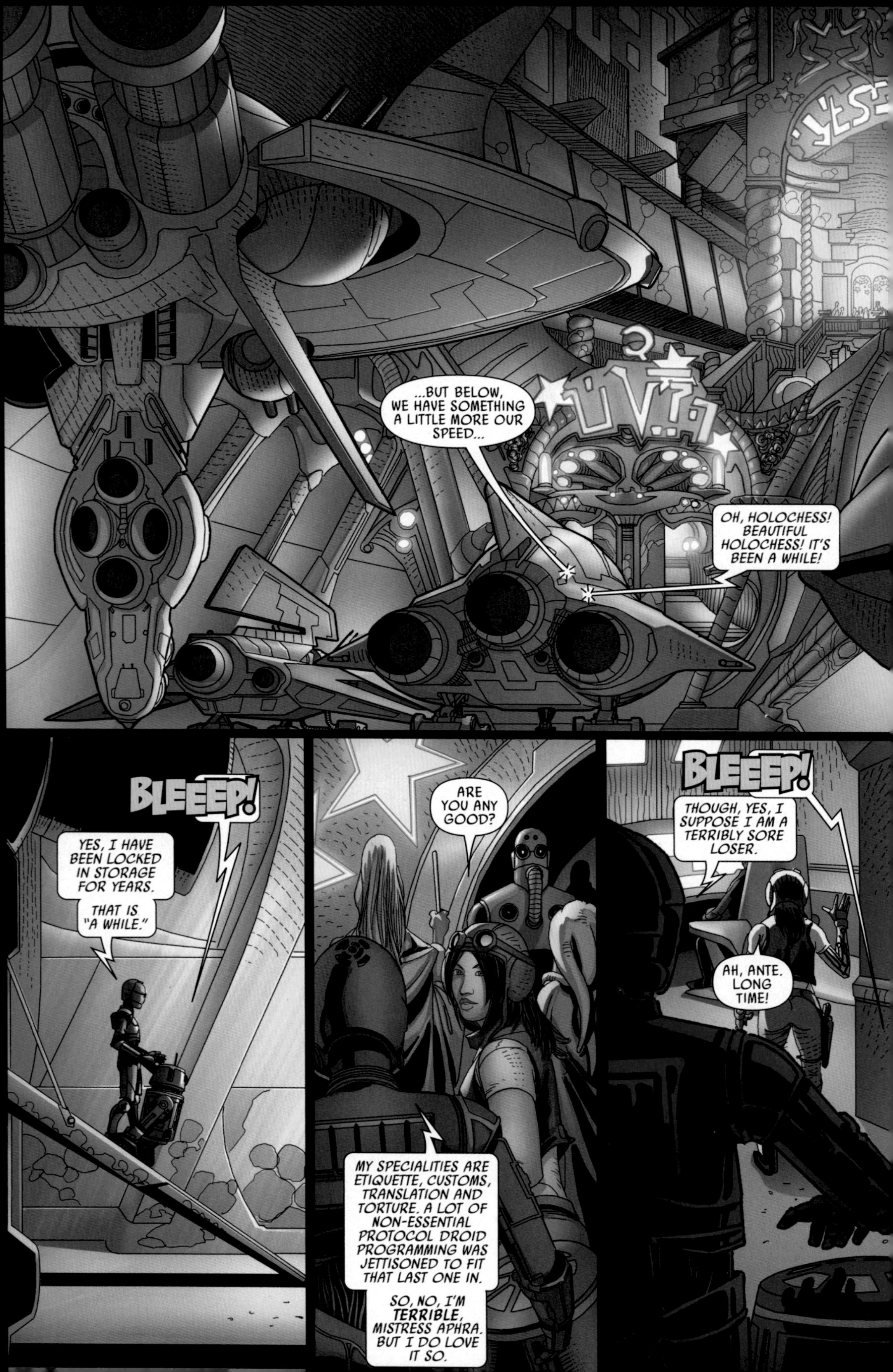
...BUT BELOW, WE HAVE SOMETHING A LITTLE MORE OUR SPEED...
OH, HOLOCHESS! BEAUTIFUL HOLOCHESS! IT'S BEEN A WHILE!
BLEEEP!
YES, I HAVE BEEN LOCKED IN STORAGE FOR YEARS.
THAT IS "A WHILE."
ARE YOU ANY GOOD?
MY SPECIALITIES ARE ETIQUETTE, CUSTOMS, TRANSLATION AND TORTURE. A LOT OF NON-ESSENTIAL PROTOCOL DROID PROGRAMMING WAS JETTISONED TO FIT THAT LAST ONE IN.
SO, NO, I'M TERRIBLE, MISTRESS APHRA. BUT I DO LOVE IT SO.
BLEEEP!
THOUGH, YES, I SUPPOSE I AM A TERRIBLY SORE LOSER.
AH, ANTE. LONG TIME!

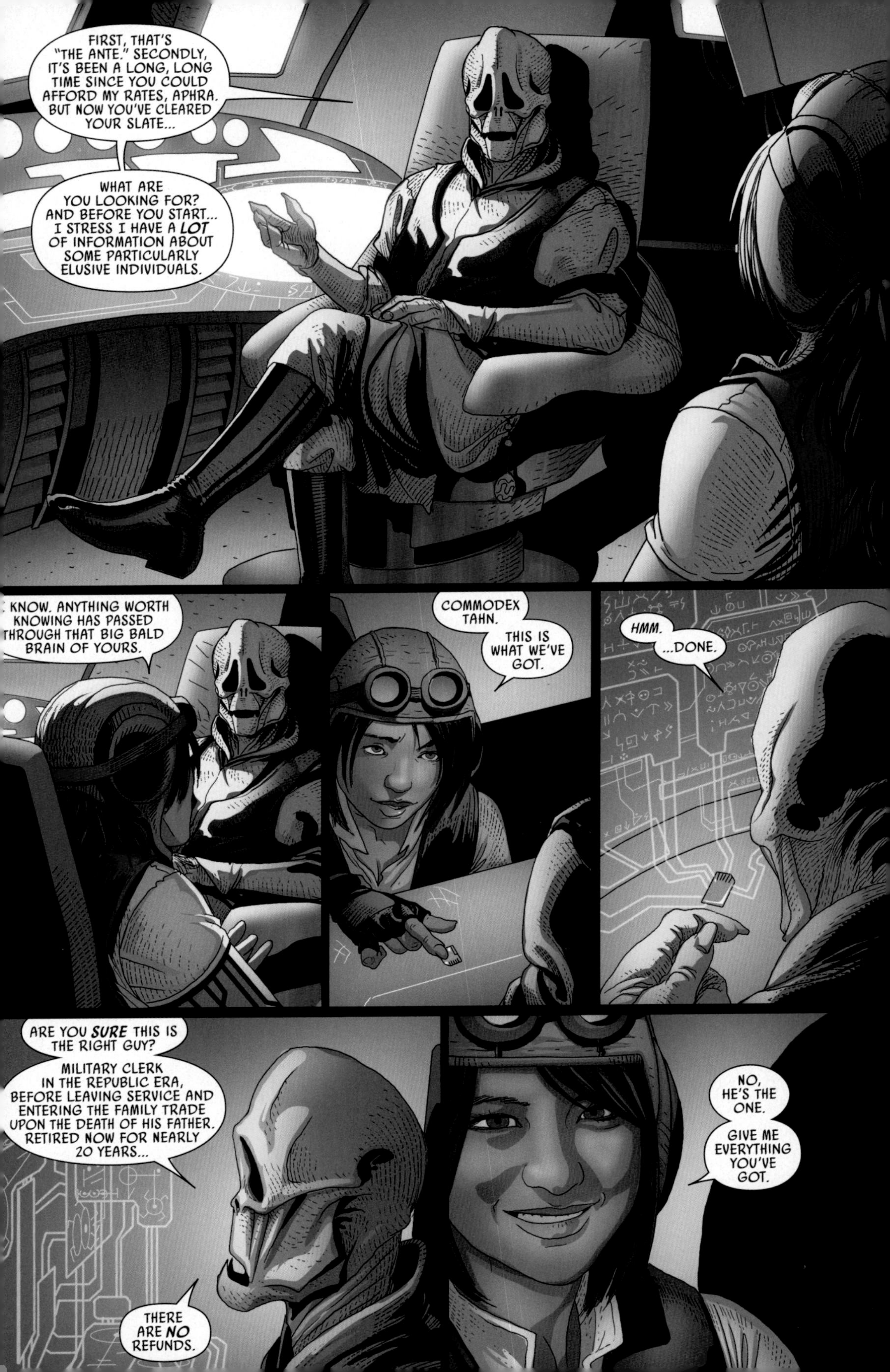
FIRST, THAT'S "THE ANTE." SECONDLY, IT'S BEEN A LONG, LONG TIME SINCE YOU COULD AFFORD MY RATES, APHRA. BUT NOW YOU'VE CLEARED YOUR SLATE...
WHAT ARE YOU LOOKING FOR? AND BEFORE YOU START... I STRESS I HAVE A *LOT* OF INFORMATION ABOUT SOME PARTICULARLY ELUSIVE INDIVIDUALS.
I KNOW. ANYTHING WORTH KNOWING HAS PASSED THROUGH THAT BIG BALD BRAIN OF YOURS.
COMMODEX TAHN.
THIS IS WHAT WE'VE GOT.
HMM.
...DONE.
ARE YOU ***SURE*** THIS IS THE RIGHT GUY?
MILITARY CLERK IN THE REPUBLIC ERA, BEFORE LEAVING SERVICE AND ENTERING THE FAMILY TRADE UPON THE DEATH OF HIS FATHER. RETIRED NOW FOR NEARLY 20 YEARS...
NO, HE'S THE ONE.
GIVE ME EVERYTHING YOU'VE GOT.
THERE ARE ***NO*** REFUNDS.

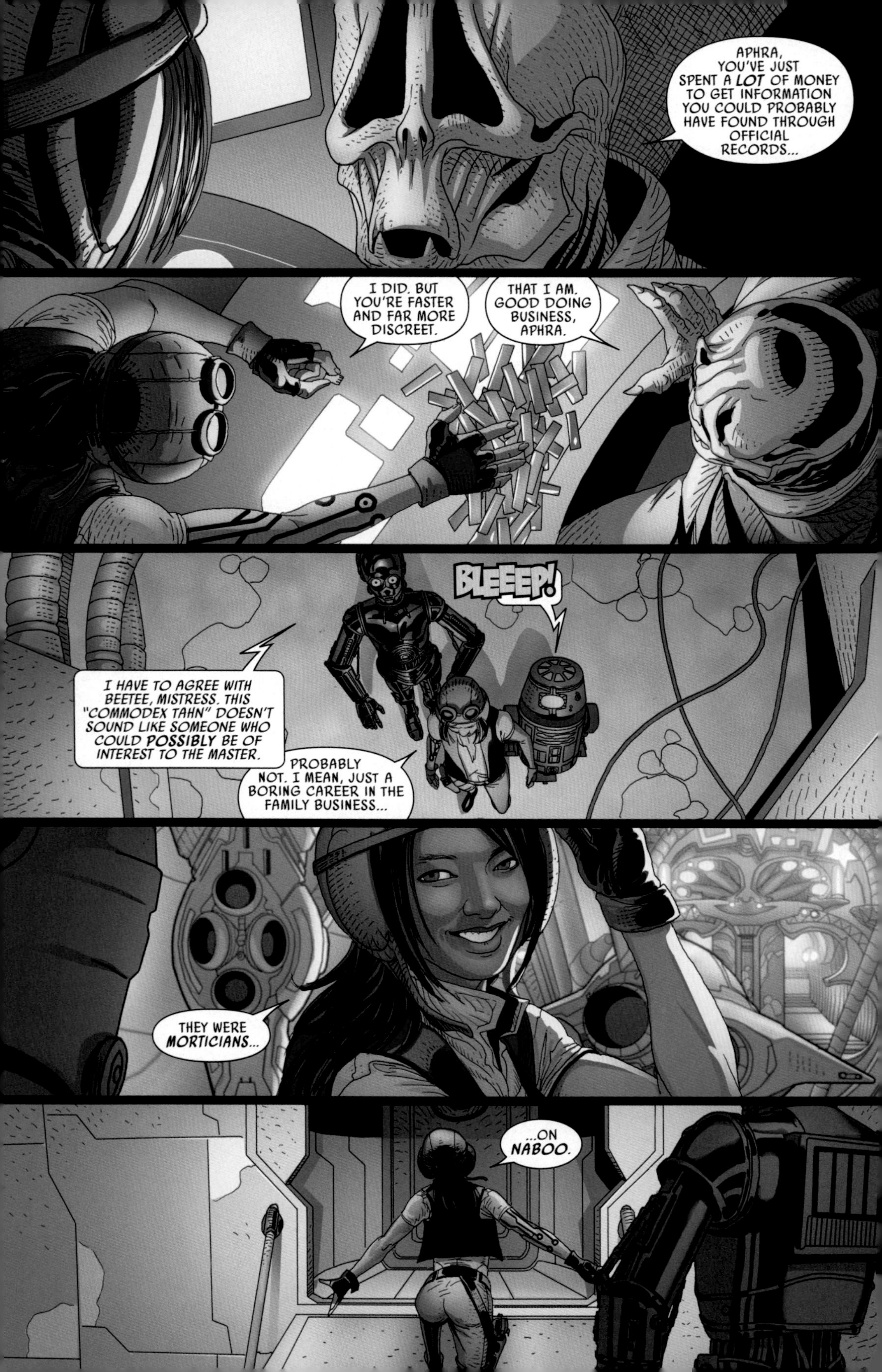

APHRA, YOU'VE JUST SPENT A LOT OF MONEY TO GET INFORMATION YOU COULD PROBABLY HAVE FOUND THROUGH OFFICIAL RECORDS...
I DID. BUT YOU'RE FASTER AND FAR MORE DISCREET.
THAT I AM. GOOD DOING BUSINESS, APHRA.
BLEEEP!
I HAVE TO AGREE WITH BEETEE, MISTRESS. THIS "COMMODEX TAHN" DOESN'T SOUND LIKE SOMEONE WHO COULD POSSIBLY BE OF INTEREST TO THE MASTER.
PROBABLY NOT. I MEAN, JUST A BORING CAREER IN THE FAMILY BUSINESS...
THEY WERE MORTICIANS...
...ON NABOO.

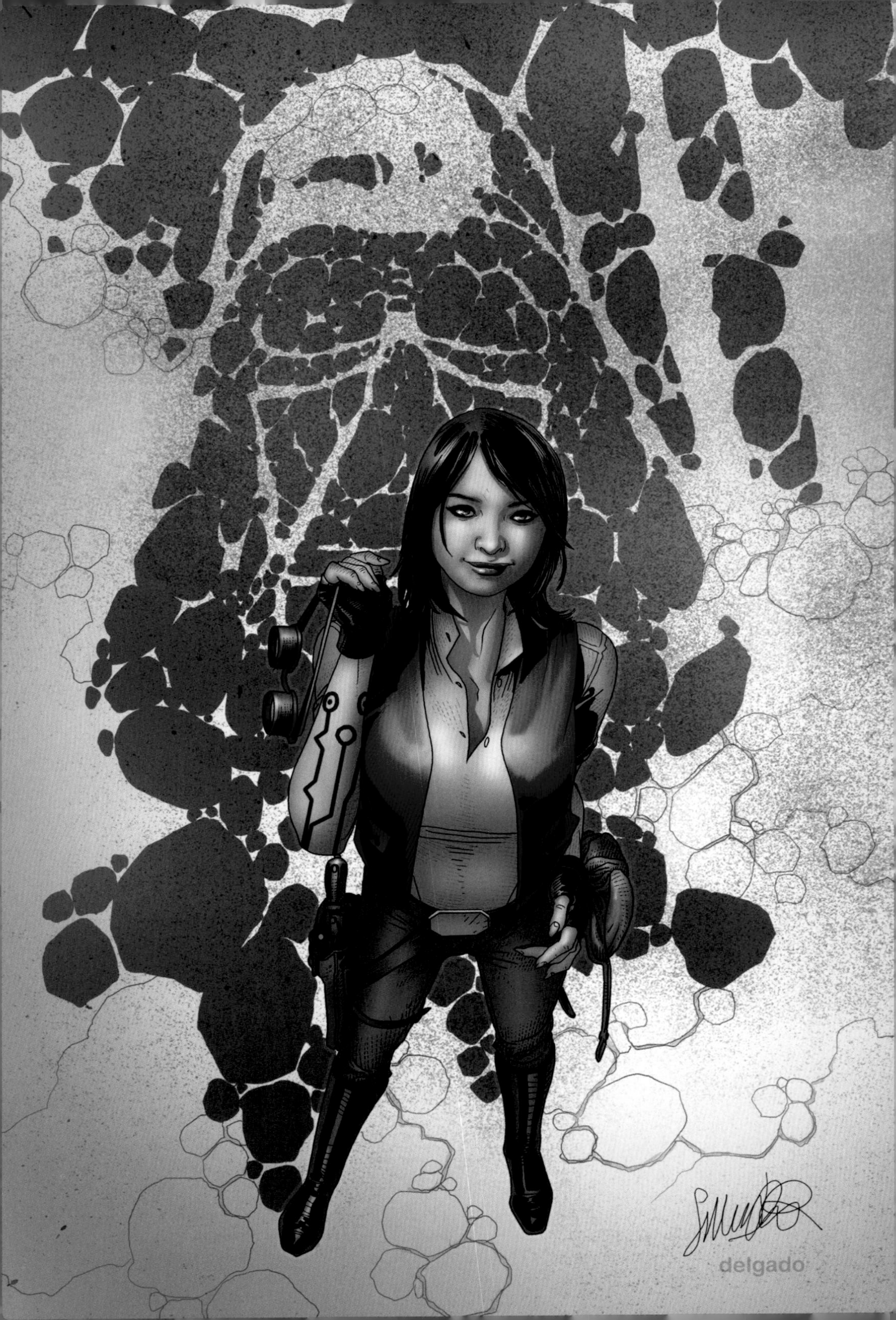
delgado

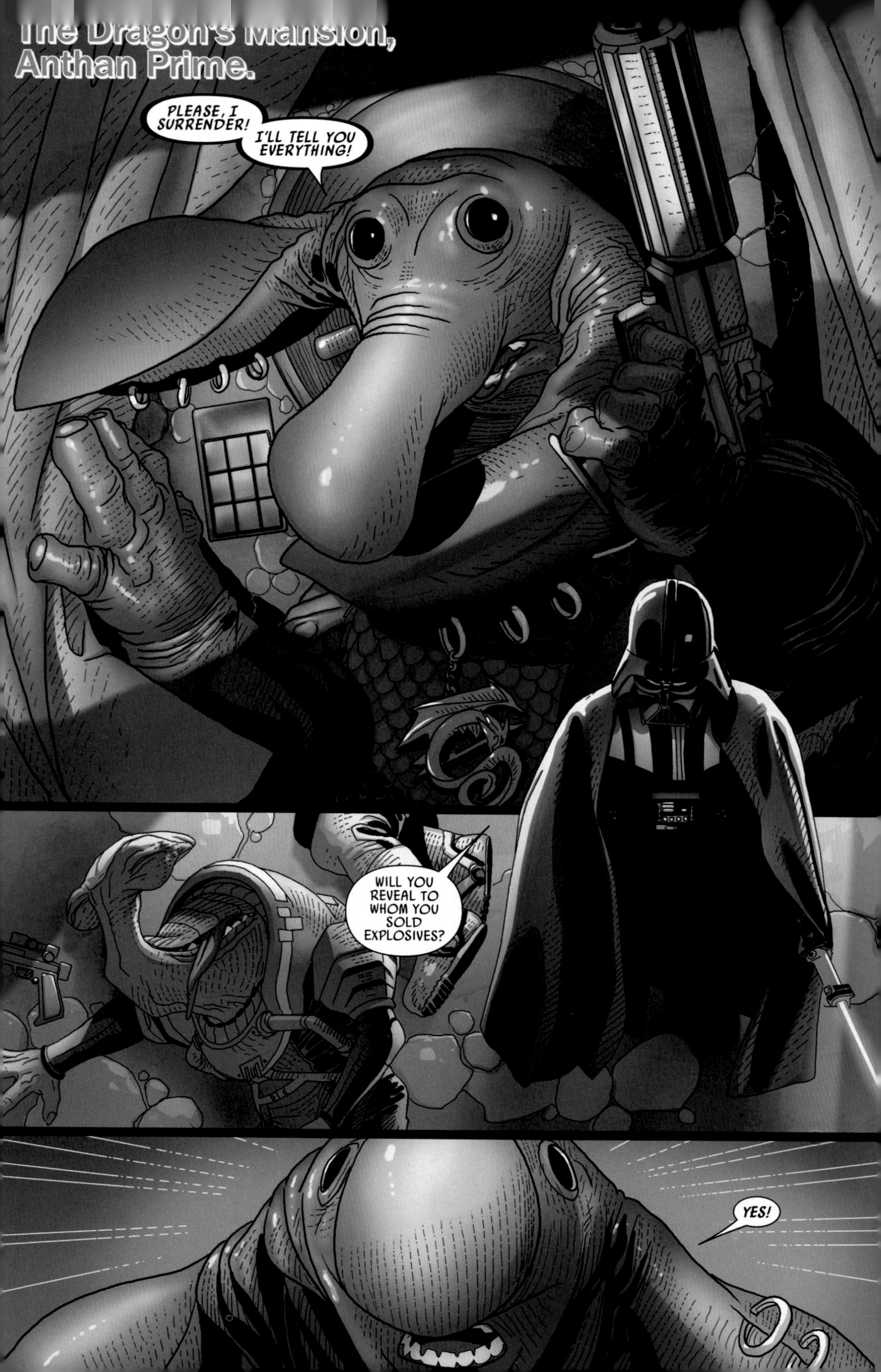
The Dragon's Mansion, Anthan Prime.
PLEASE, I SURRENDER!
I'LL TELL YOU EVERYTHING!
WILL YOU REVEAL TO WHOM YOU SOLD EXPLOSIVES?
YES!

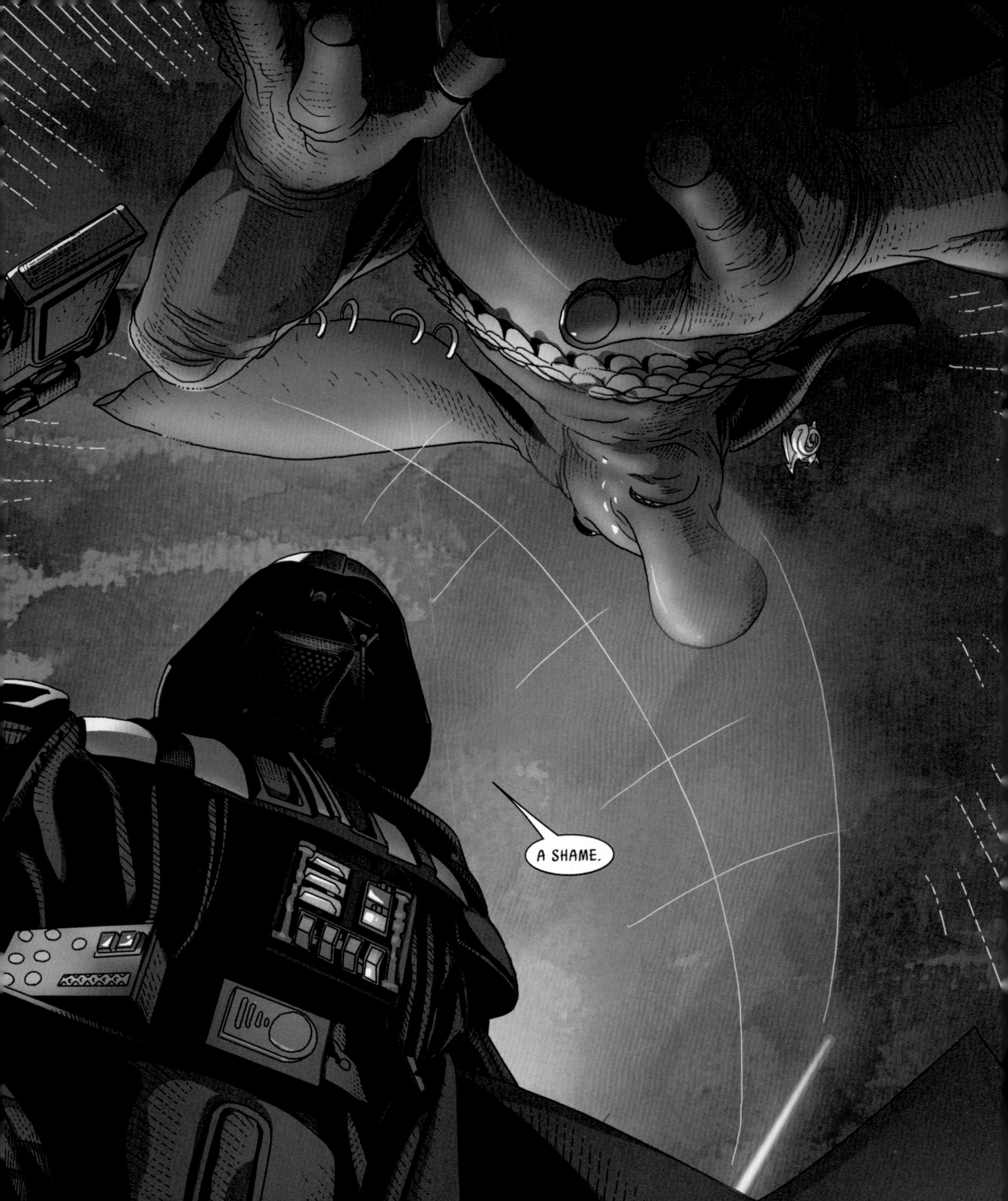
A SHAME.

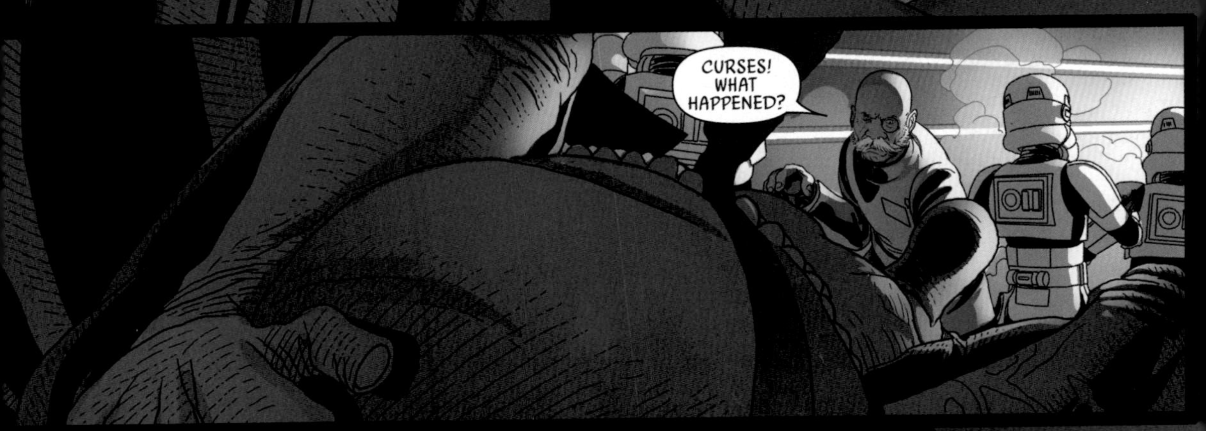
CURSES! WHAT HAPPENED?

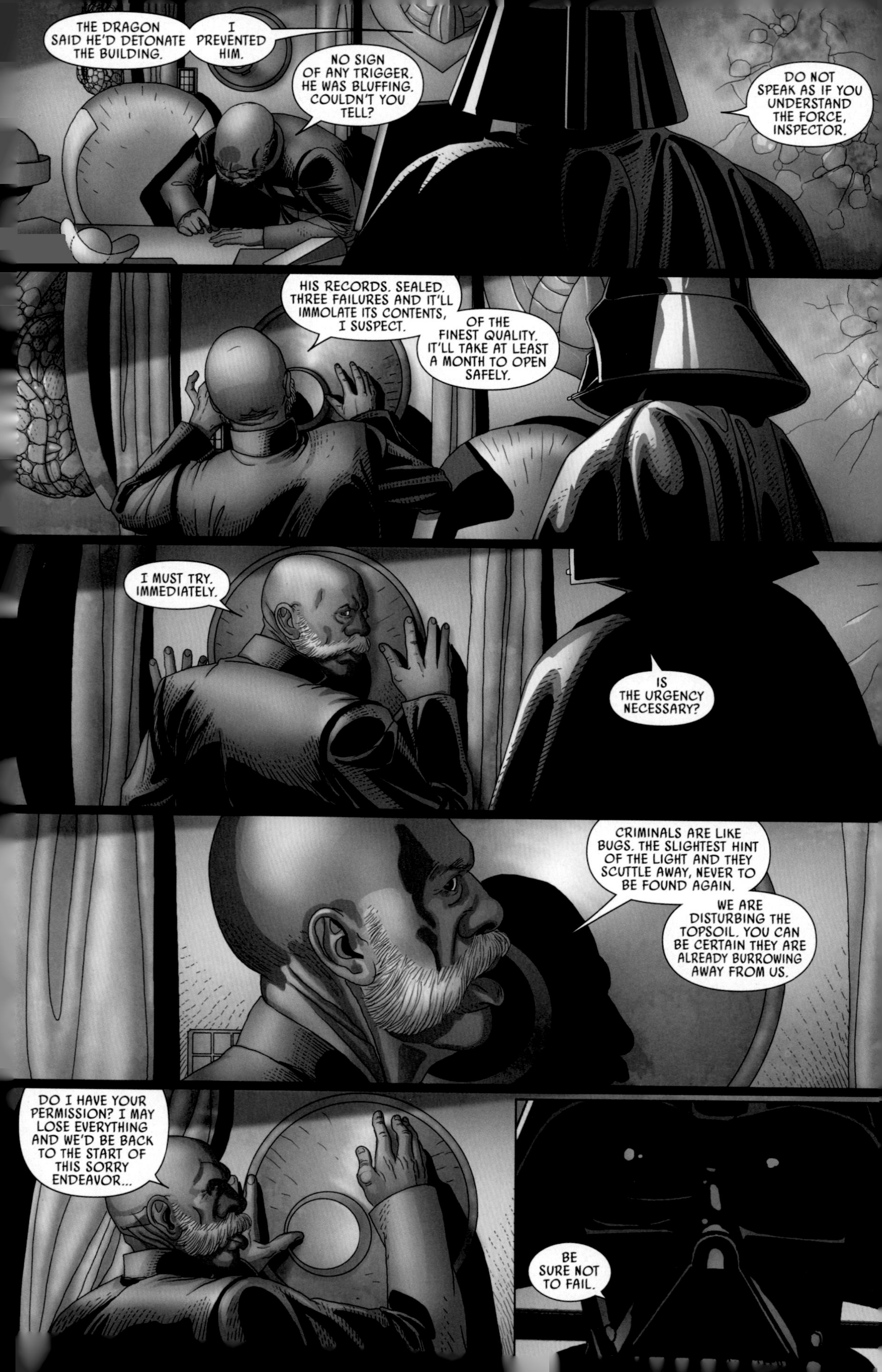
THE DRAGON SAID HE'D DETONATE THE BUILDING.
I PREVENTED HIM.
NO SIGN OF ANY TRIGGER. HE WAS BLUFFING. COULDN'T YOU TELL?
DO NOT SPEAK AS IF YOU UNDERSTAND THE FORCE, INSPECTOR.
HIS RECORDS. SEALED. THREE FAILURES AND IT'LL IMMOLATE ITS CONTENTS, I SUSPECT.
OF THE FINEST QUALITY. IT'LL TAKE AT LEAST A MONTH TO OPEN SAFELY.
I MUST TRY. IMMEDIATELY.
IS THE URGENCY NECESSARY?
CRIMINALS ARE LIKE BUGS. THE SLIGHTEST HINT OF THE LIGHT AND THEY SCUTTLE AWAY, NEVER TO BE FOUND AGAIN.
WE ARE DISTURBING THE TOPSOIL. YOU CAN BE CERTAIN THEY ARE ALREADY BURROWING AWAY FROM US.
DO I HAVE YOUR PERMISSION? I MAY LOSE EVERYTHING AND WE'D BE BACK TO THE START OF THIS SORRY ENDEAVOR...
BE SURE NOT TO FAIL.

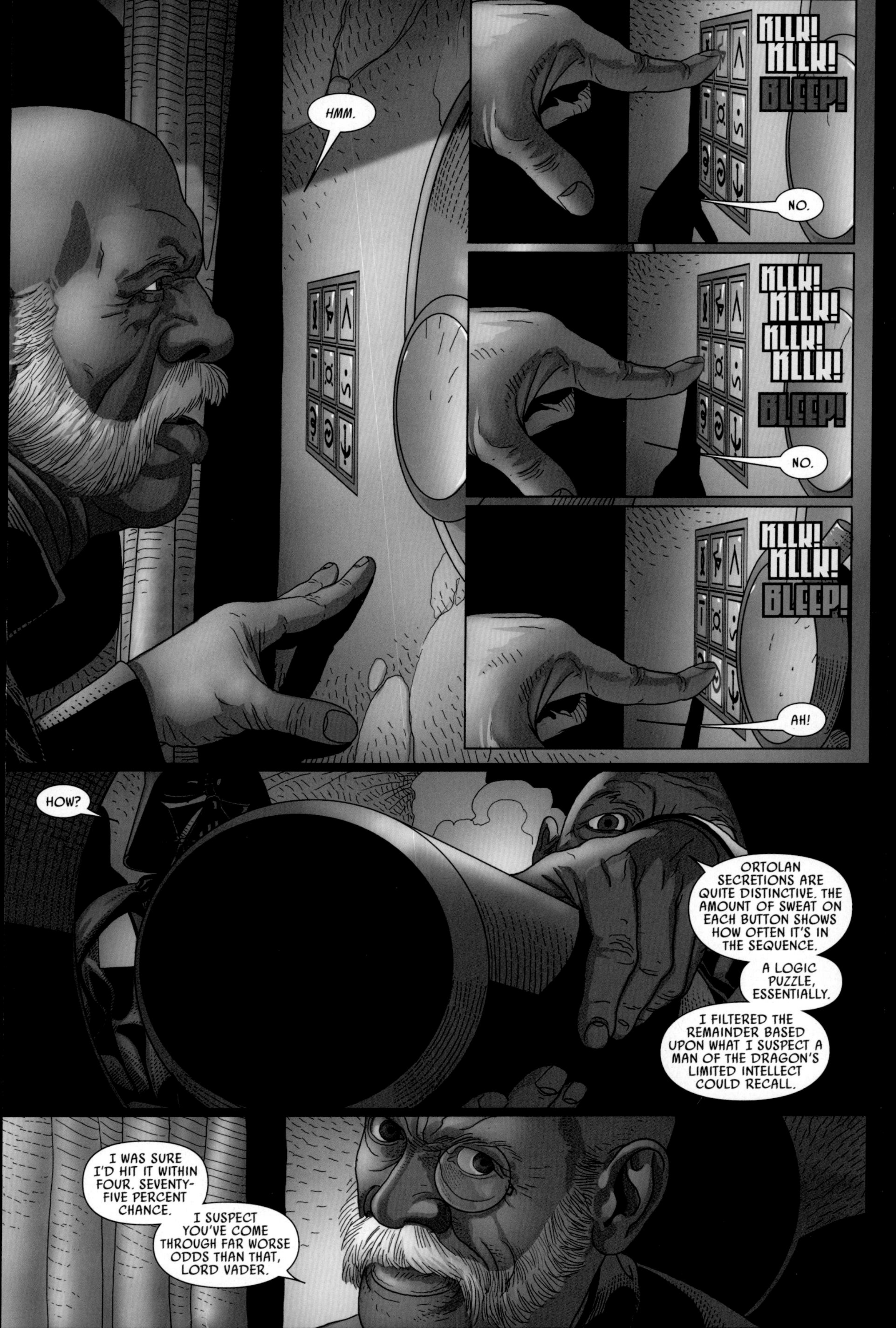
HMM.
KLLK!
KLLK!
BLEEP!
NO.
KLLK!
KLLK!
KLLK!
KLLK!
BLEEP!
NO.
KLLK!
KLLK!
BLEEP!
AH!
HOW?
ORTOLAN SECRETIONS ARE QUITE DISTINCTIVE. THE AMOUNT OF SWEAT ON EACH BUTTON SHOWS HOW OFTEN IT'S IN THE SEQUENCE.
A LOGIC PUZZLE, ESSENTIALLY.
I FILTERED THE REMAINDER BASED UPON WHAT I SUSPECT A MAN OF THE DRAGON'S LIMITED INTELLECT COULD RECALL.
I WAS SURE I'D HIT IT WITHIN FOUR. SEVENTY-FIVE PERCENT CHANCE.
I SUSPECT YOU'VE COME THROUGH FAR WORSE ODDS THAN THAT, LORD VADER.

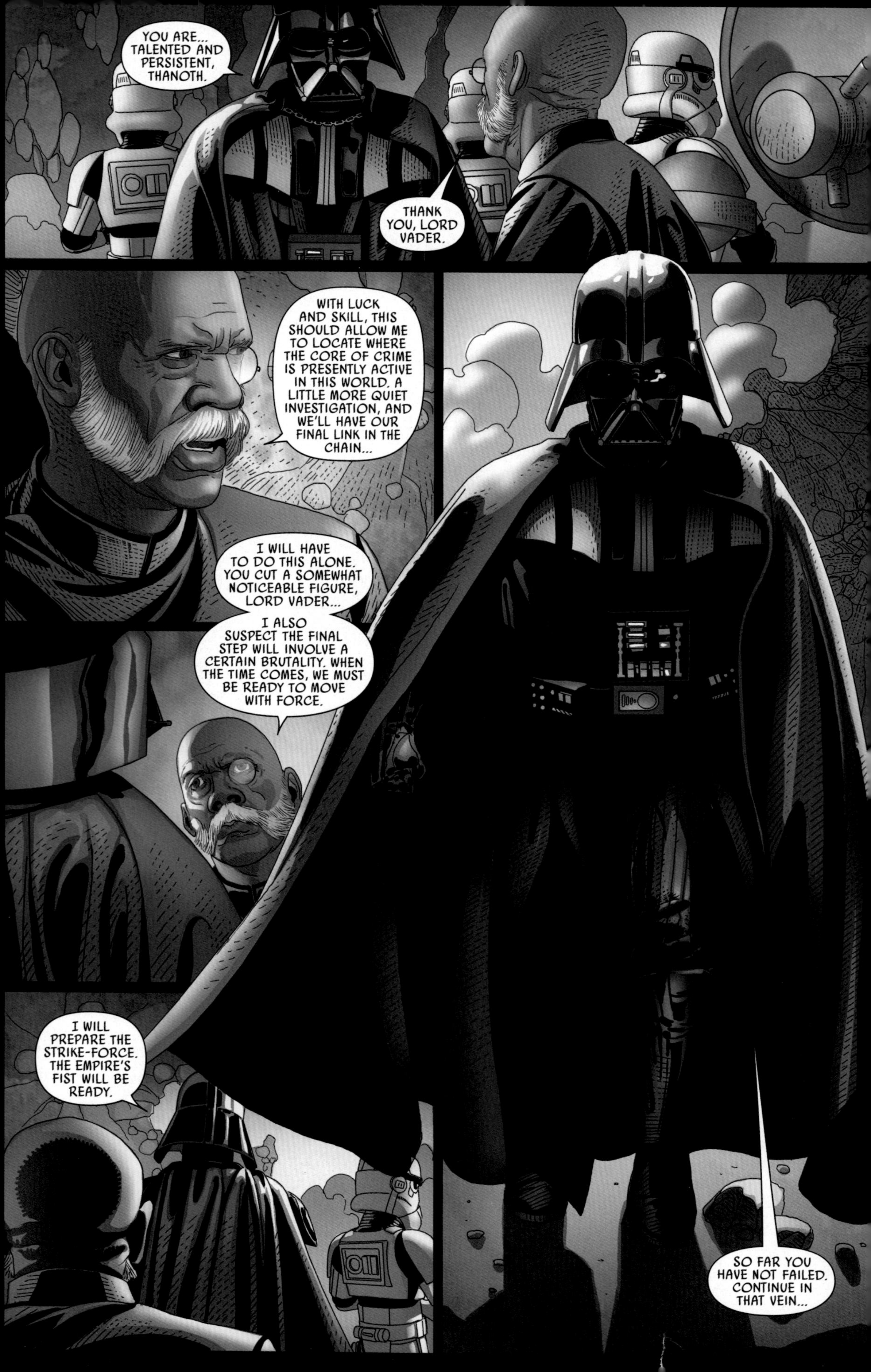
YOU ARE... TALENTED AND PERSISTENT, THANOTH.
THANK YOU, LORD VADER.
WITH LUCK AND SKILL, THIS SHOULD ALLOW ME TO LOCATE WHERE THE CORE OF CRIME IS PRESENTLY ACTIVE IN THIS WORLD. A LITTLE MORE QUIET INVESTIGATION, AND WE'LL HAVE OUR FINAL LINK IN THE CHAIN...
I WILL HAVE TO DO THIS ALONE. YOU CUT A SOMEWHAT NOTICEABLE FIGURE, LORD VADER...
I ALSO SUSPECT THE FINAL STEP WILL INVOLVE A CERTAIN BRUTALITY. WHEN THE TIME COMES, WE MUST BE READY TO MOVE WITH FORCE.
SO FAR YOU HAVE NOT FAILED. CONTINUE IN THAT VEIN...
I WILL PREPARE THE STRIKE-FORCE. THE EMPIRE'S FIST WILL BE READY.

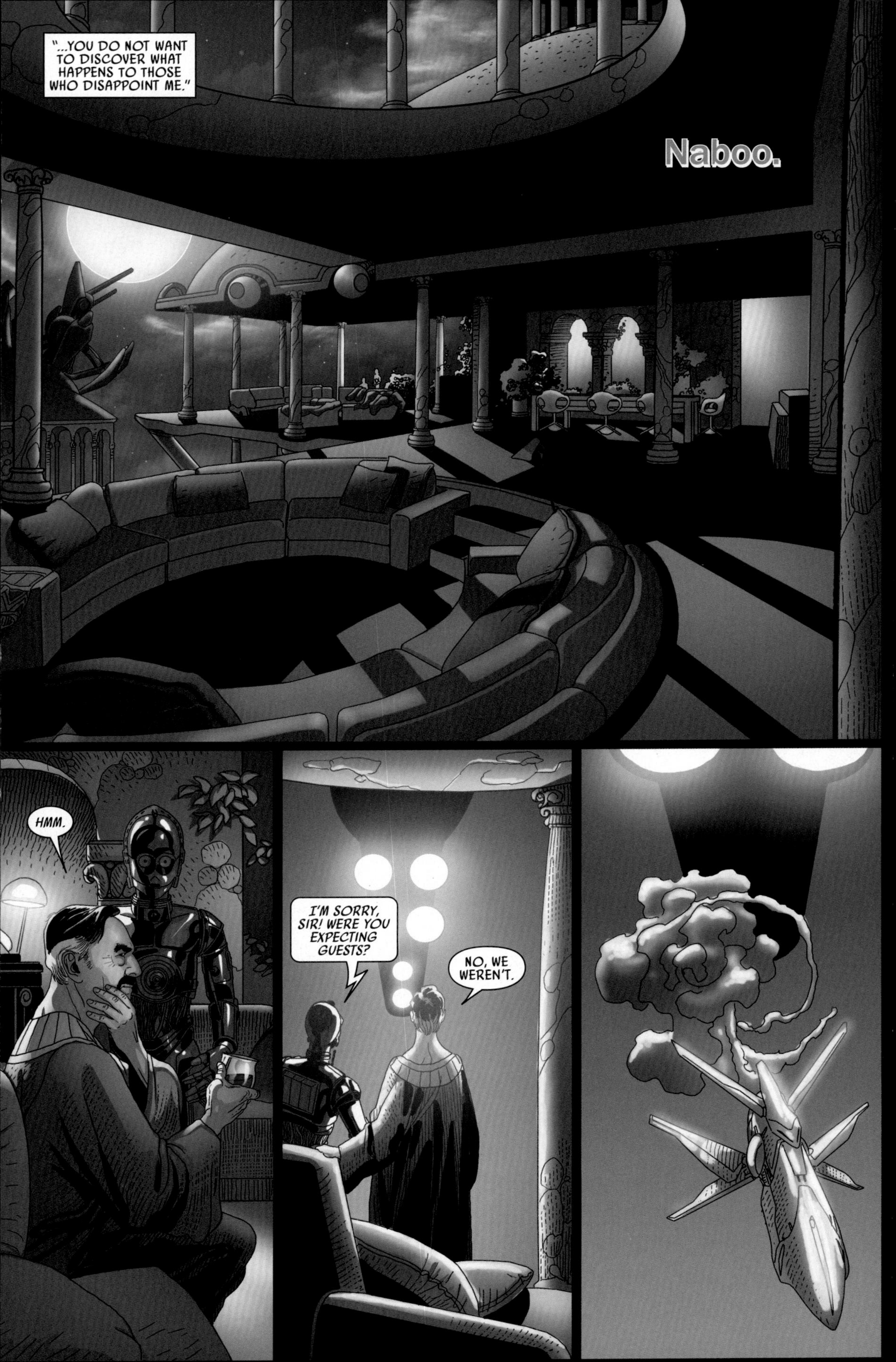
"...YOU DO NOT WANT TO DISCOVER WHAT HAPPENS TO THOSE WHO DISAPPOINT ME."
Naboo.
HMM.
I'M SORRY, SIR! WERE YOU EXPECTING GUESTS?
NO, WE WEREN'T.

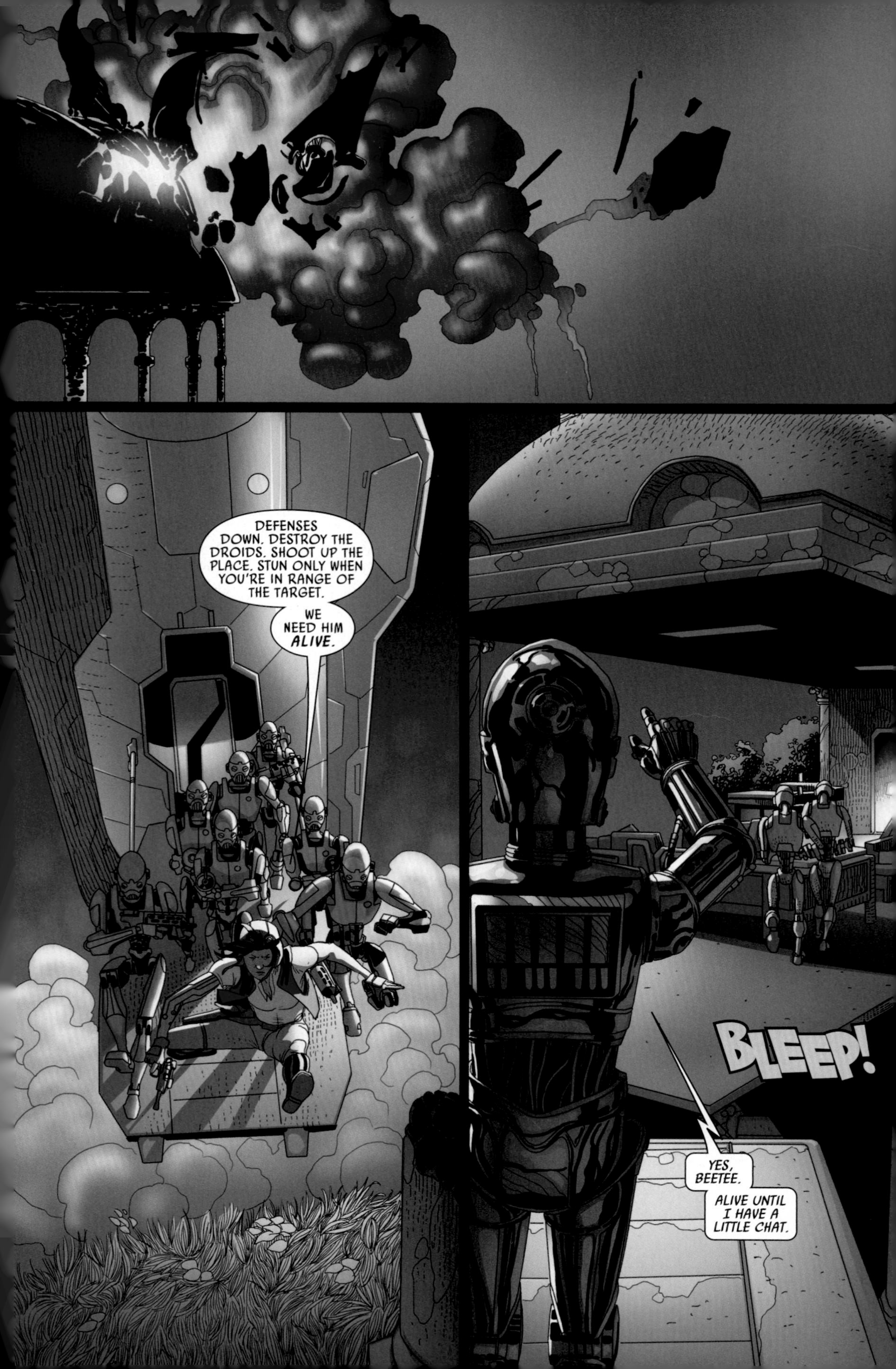

DEFENSES DOWN. DESTROY THE DROIDS. SHOOT UP THE PLACE. STUN ONLY WHEN YOU'RE IN RANGE OF THE TARGET.
WE NEED HIM *ALIVE*.
BLEEP!
YES, BEETEE.
ALIVE UNTIL I HAVE A LITTLE CHAT.

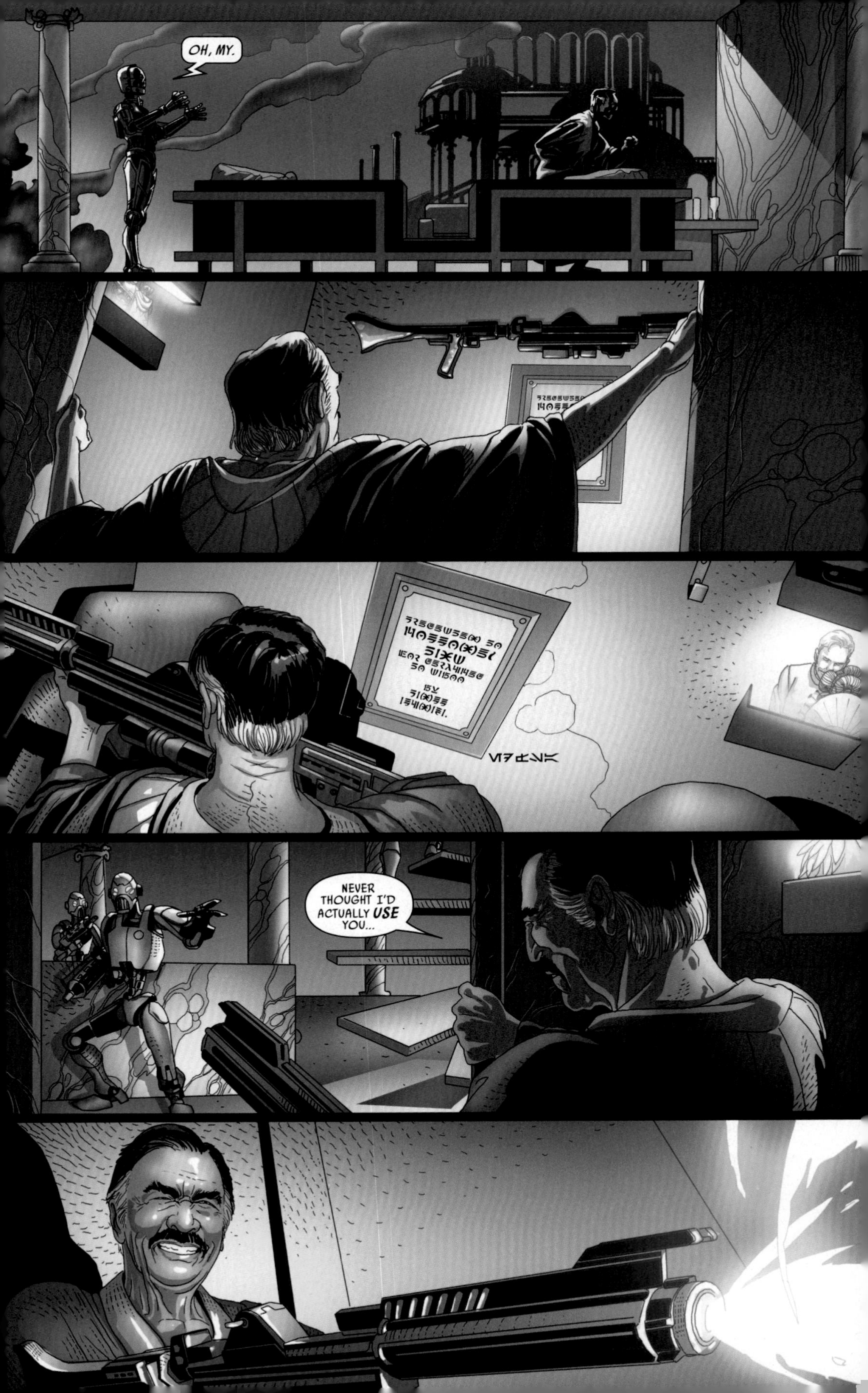
OH, MY.
NEVER THOUGHT I'D ACTUALLY USE YOU...

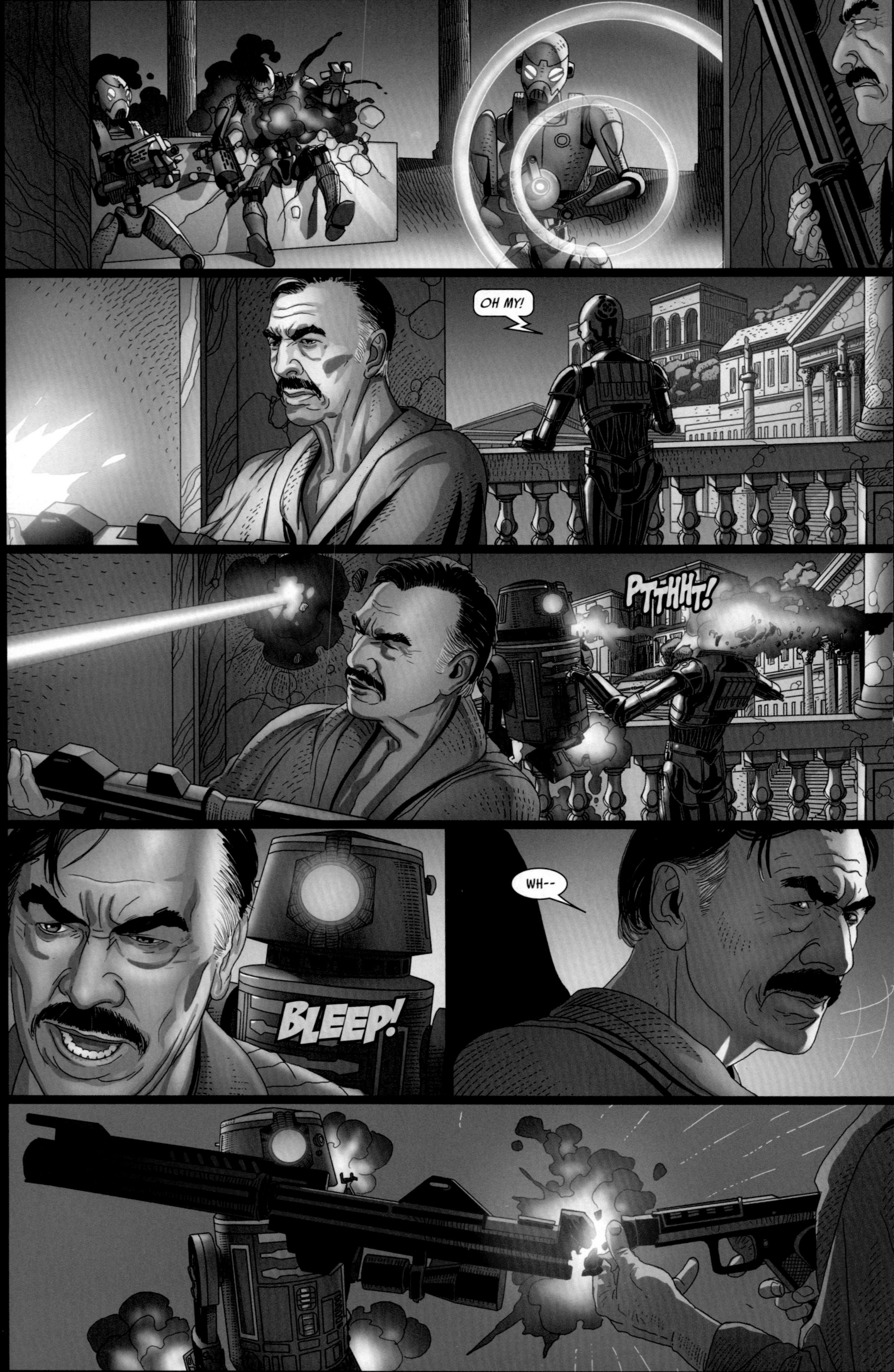
OH MY!
PTTHHT!
BLEEP!
WH--

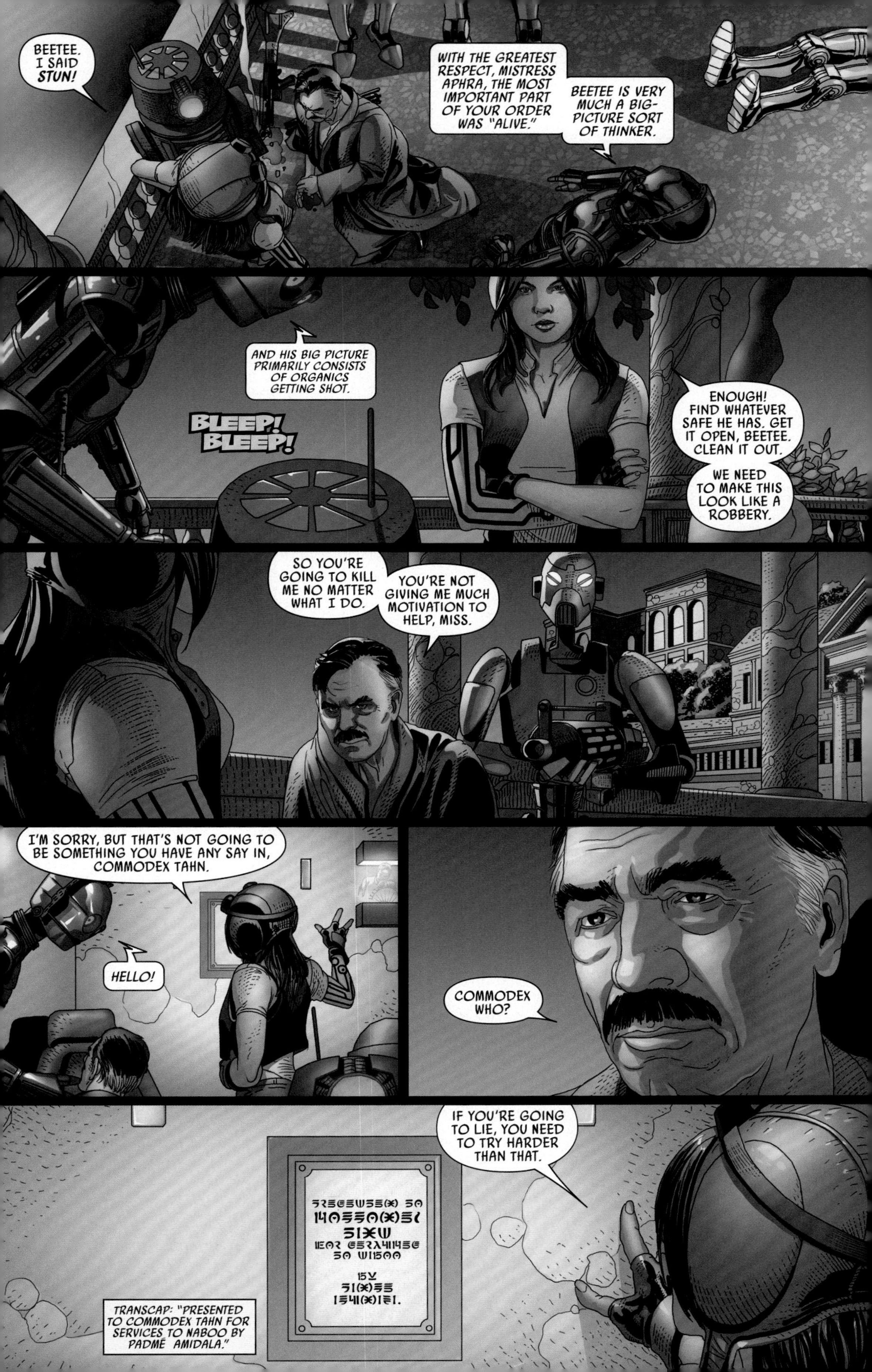

BEETEE. I SAID STUN!
WITH THE GREATEST RESPECT, MISTRESS APHRA, THE MOST IMPORTANT PART OF YOUR ORDER WAS "ALIVE."
BEETEE IS VERY MUCH A BIG-PICTURE SORT OF THINKER.
AND HIS BIG PICTURE PRIMARILY CONSISTS OF ORGANICS GETTING SHOT.
BLEEP! BLEEP!
ENOUGH! FIND WHATEVER SAFE HE HAS. GET IT OPEN, BEETEE. CLEAN IT OUT.
WE NEED TO MAKE THIS LOOK LIKE A ROBBERY.
SO YOU'RE GOING TO KILL ME NO MATTER WHAT I DO.
YOU'RE NOT GIVING ME MUCH MOTIVATION TO HELP, MISS.
I'M SORRY, BUT THAT'S NOT GOING TO BE SOMETHING YOU HAVE ANY SAY IN, COMMODEX TAHN.
HELLO!
COMMODEX WHO?
IF YOU'RE GOING TO LIE, YOU NEED TO TRY HARDER THAN THAT.
TRANSCAP: "PRESENTED TO COMMODEX TAHN FOR SERVICES TO NABOO BY PADMÉ AMIDALA."

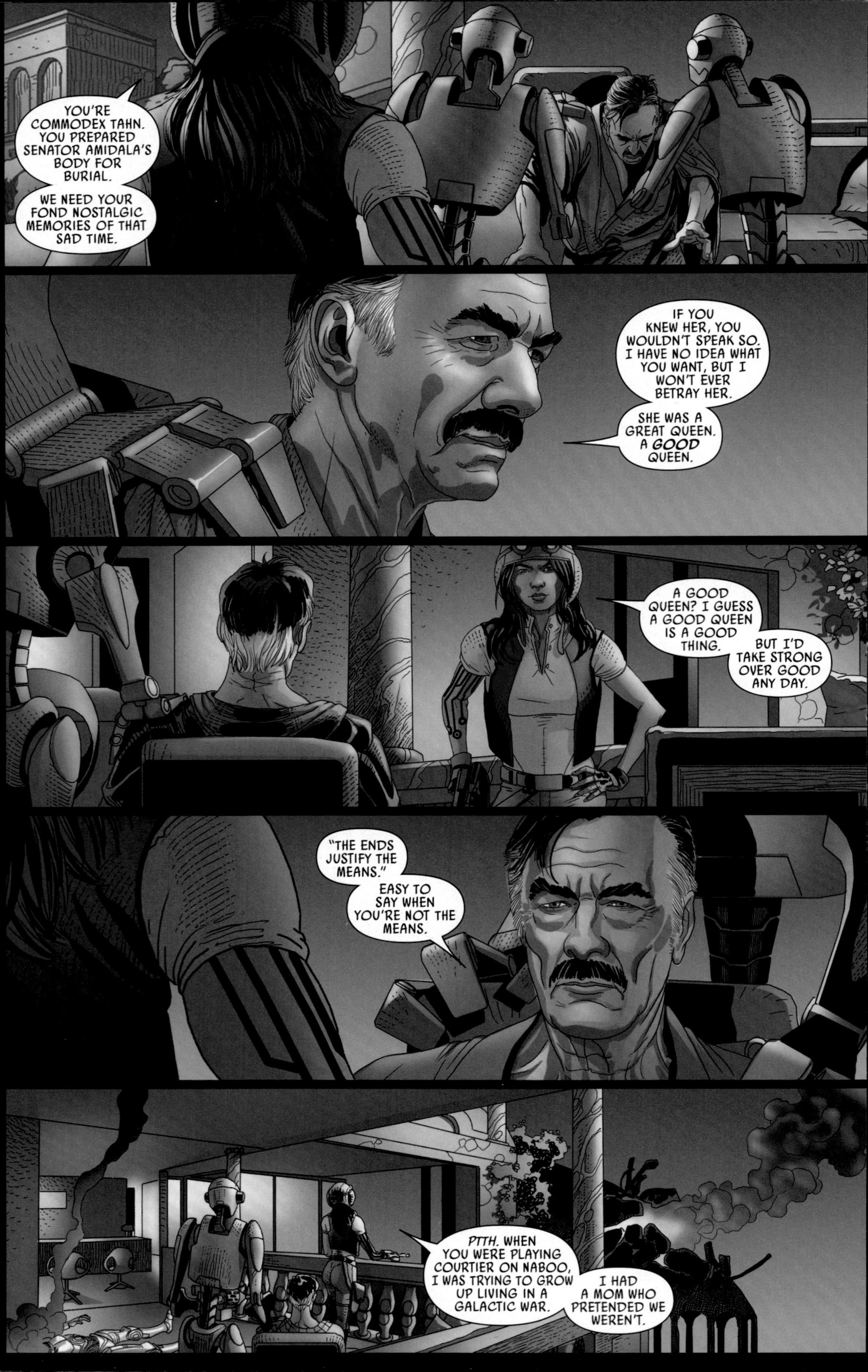
YOU'RE COMMODEX TAHN. YOU PREPARED SENATOR AMIDALA'S BODY FOR BURIAL.
WE NEED YOUR FOND NOSTALGIC MEMORIES OF THAT SAD TIME.
IF YOU KNEW HER, YOU WOULDN'T SPEAK SO. I HAVE NO IDEA WHAT YOU WANT, BUT I WON'T EVER BETRAY HER.
SHE WAS A GREAT QUEEN. A *GOOD* QUEEN.
A GOOD QUEEN? I GUESS A GOOD QUEEN IS A GOOD THING.
BUT I'D TAKE STRONG OVER GOOD ANY DAY.
"THE ENDS JUSTIFY THE MEANS."
EASY TO SAY WHEN YOU'RE NOT THE MEANS.
PTTH. WHEN YOU WERE PLAYING COURTIER ON NABOO, I WAS TRYING TO GROW UP LIVING IN A GALACTIC WAR.
I HAD A MOM WHO PRETENDED WE WEREN'T.

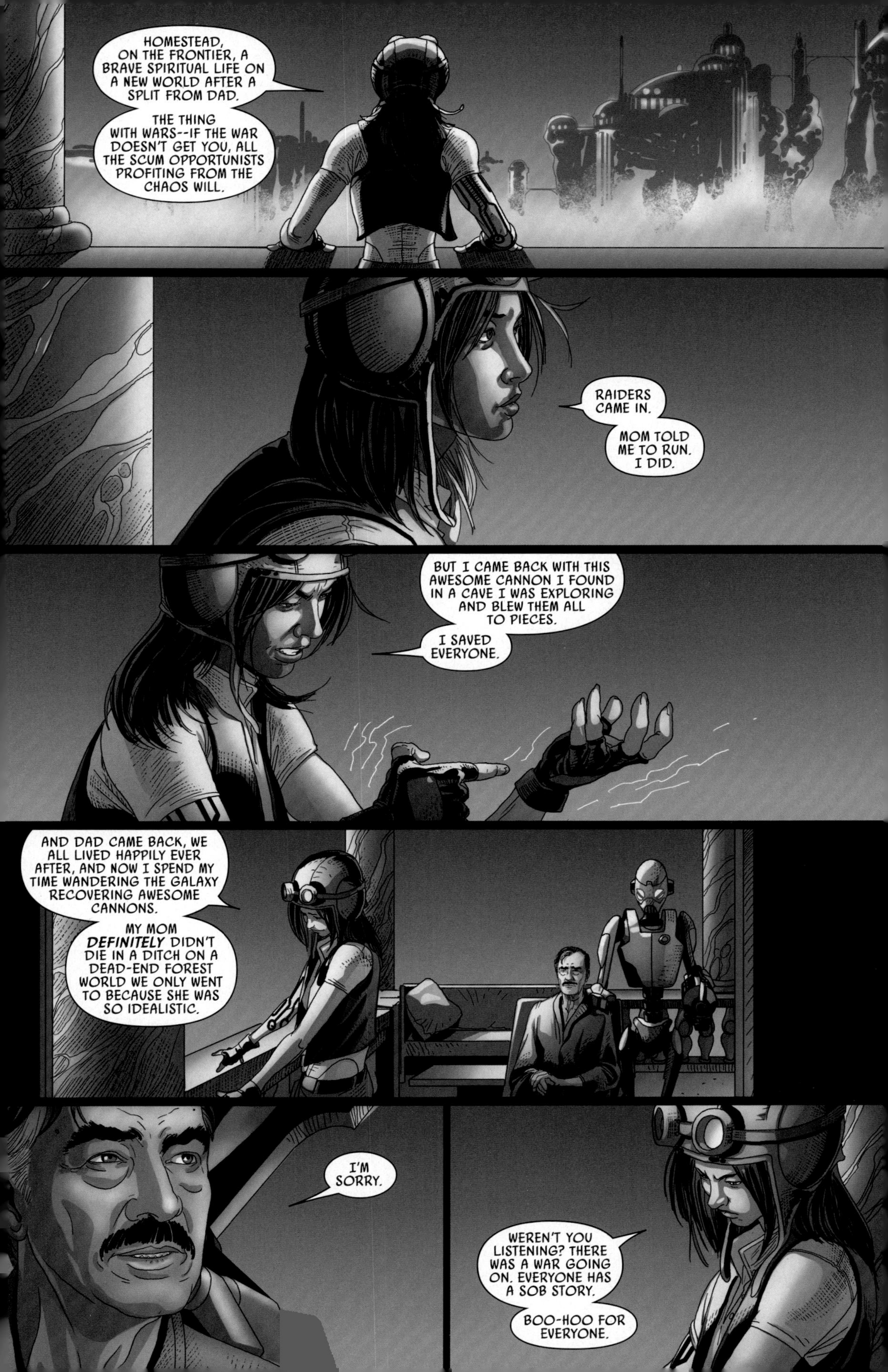
HOMESTEAD, ON THE FRONTIER, A BRAVE SPIRITUAL LIFE ON A NEW WORLD AFTER A SPLIT FROM DAD.
THE THING WITH WARS--IF THE WAR DOESN'T GET YOU, ALL THE SCUM OPPORTUNISTS PROFITING FROM THE CHAOS WILL.
RAIDERS CAME IN.
MOM TOLD ME TO RUN. I DID.
BUT I CAME BACK WITH THIS AWESOME CANNON I FOUND IN A CAVE I WAS EXPLORING AND BLEW THEM ALL TO PIECES.
I SAVED EVERYONE.
AND DAD CAME BACK, WE ALL LIVED HAPPILY EVER AFTER, AND NOW I SPEND MY TIME WANDERING THE GALAXY RECOVERING AWESOME CANNONS.
MY MOM ***DEFINITELY*** DIDN'T DIE IN A DITCH ON A DEAD-END FOREST WORLD WE ONLY WENT TO BECAUSE SHE WAS SO IDEALISTIC.
I'M SORRY.
WEREN'T YOU LISTENING? THERE WAS A WAR GOING ON. EVERYONE HAS A SOB STORY.
BOO-HOO FOR EVERYONE.

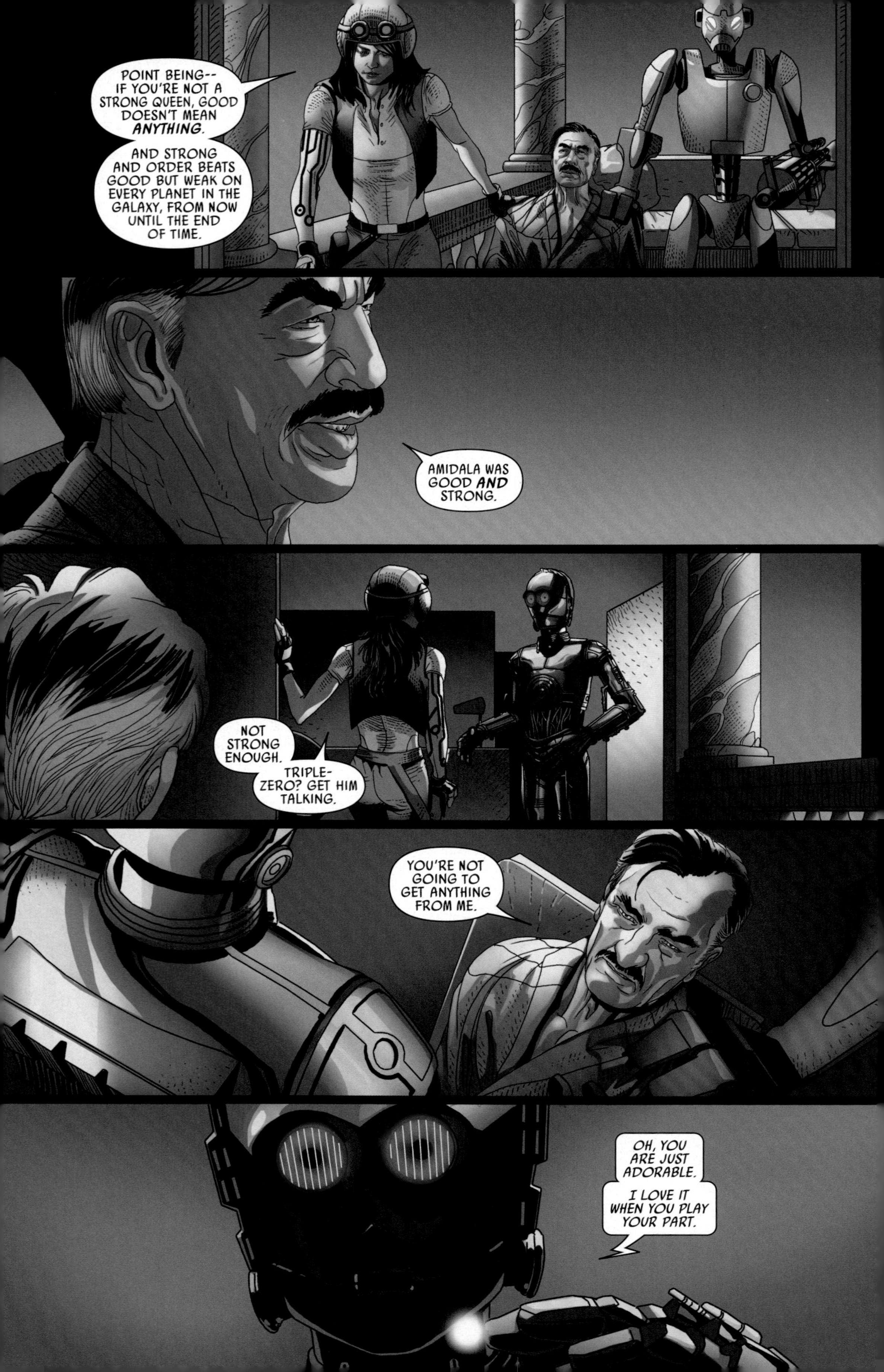
POINT BEING-- IF YOU'RE NOT A STRONG QUEEN, GOOD DOESN'T MEAN *ANYTHING*.
AND STRONG AND ORDER BEATS GOOD BUT WEAK ON EVERY PLANET IN THE GALAXY, FROM NOW UNTIL THE END OF TIME.
AMIDALA WAS GOOD *AND* STRONG.
NOT STRONG ENOUGH.
TRIPLE-ZERO? GET HIM TALKING.
YOU'RE NOT GOING TO GET ANYTHING FROM ME.
OH, YOU ARE JUST ADORABLE.
I LOVE IT WHEN YOU PLAY YOUR PART.

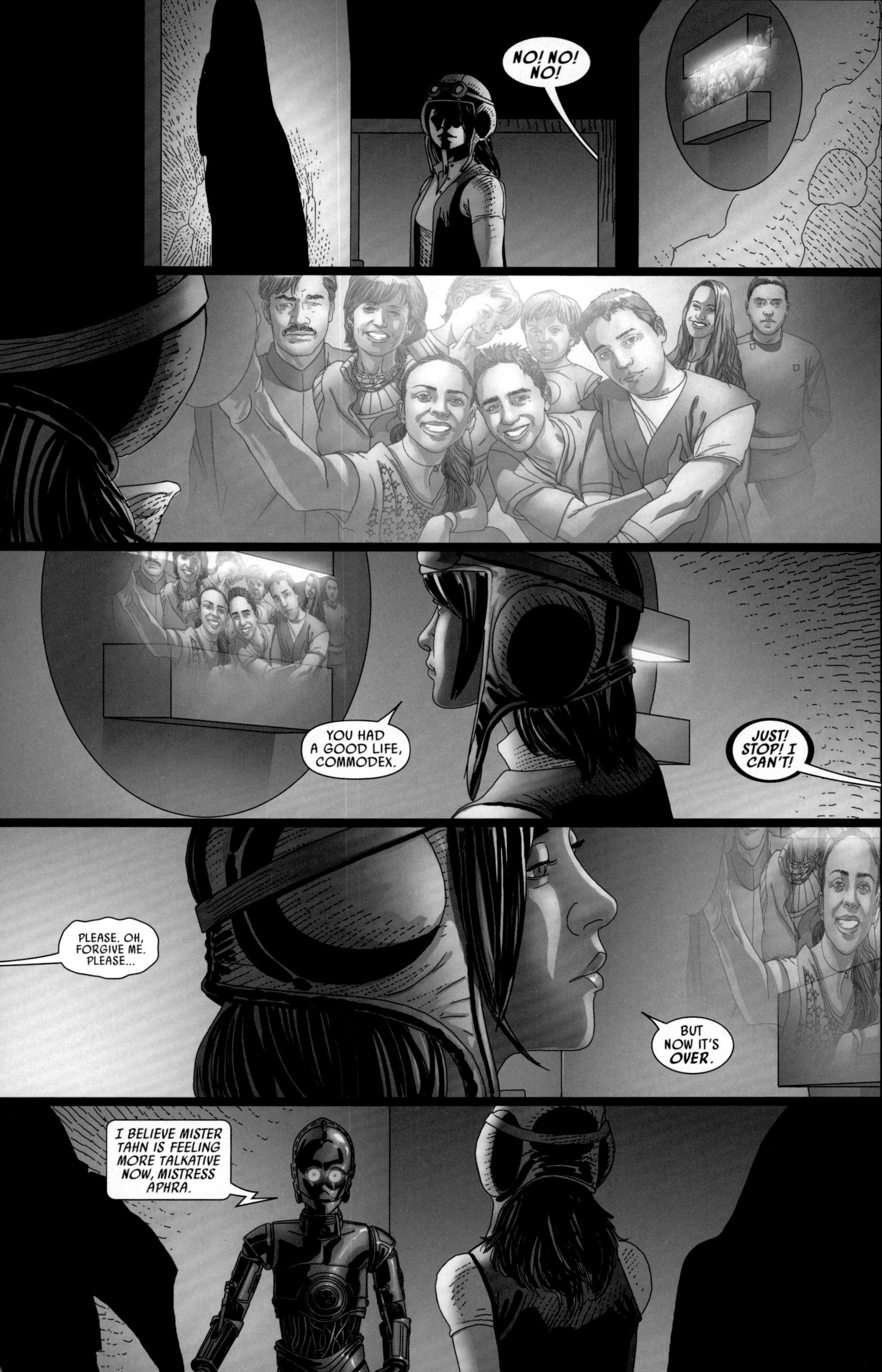
NO! NO! NO!
YOU HAD A GOOD LIFE, COMMODEX.
JUST! STOP! I CAN'T!
PLEASE. OH, FORGIVE ME. PLEASE...
BUT NOW IT'S OVER.
I BELIEVE MISTER TAHN IS FEELING MORE TALKATIVE NOW, MISTRESS APHRA.

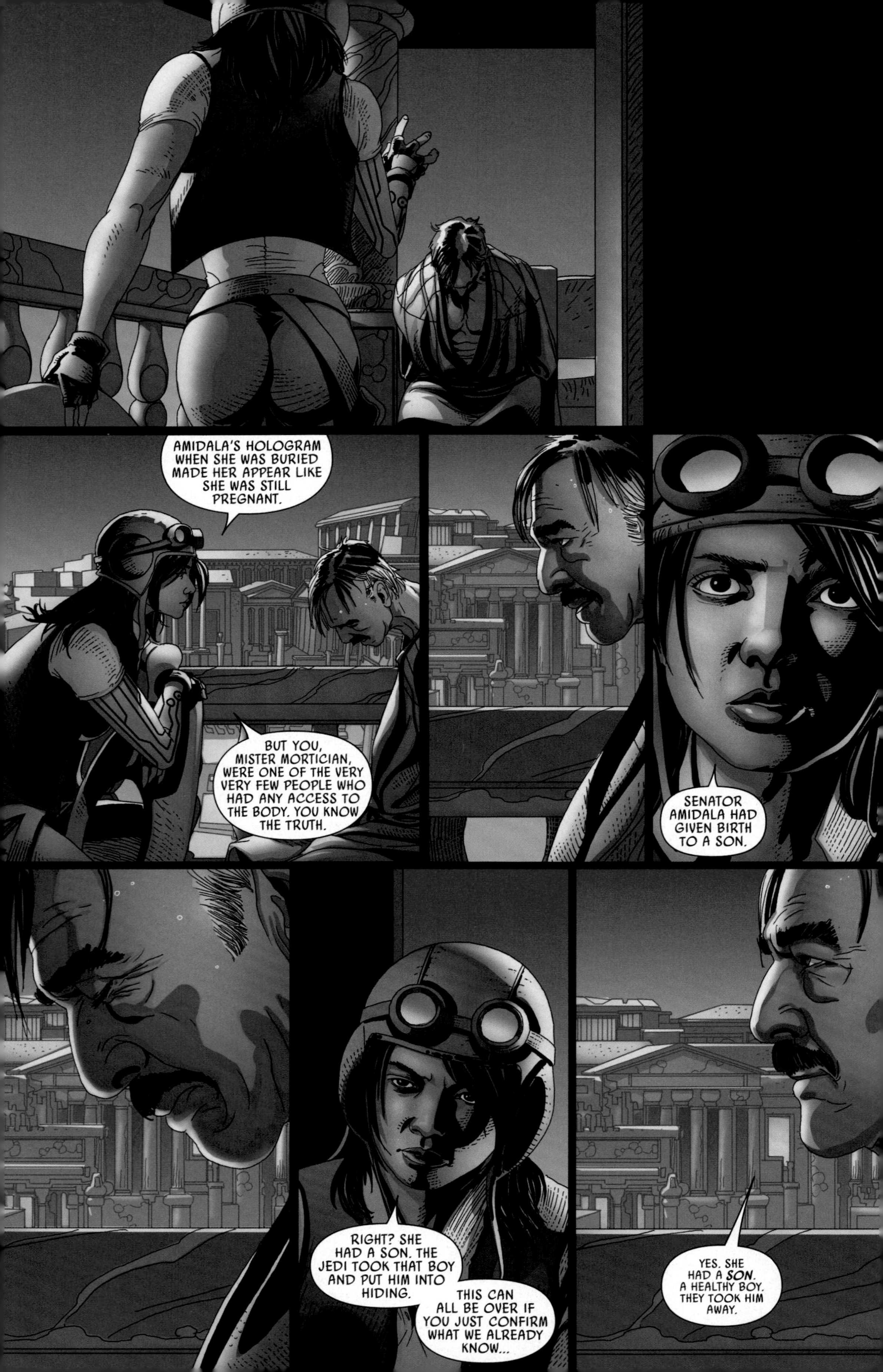
AMIDALA'S HOLOGRAM WHEN SHE WAS BURIED MADE HER APPEAR LIKE SHE WAS STILL PREGNANT.
BUT YOU, MISTER MORTICIAN, WERE ONE OF THE VERY VERY FEW PEOPLE WHO HAD ANY ACCESS TO THE BODY. YOU KNOW THE TRUTH.
SENATOR AMIDALA HAD GIVEN BIRTH TO A SON.
RIGHT? SHE HAD A SON. THE JEDI TOOK THAT BOY AND PUT HIM INTO HIDING.
THIS CAN ALL BE OVER IF YOU JUST CONFIRM WHAT WE ALREADY KNOW...
YES. SHE HAD A SON. A HEALTHY BOY. THEY TOOK HIM AWAY.

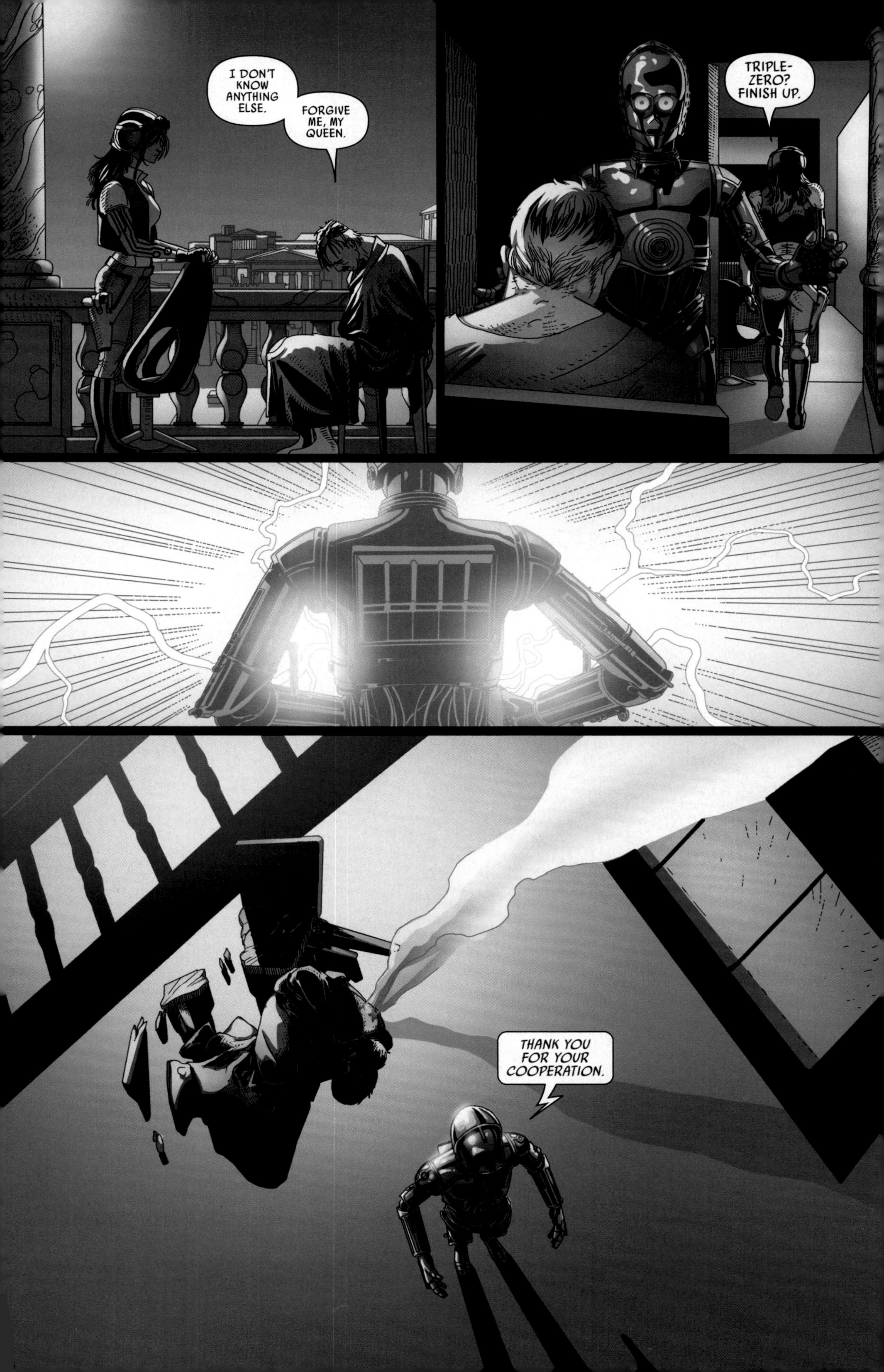
I DON'T KNOW ANYTHING ELSE.
FORGIVE ME, MY QUEEN.
TRIPLE-ZERO? FINISH UP.
THANK YOU FOR YOUR COOPERATION.

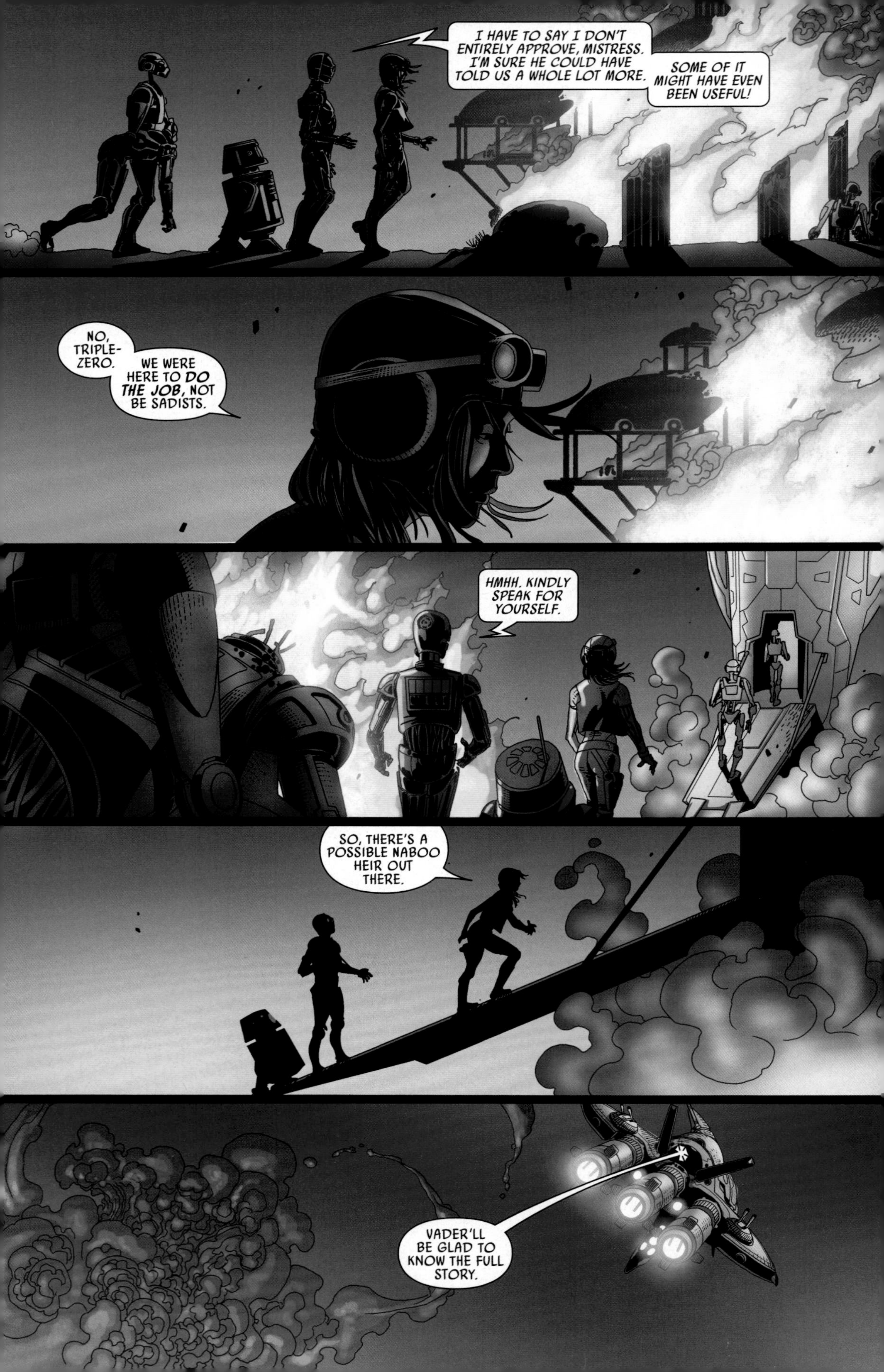
I HAVE TO SAY I DON'T ENTIRELY APPROVE, MISTRESS. I'M SURE HE COULD HAVE TOLD US A WHOLE LOT MORE.
SOME OF IT MIGHT HAVE EVEN BEEN USEFUL!
NO, TRIPLE-ZERO.
WE WERE HERE TO DO THE JOB, NOT BE SADISTS.
HMHH. KINDLY SPEAK FOR YOURSELF.
SO, THERE'S A POSSIBLE NABOO HEIR OUT THERE.
VADER'LL BE GLAD TO KNOW THE FULL STORY.

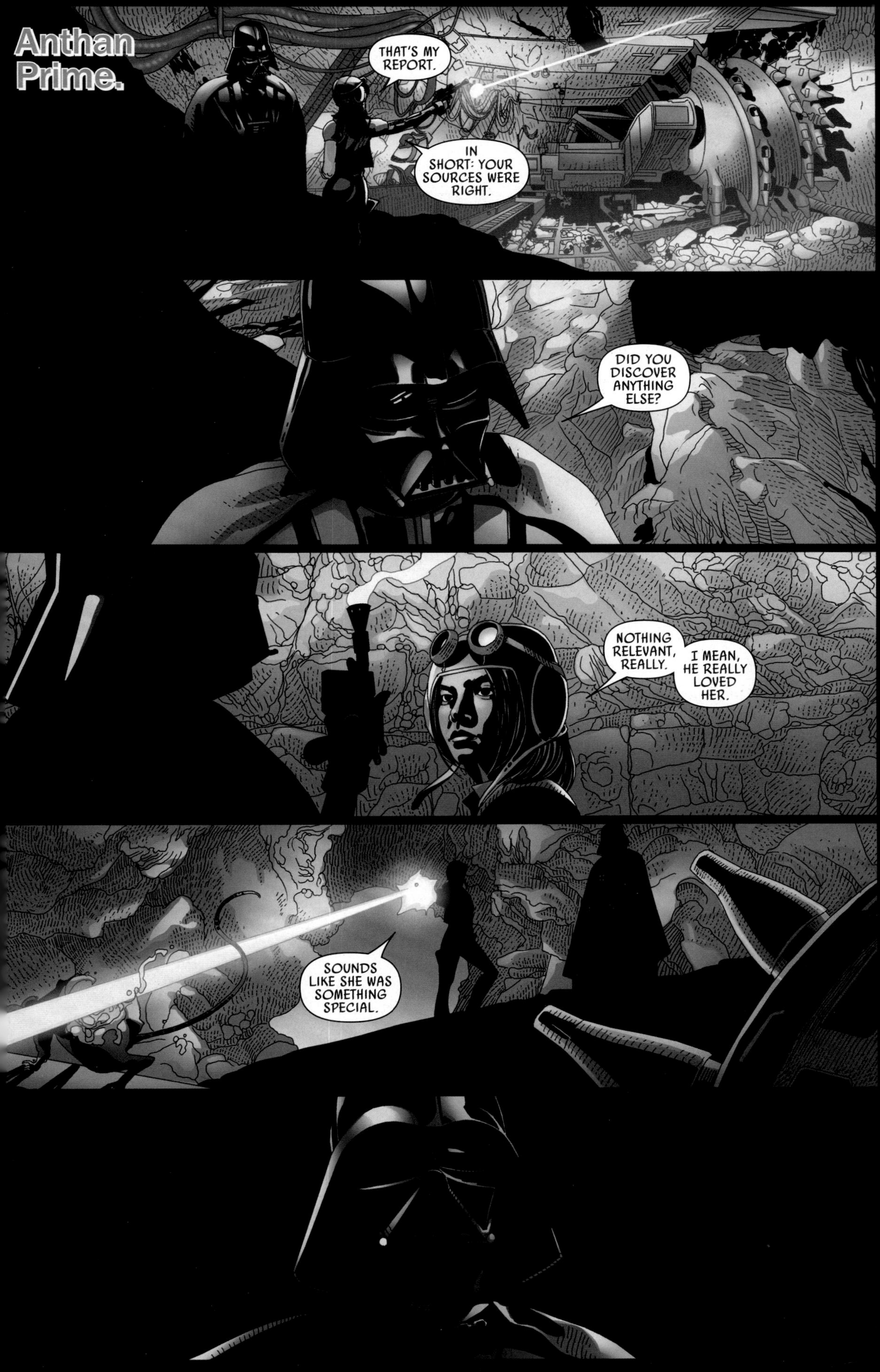

Anthan Prime.
THAT'S MY REPORT.
IN SHORT: YOUR SOURCES WERE RIGHT.
DID YOU DISCOVER ANYTHING ELSE?
NOTHING RELEVANT, REALLY.
I MEAN, HE REALLY LOVED HER.
SOUNDS LIKE SHE WAS SOMETHING SPECIAL.

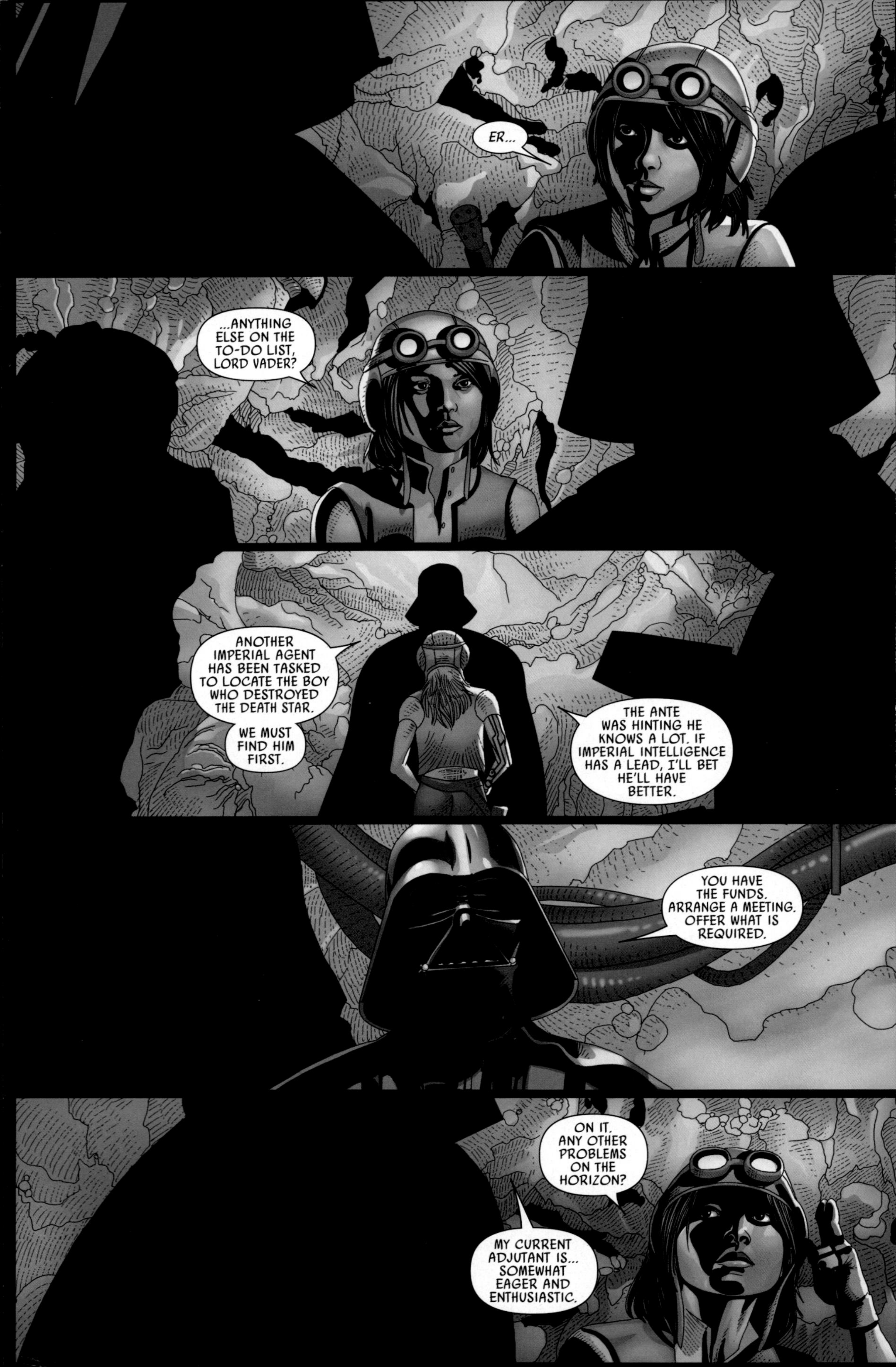
ER...
...ANYTHING ELSE ON THE TO-DO LIST, LORD VADER?
ANOTHER IMPERIAL AGENT HAS BEEN TASKED TO LOCATE THE BOY WHO DESTROYED THE DEATH STAR.
WE MUST FIND HIM FIRST.
THE ANTE WAS HINTING HE KNOWS A LOT. IF IMPERIAL INTELLIGENCE HAS A LEAD, I'LL BET HE'LL HAVE BETTER.
YOU HAVE THE FUNDS. ARRANGE A MEETING. OFFER WHAT IS REQUIRED.
ON IT. ANY OTHER PROBLEMS ON THE HORIZON?
MY CURRENT ADJUTANT IS... SOMEWHAT EAGER AND ENTHUSIASTIC.

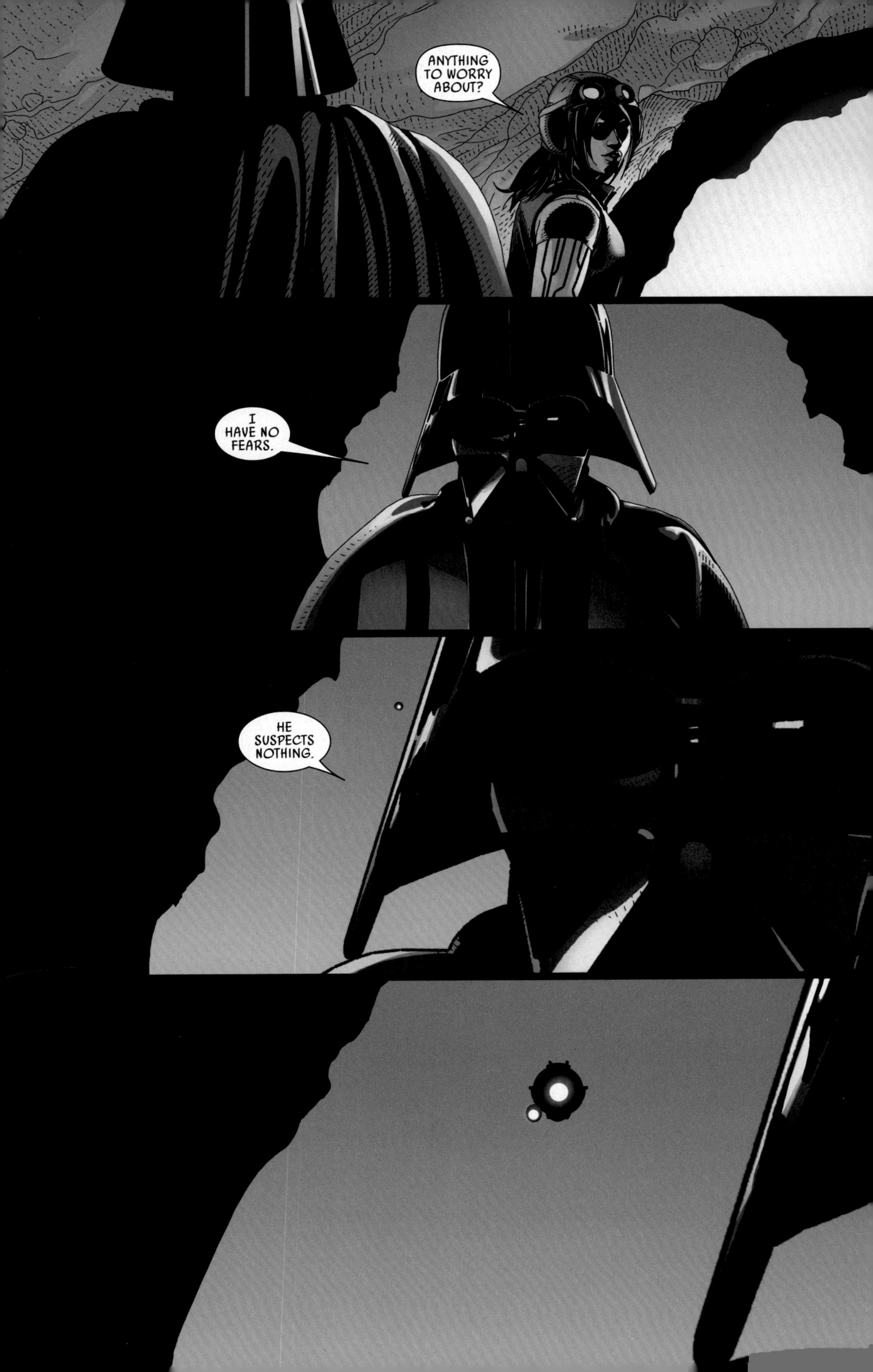
ANYTHING TO WORRY ABOUT?
I HAVE NO FEARS.
HE SUSPECTS NOTHING.

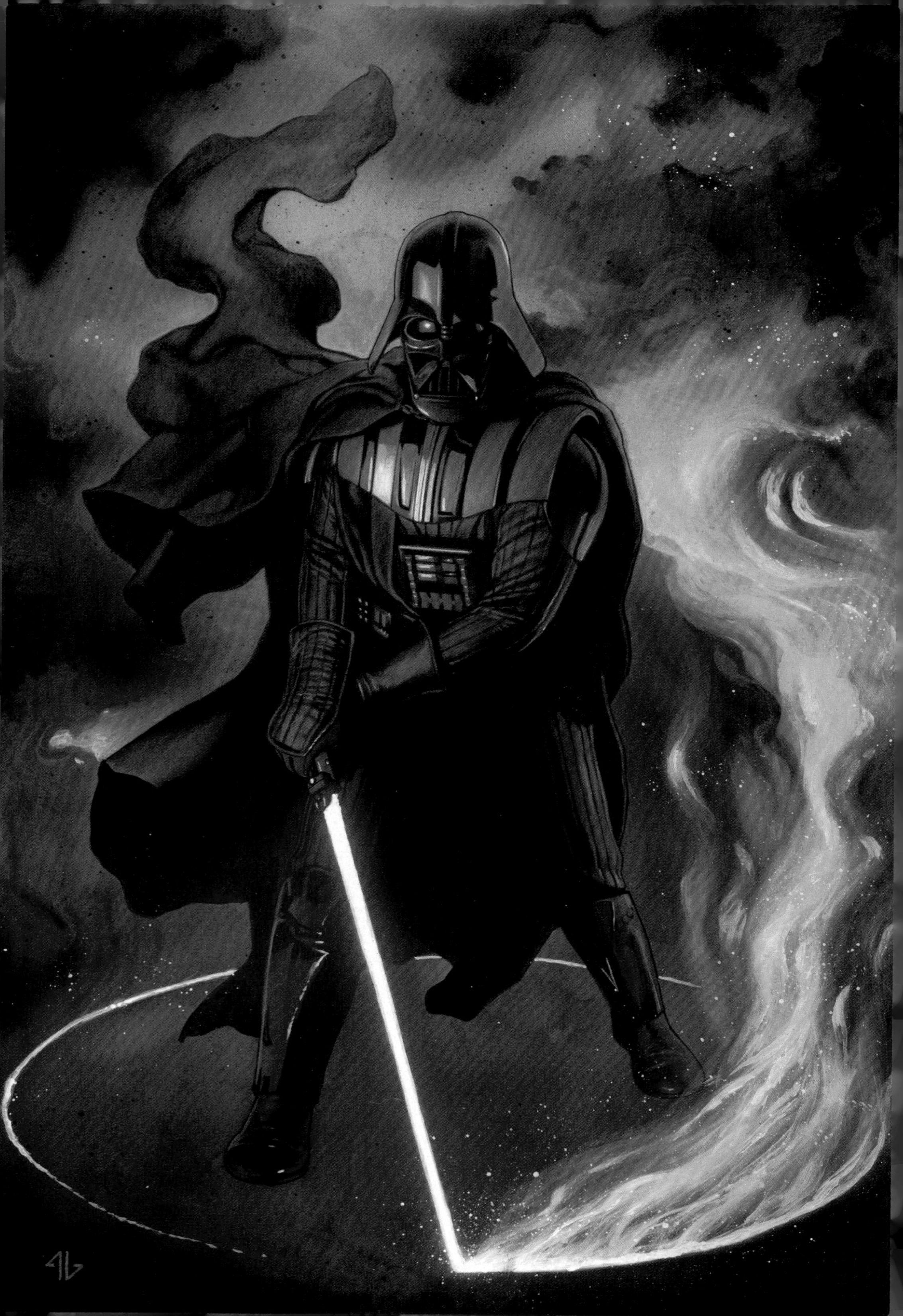

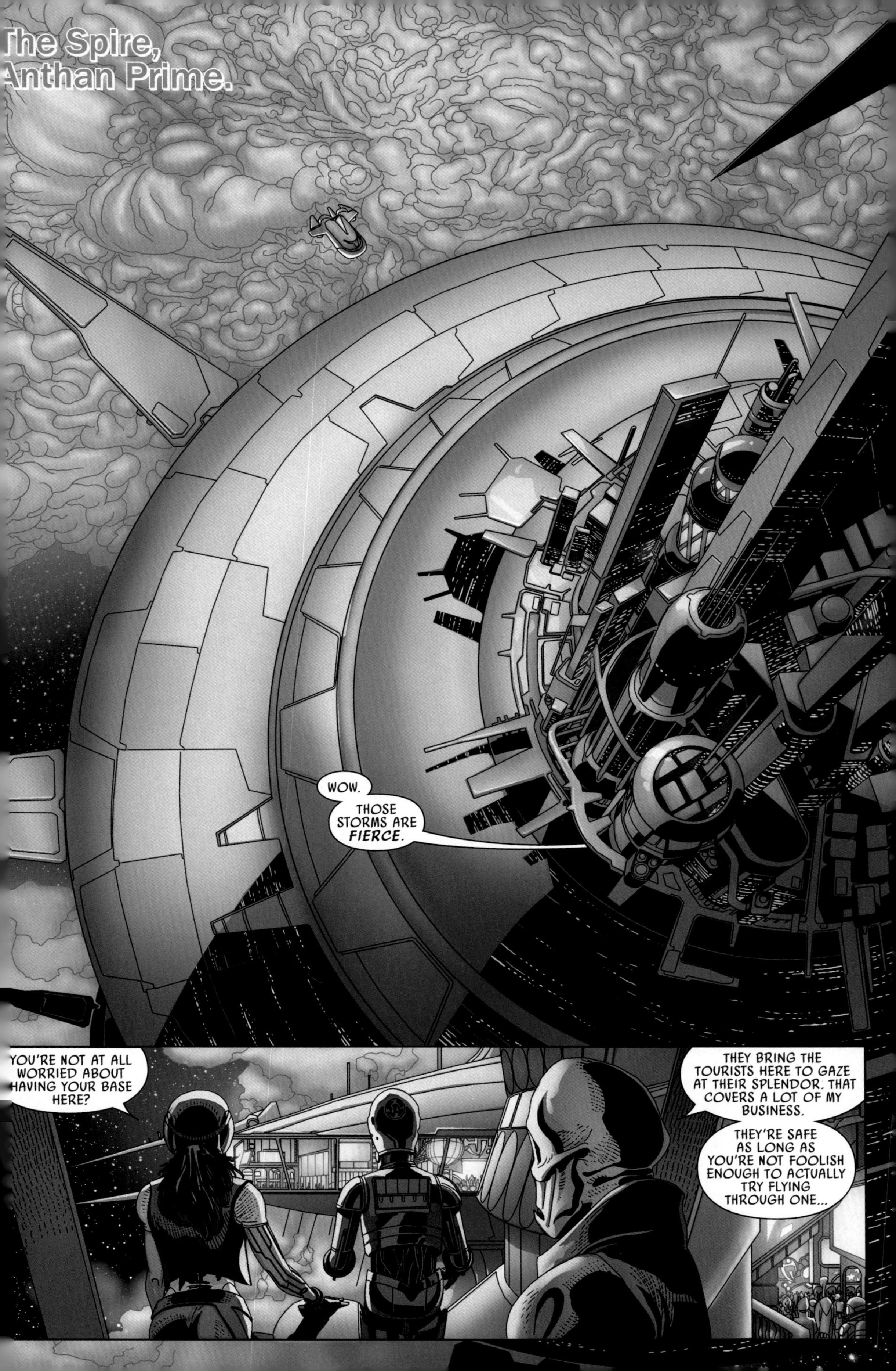
The Spire, Anthan Prime.
WOW.
THOSE STORMS ARE FIERCE.
YOU'RE NOT AT ALL WORRIED ABOUT HAVING YOUR BASE HERE?
THEY BRING THE TOURISTS HERE TO GAZE AT THEIR SPLENDOR. THAT COVERS A LOT OF MY BUSINESS.
THEY'RE SAFE AS LONG AS YOU'RE NOT FOOLISH ENOUGH TO ACTUALLY TRY FLYING THROUGH ONE...

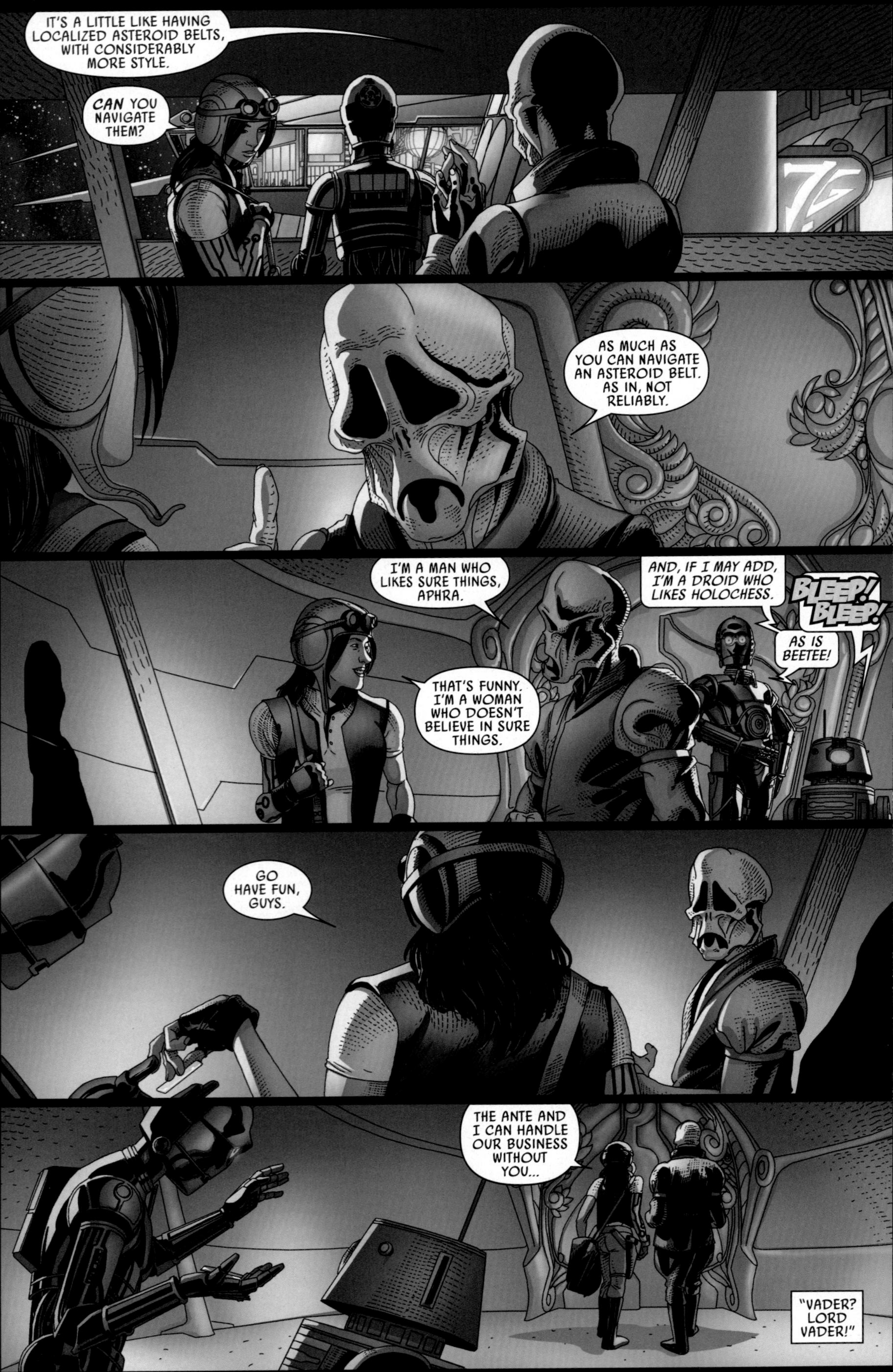
IT'S A LITTLE LIKE HAVING LOCALIZED ASTEROID BELTS, WITH CONSIDERABLY MORE STYLE.
CAN YOU NAVIGATE THEM?
AS MUCH AS YOU CAN NAVIGATE AN ASTEROID BELT. AS IN, NOT RELIABLY.
I'M A MAN WHO LIKES SURE THINGS, APHRA.
THAT'S FUNNY. I'M A WOMAN WHO DOESN'T BELIEVE IN SURE THINGS.
AND, IF I MAY ADD, I'M A DROID WHO LIKES HOLOCHESS.
BLEEP! BLEEP!
AS IS BEETEE!
GO HAVE FUN, GUYS.
THE ANTE AND I CAN HANDLE OUR BUSINESS WITHOUT YOU...
"VADER? LORD VADER!"

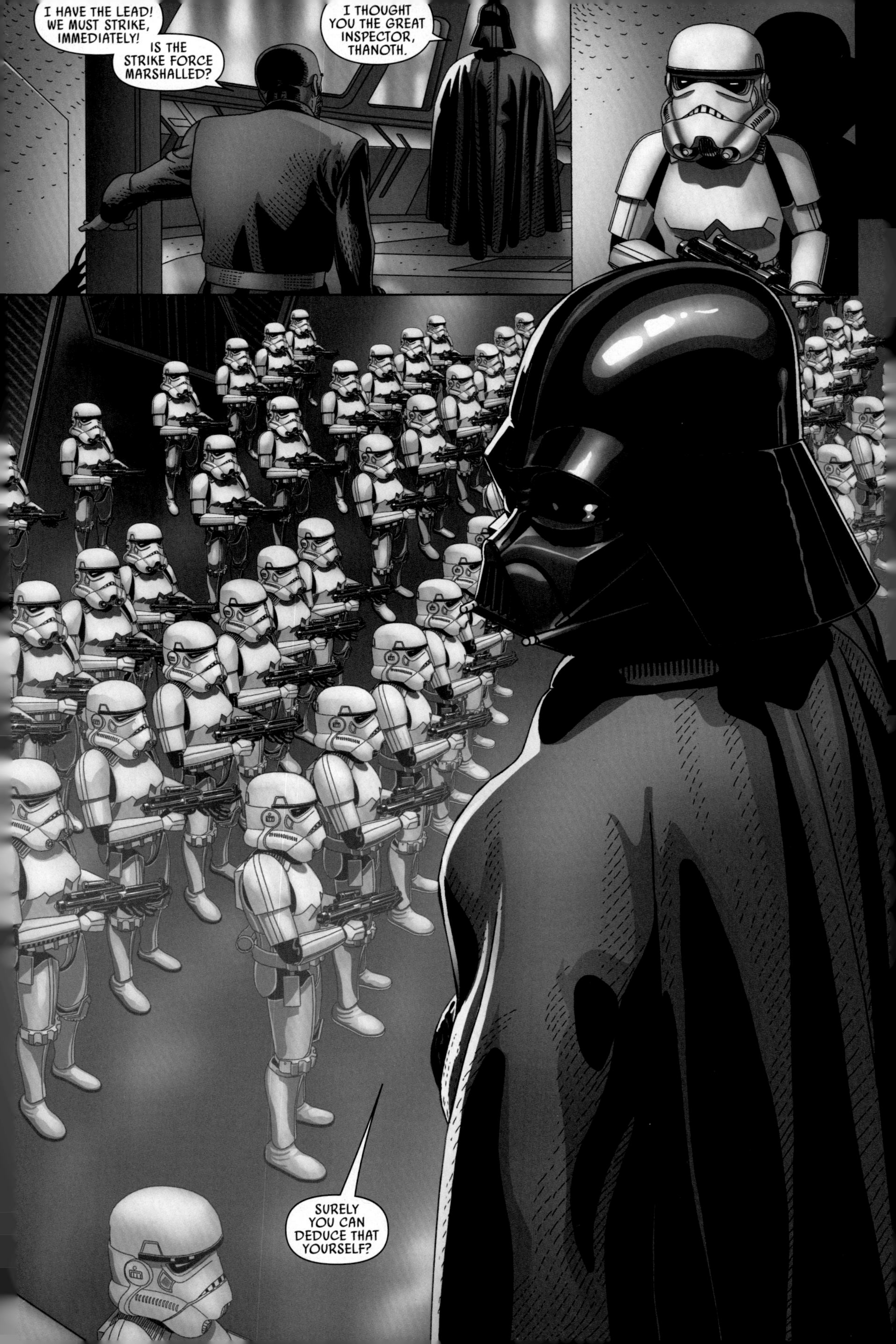

I HAVE THE LEAD! WE MUST STRIKE, IMMEDIATELY!
IS THE STRIKE FORCE MARSHALLED?
I THOUGHT YOU THE GREAT INSPECTOR, THANOTH.
SURELY YOU CAN DEDUCE THAT YOURSELF?

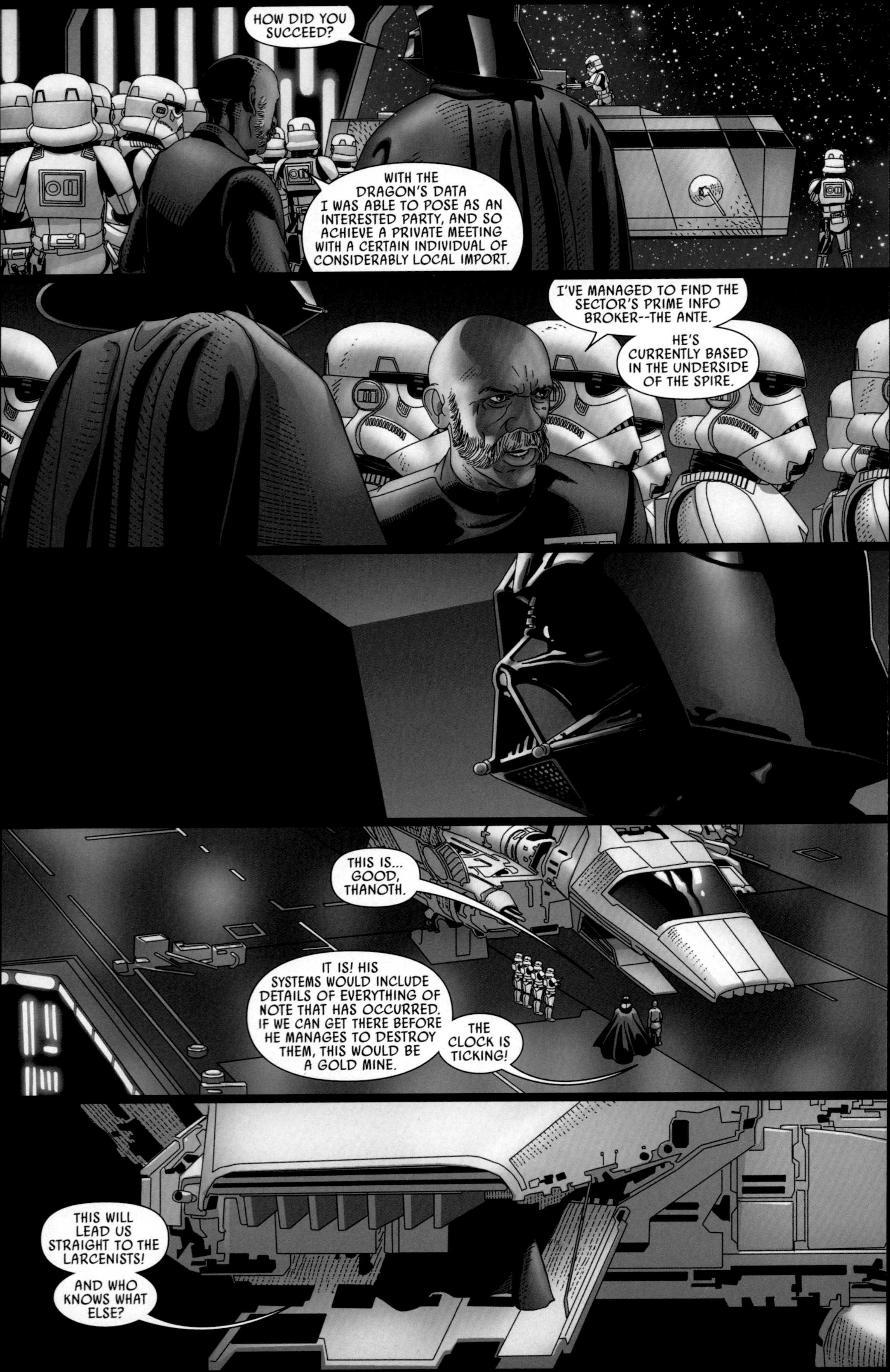
HOW DID YOU SUCCEED?
WITH THE DRAGON'S DATA I WAS ABLE TO POSE AS AN INTERESTED PARTY, AND SO ACHIEVE A PRIVATE MEETING WITH A CERTAIN INDIVIDUAL OF CONSIDERABLY LOCAL IMPORT.
I'VE MANAGED TO FIND THE SECTOR'S PRIME INFO BROKER--THE ANTE.
HE'S CURRENTLY BASED IN THE UNDERSIDE OF THE SPIRE.
THIS IS... GOOD, THANOTH.
IT IS! HIS SYSTEMS WOULD INCLUDE DETAILS OF EVERYTHING OF NOTE THAT HAS OCCURRED. IF WE CAN GET THERE BEFORE HE MANAGES TO DESTROY THEM, THIS WOULD BE A GOLD MINE.
THE CLOCK IS TICKING!
THIS WILL LEAD US STRAIGHT TO THE LARCENISTS!
AND WHO KNOWS WHAT ELSE?

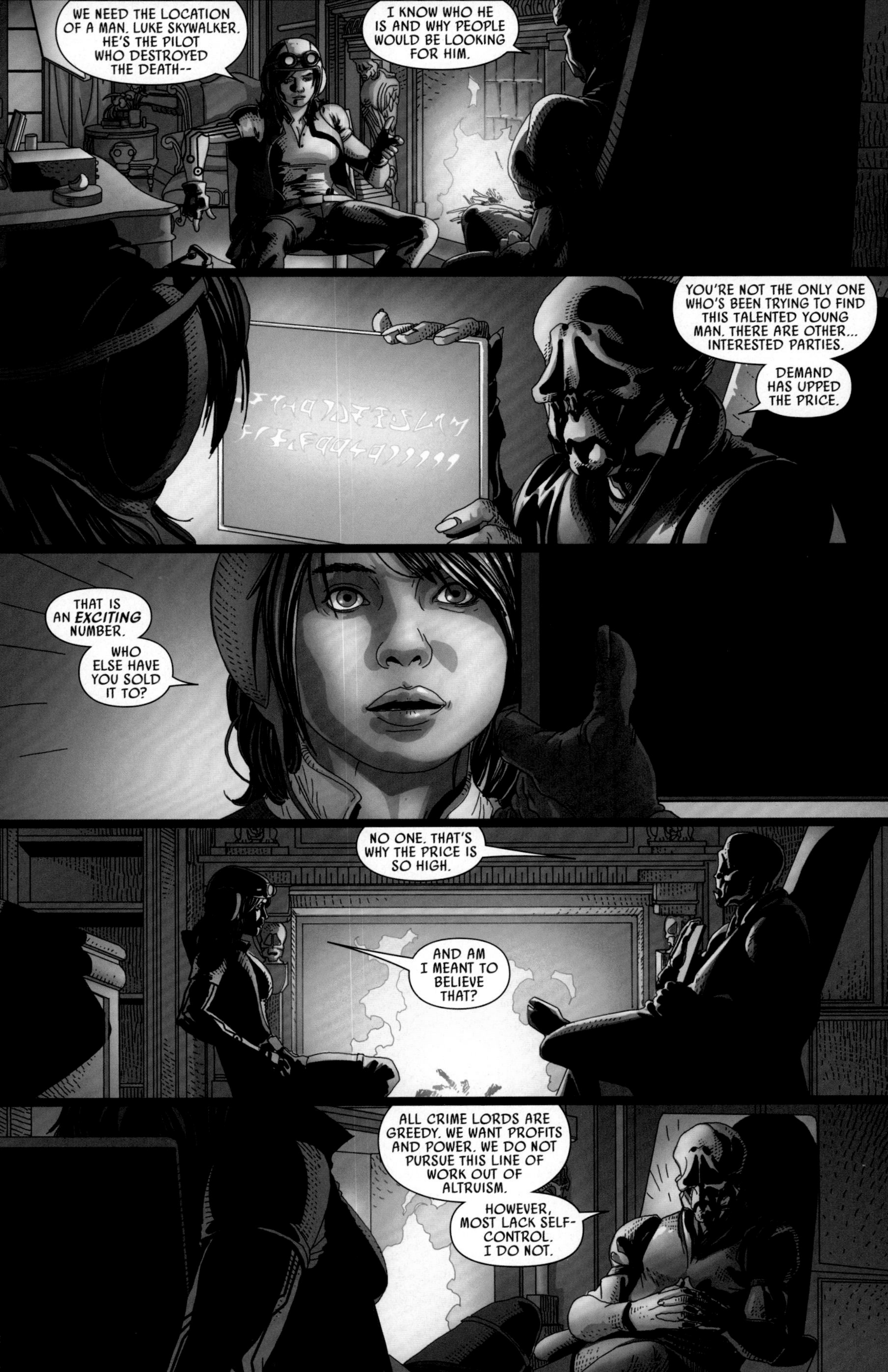
WE NEED THE LOCATION OF A MAN. LUKE SKYWALKER. HE'S THE PILOT WHO DESTROYED THE DEATH--
I KNOW WHO HE IS AND WHY PEOPLE WOULD BE LOOKING FOR HIM.
YOU'RE NOT THE ONLY ONE WHO'S BEEN TRYING TO FIND THIS TALENTED YOUNG MAN. THERE ARE OTHER... INTERESTED PARTIES.
DEMAND HAS UPPED THE PRICE.
THAT IS AN *EXCITING* NUMBER.
WHO ELSE HAVE YOU SOLD IT TO?
NO ONE. THAT'S WHY THE PRICE IS SO HIGH.
AND AM I MEANT TO BELIEVE THAT?
ALL CRIME LORDS ARE GREEDY. WE WANT PROFITS AND POWER. WE DO NOT PURSUE THIS LINE OF WORK OUT OF ALTRUISM.
HOWEVER, MOST LACK SELF-CONTROL. I DO NOT.

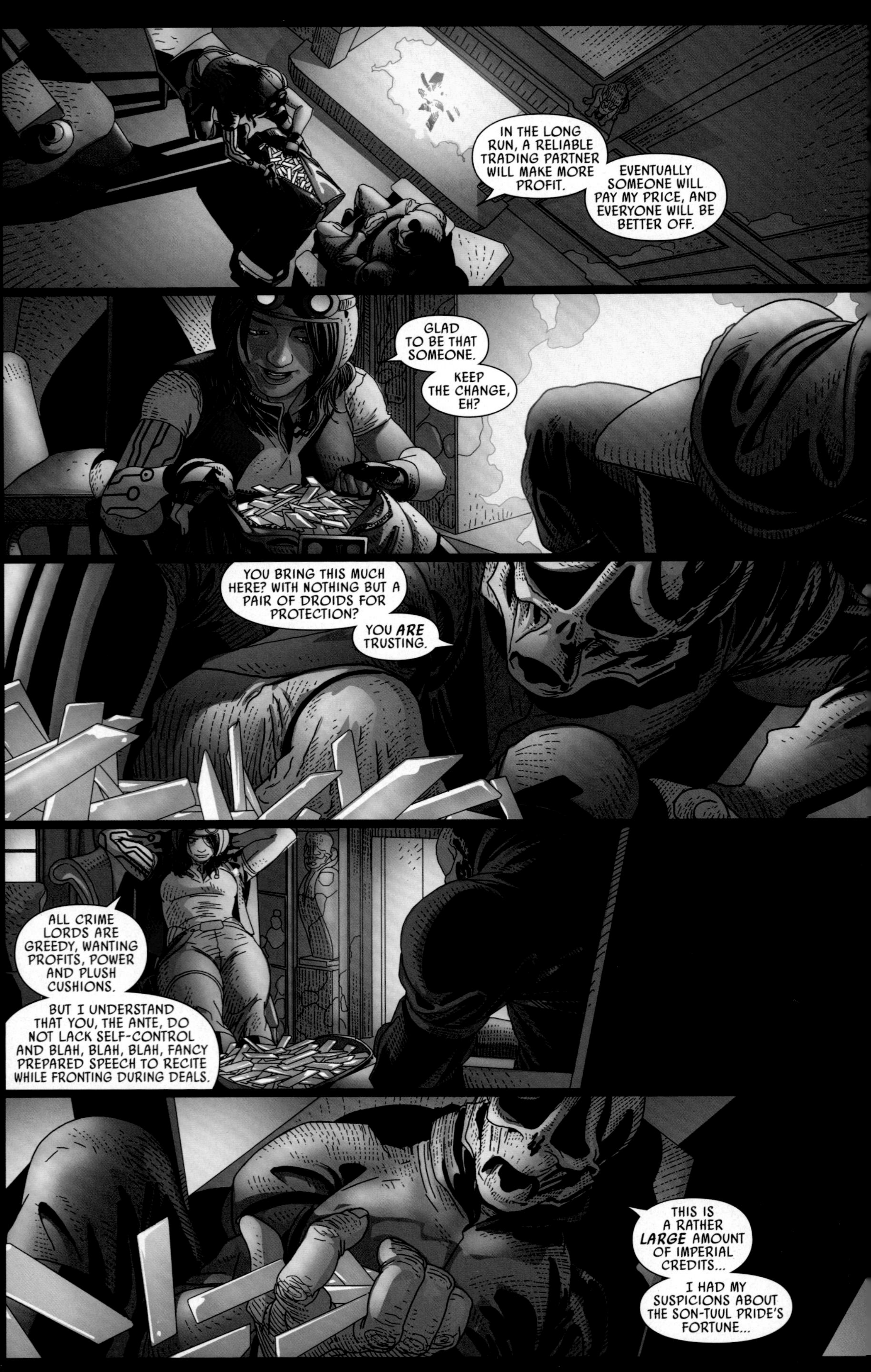
IN THE LONG RUN, A RELIABLE TRADING PARTNER WILL MAKE MORE PROFIT.
EVENTUALLY SOMEONE WILL PAY MY PRICE, AND EVERYONE WILL BE BETTER OFF.
GLAD TO BE THAT SOMEONE.
KEEP THE CHANGE, EH?
YOU BRING THIS MUCH HERE? WITH NOTHING BUT A PAIR OF DROIDS FOR PROTECTION?
YOU *ARE* TRUSTING.
ALL CRIME LORDS ARE GREEDY, WANTING PROFITS, POWER AND PLUSH CUSHIONS.
BUT I UNDERSTAND THAT YOU, THE ANTE, DO NOT LACK SELF-CONTROL AND BLAH, BLAH, BLAH, FANCY PREPARED SPEECH TO RECITE WHILE FRONTING DURING DEALS.
THIS IS A RATHER *LARGE* AMOUNT OF IMPERIAL CREDITS...
I HAD MY SUSPICIONS ABOUT THE SON-TUUL PRIDE'S FORTUNE...

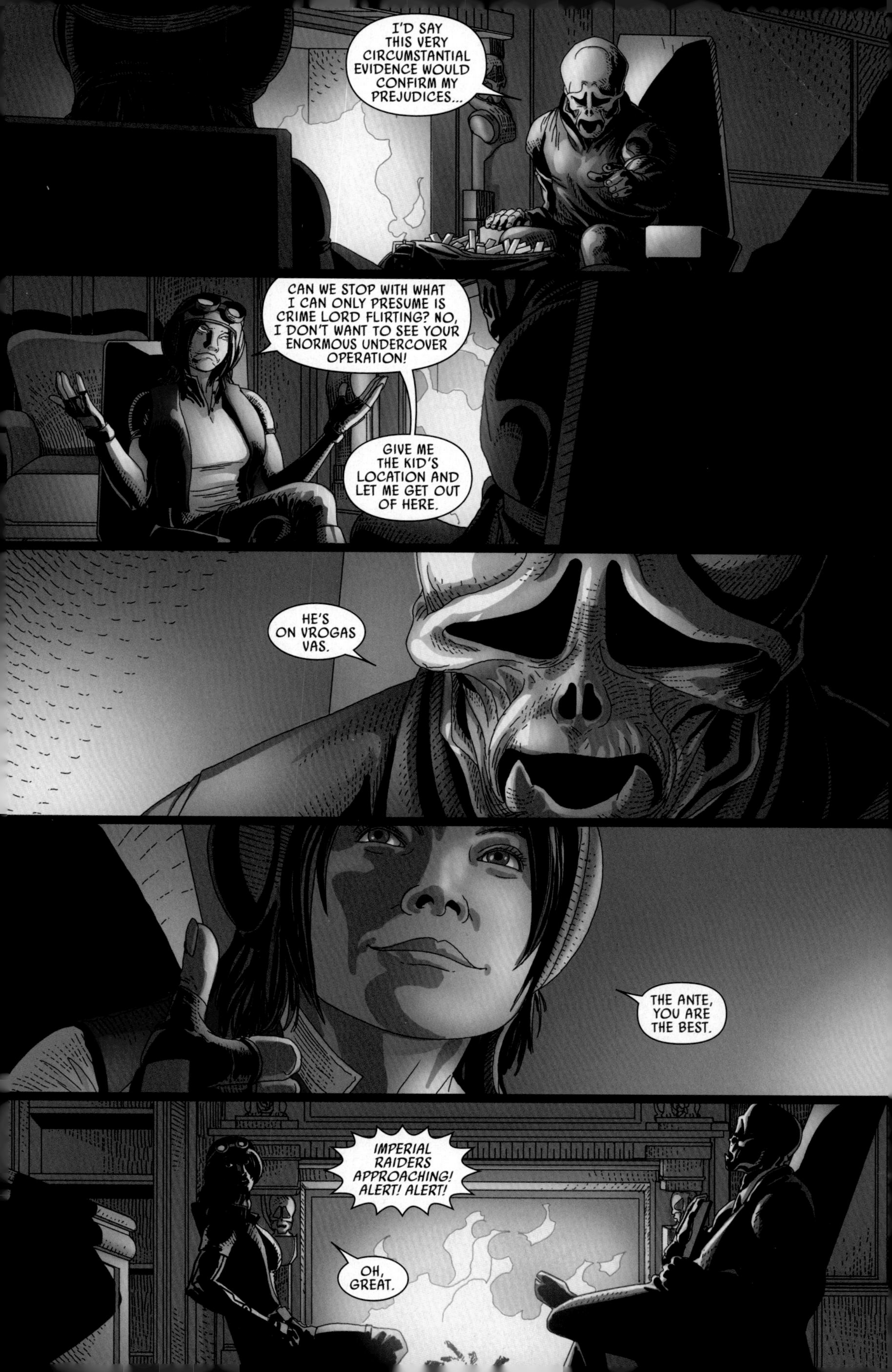
I'D SAY THIS VERY CIRCUMSTANTIAL EVIDENCE WOULD CONFIRM MY PREJUDICES...
CAN WE STOP WITH WHAT I CAN ONLY PRESUME IS CRIME LORD FLIRTING? NO, I DON'T WANT TO SEE YOUR ENORMOUS UNDERCOVER OPERATION!
GIVE ME THE KID'S LOCATION AND LET ME GET OUT OF HERE.
HE'S ON VROGAS VAS.
THE ANTE, YOU ARE THE BEST.
IMPERIAL RAIDERS APPROACHING! ALERT! ALERT!
OH, GREAT.

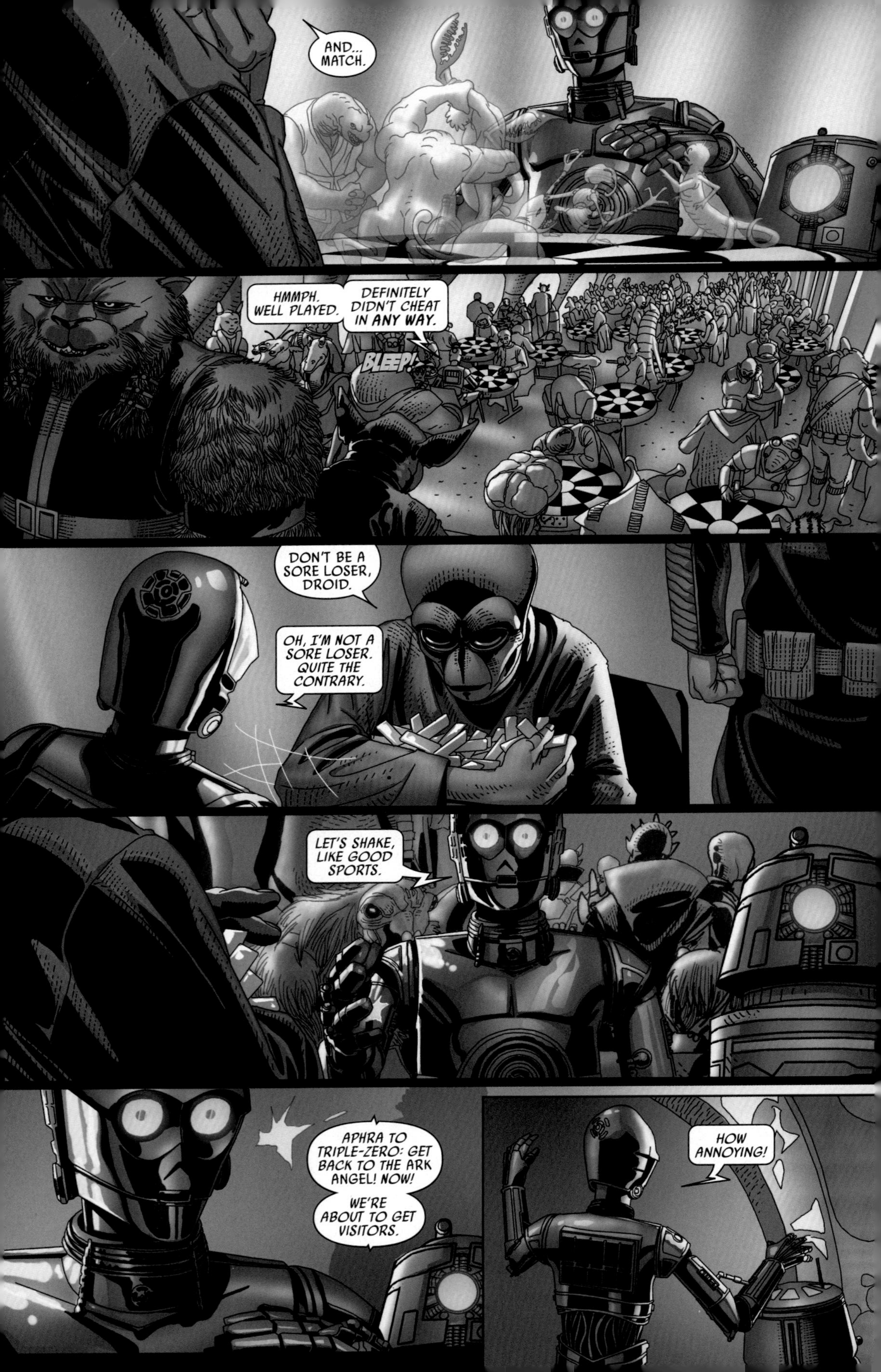
AND... MATCH.
HMMPH. WELL PLAYED.
DEFINITELY DIDN'T CHEAT IN ANY WAY.
BLEEP!
DON'T BE A SORE LOSER, DROID.
OH, I'M NOT A SORE LOSER. QUITE THE CONTRARY.
LET'S SHAKE, LIKE GOOD SPORTS.
APHRA TO TRIPLE-ZERO: GET BACK TO THE ARK ANGEL! NOW!
WE'RE ABOUT TO GET VISITORS.
HOW ANNOYING!

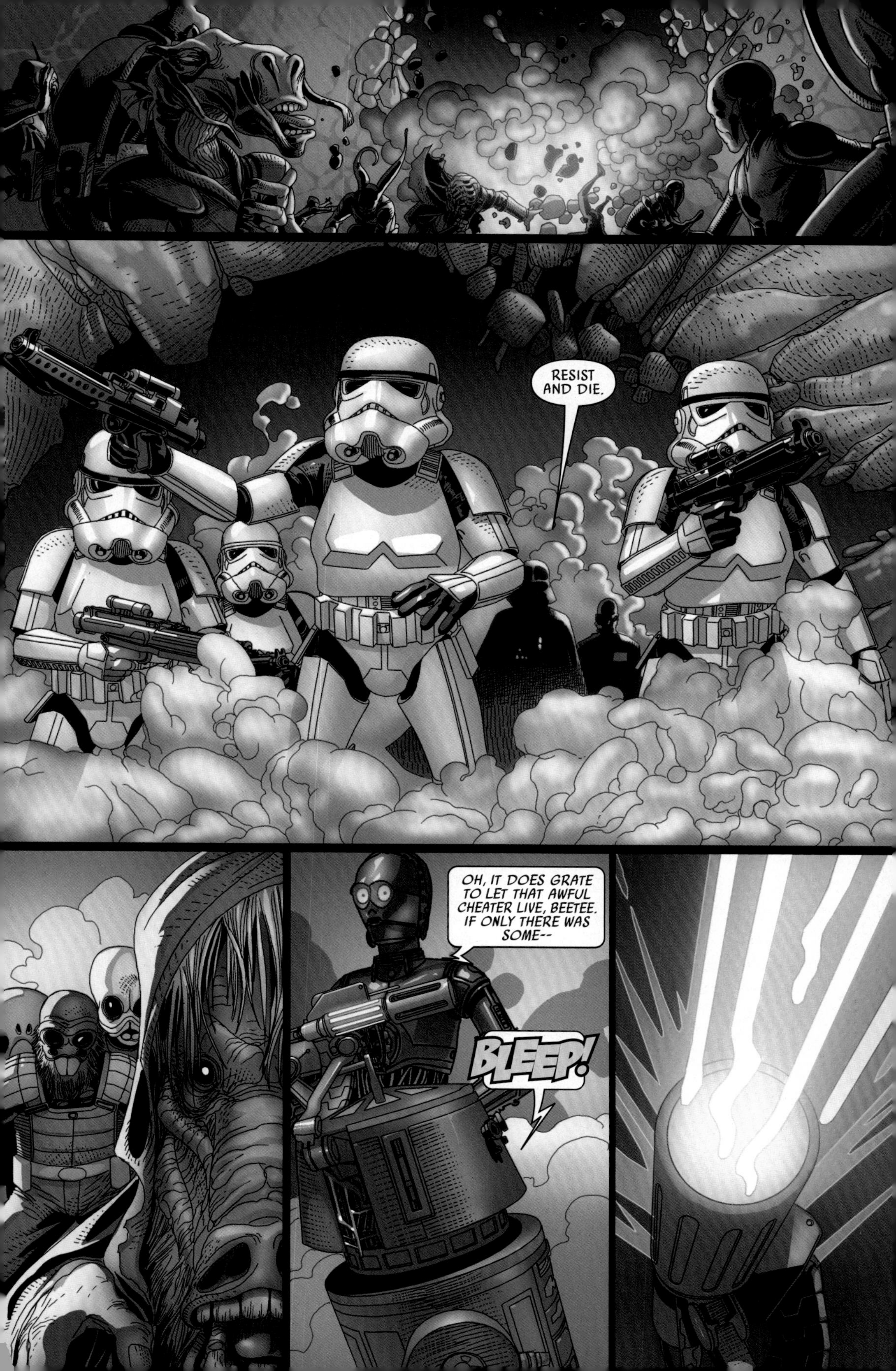
RESIST AND DIE.
OH, IT DOES GRATE TO LET THAT AWFUL CHEATER LIVE, BEETEE. IF ONLY THERE WAS SOME--
BLEEP!

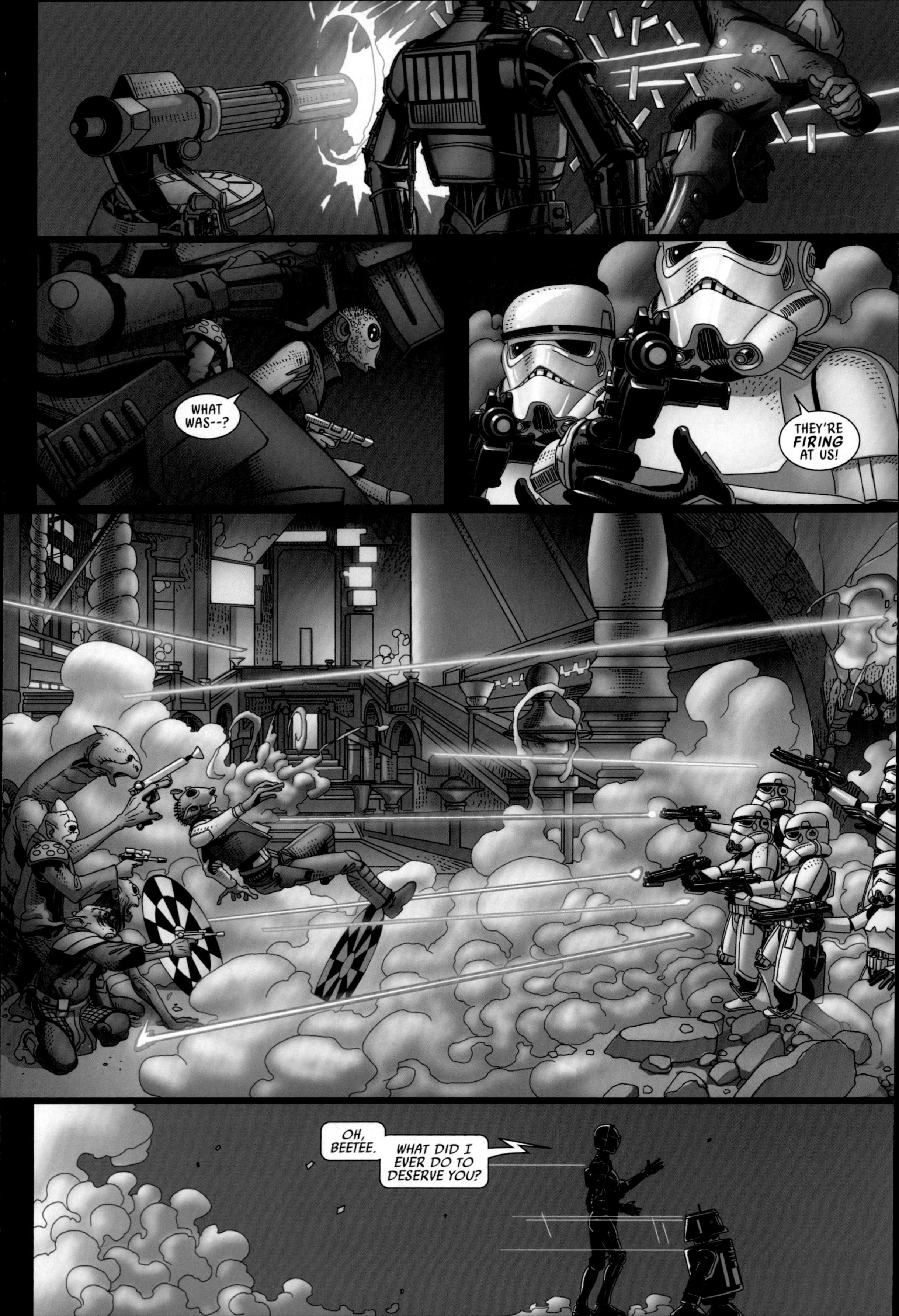
WHAT WAS--?
THEY'RE FIRING AT US!
OH, BEETEE.
WHAT DID I EVER DO TO DESERVE YOU?

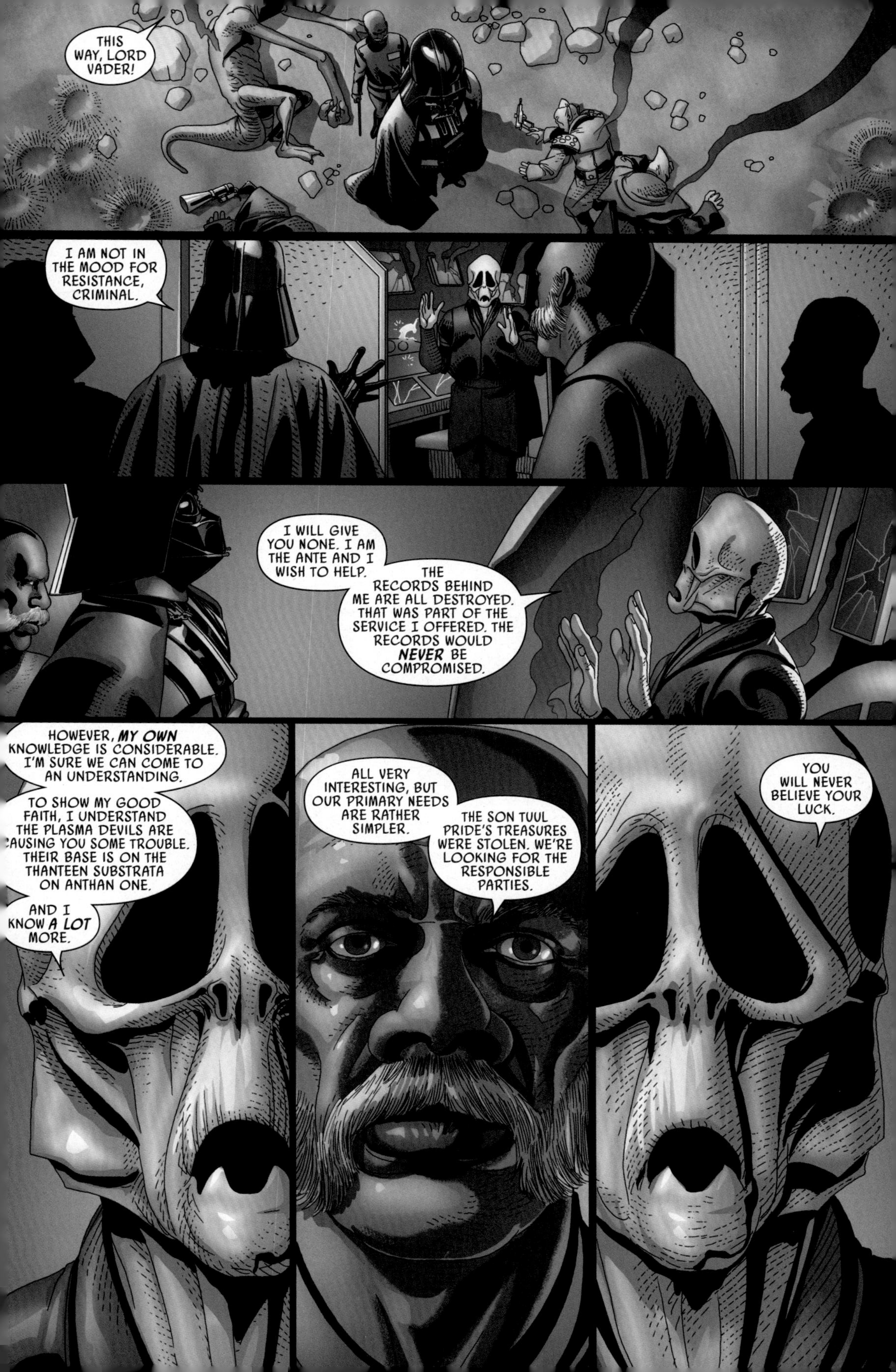
THIS WAY, LORD VADER!
I AM NOT IN THE MOOD FOR RESISTANCE, CRIMINAL.
I WILL GIVE YOU NONE. I AM THE ANTE AND I WISH TO HELP.
THE RECORDS BEHIND ME ARE ALL DESTROYED. THAT WAS PART OF THE SERVICE I OFFERED. THE RECORDS WOULD NEVER BE COMPROMISED.
HOWEVER, MY OWN KNOWLEDGE IS CONSIDERABLE. I'M SURE WE CAN COME TO AN UNDERSTANDING.
TO SHOW MY GOOD FAITH, I UNDERSTAND THE PLASMA DEVILS ARE CAUSING YOU SOME TROUBLE. THEIR BASE IS ON THE THANTEEN SUBSTRATA ON ANTHAN ONE.
AND I KNOW A LOT MORE.
ALL VERY INTERESTING, BUT OUR PRIMARY NEEDS ARE RATHER SIMPLER.
THE SON TUUL PRIDE'S TREASURES WERE STOLEN. WE'RE LOOKING FOR THE RESPONSIBLE PARTIES.
YOU WILL NEVER BELIEVE YOUR LUCK.

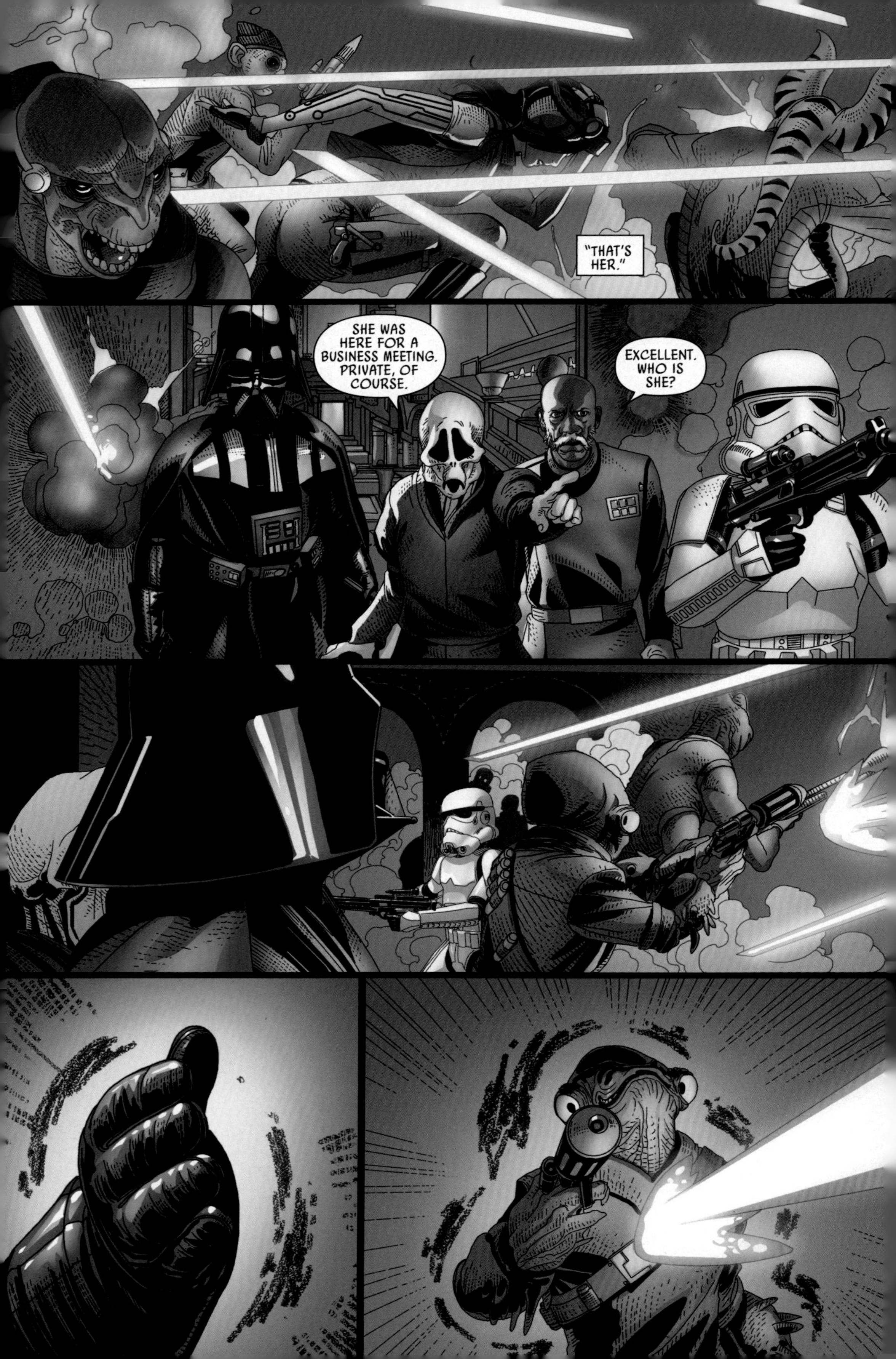
"THAT'S HER."
SHE WAS HERE FOR A BUSINESS MEETING. PRIVATE, OF COURSE.
EXCELLENT. WHO IS SHE?

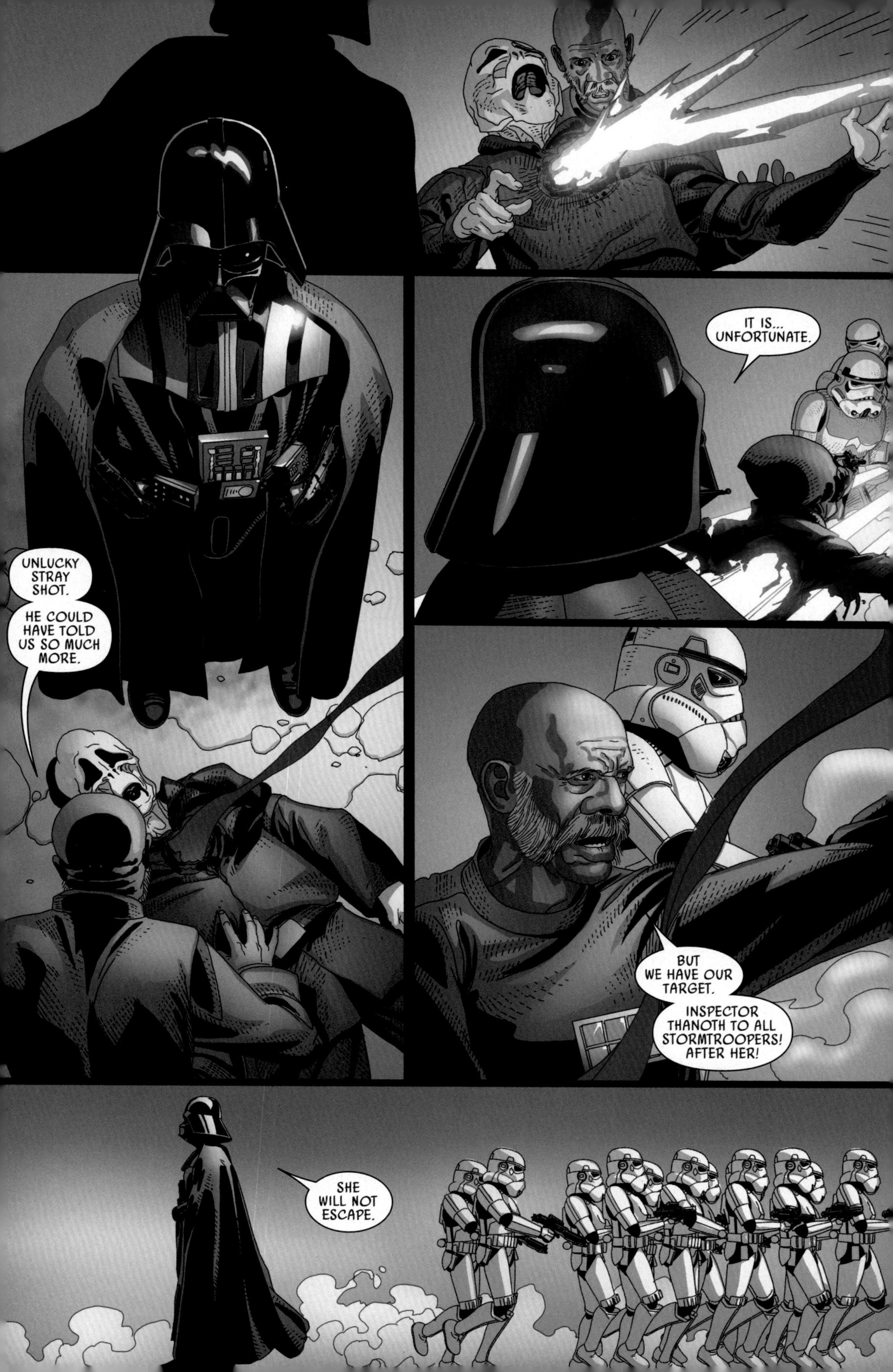
UNLUCKY STRAY SHOT.
HE COULD HAVE TOLD US SO MUCH MORE.
IT IS... UNFORTUNATE.
BUT WE HAVE OUR TARGET.
INSPECTOR THANOTH TO ALL STORMTROOPERS! AFTER HER!
SHE WILL NOT ESCAPE.

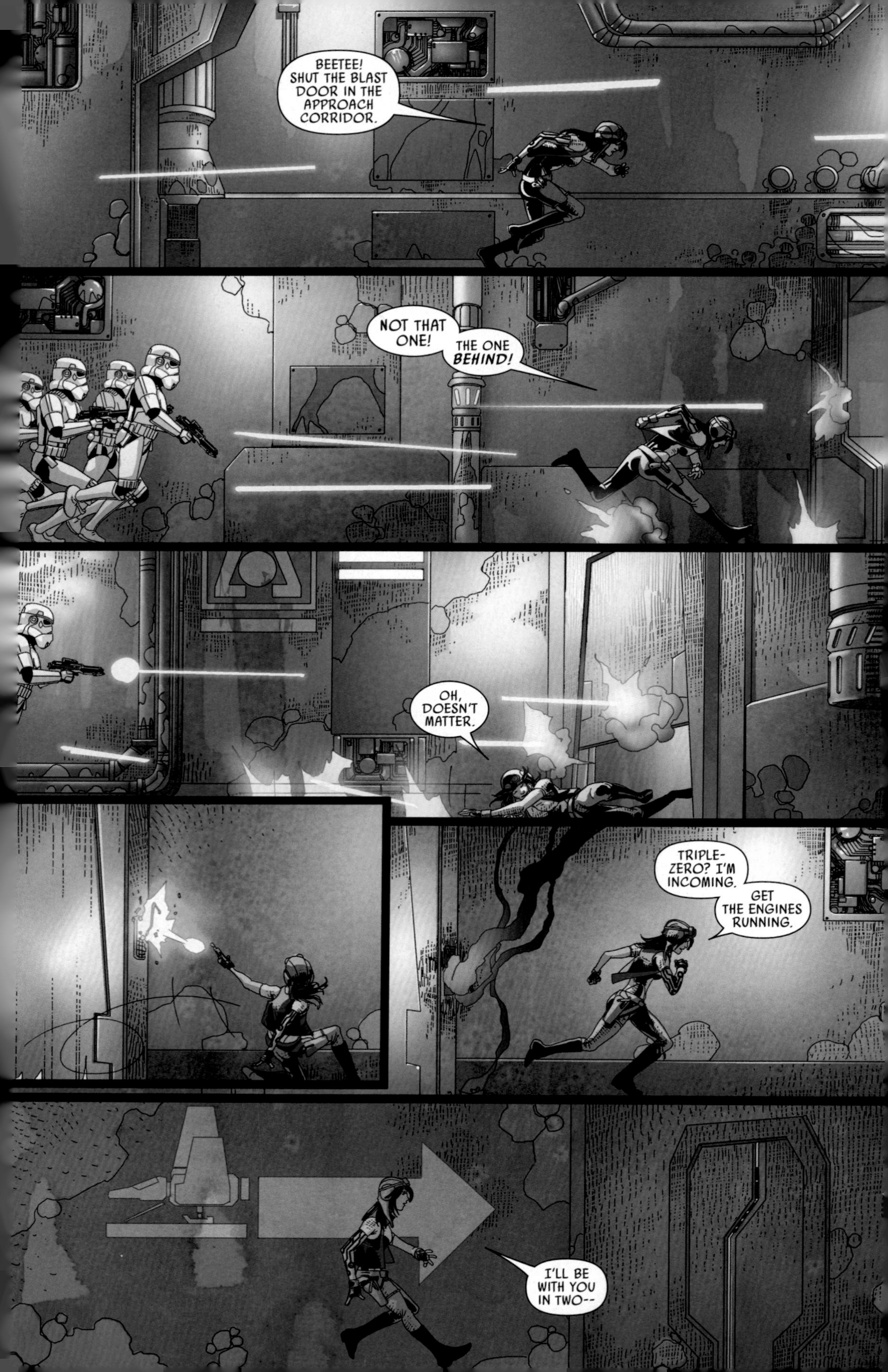
BEETEE! SHUT THE BLAST DOOR IN THE APPROACH CORRIDOR.
NOT THAT ONE!
THE ONE *BEHIND!*
OH, DOESN'T MATTER.
TRIPLE-ZERO? I'M INCOMING.
GET THE ENGINES RUNNING.
I'LL BE WITH YOU IN TWO--

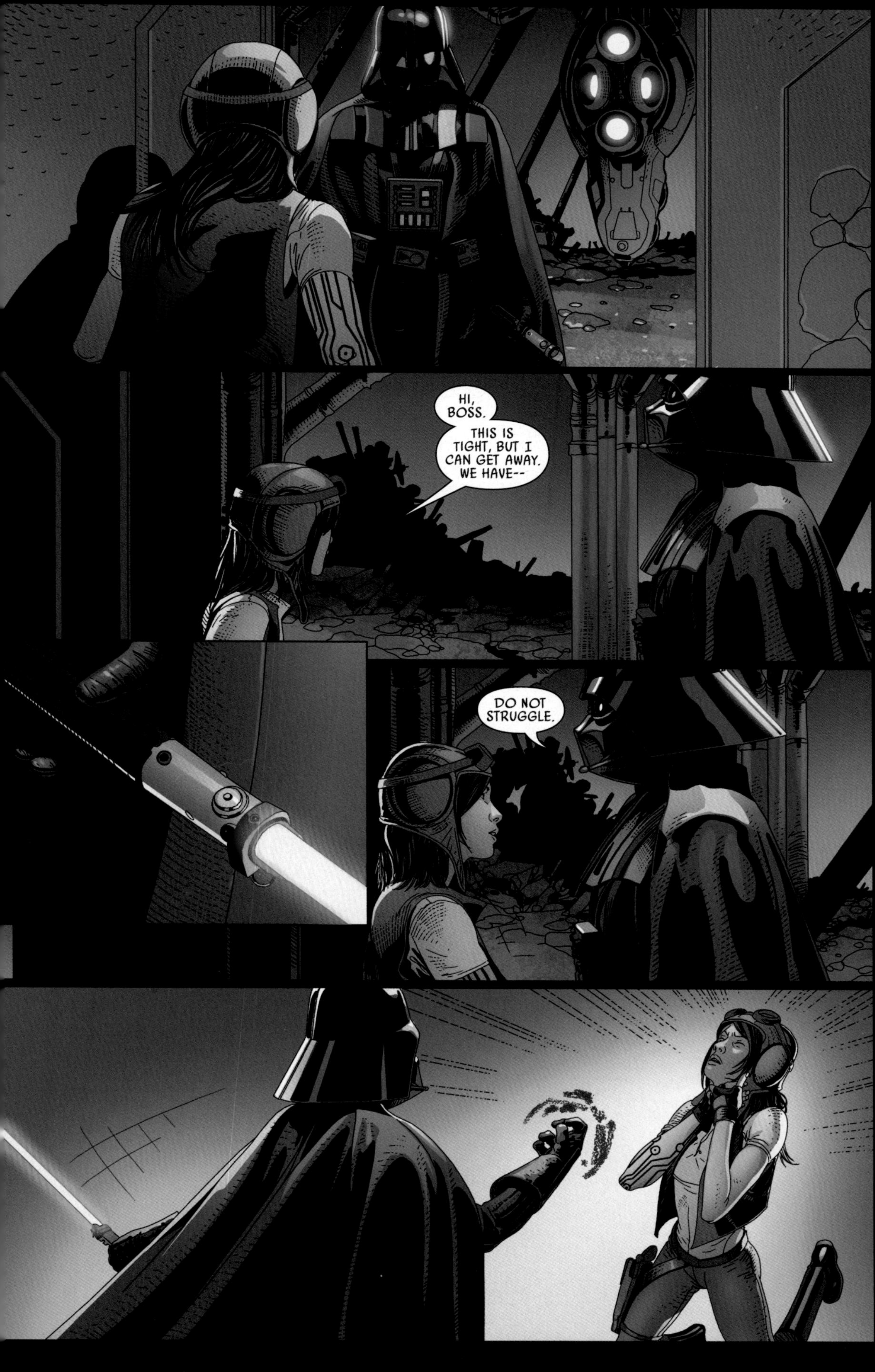
HI, BOSS.
THIS IS TIGHT, BUT I CAN GET AWAY. WE HAVE--
DO NOT STRUGGLE.

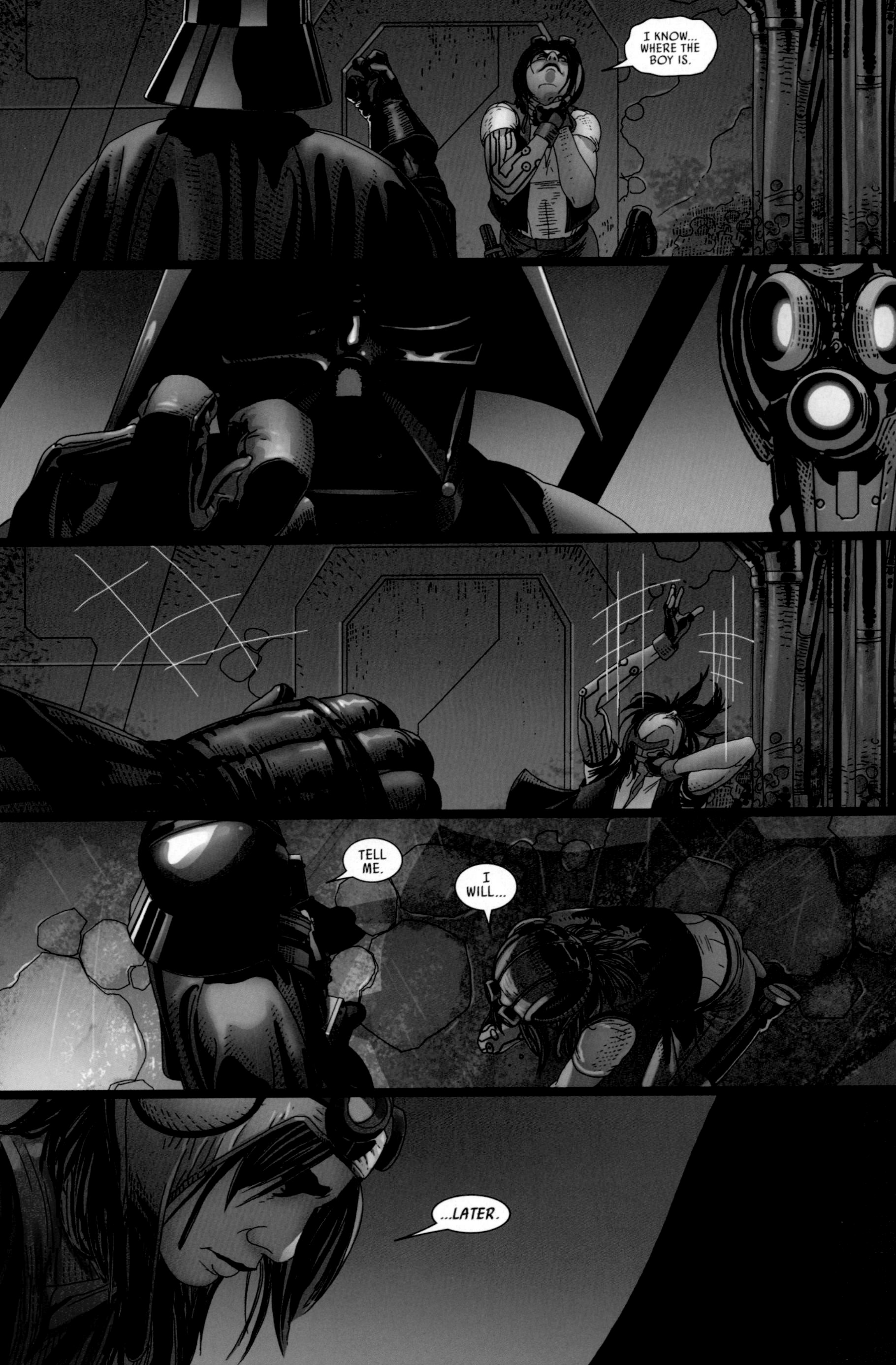
I KNOW... WHERE THE BOY IS.
TELL ME.
I WILL...
...LATER.

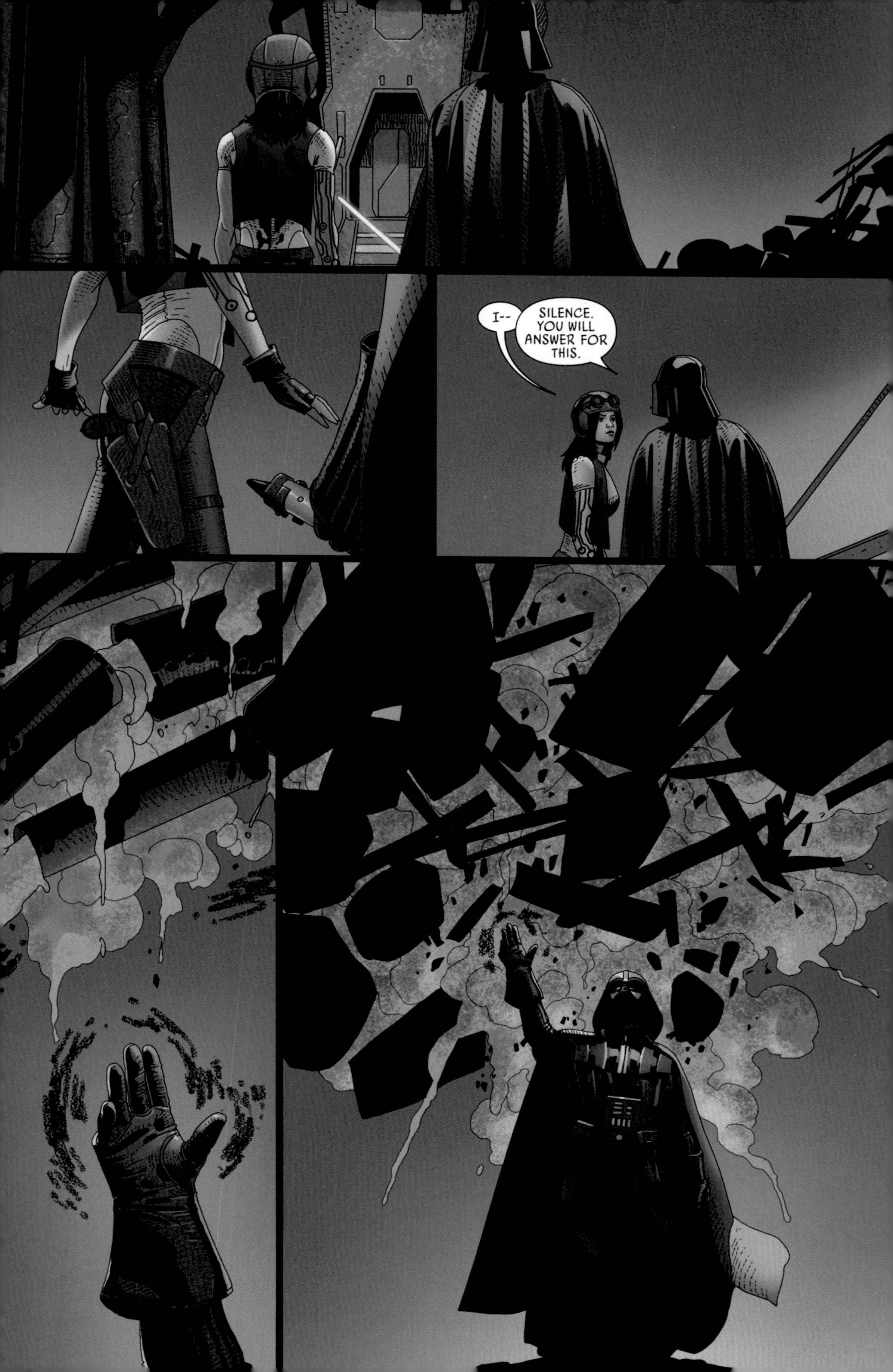
I--
SILENCE. YOU WILL ANSWER FOR THIS.

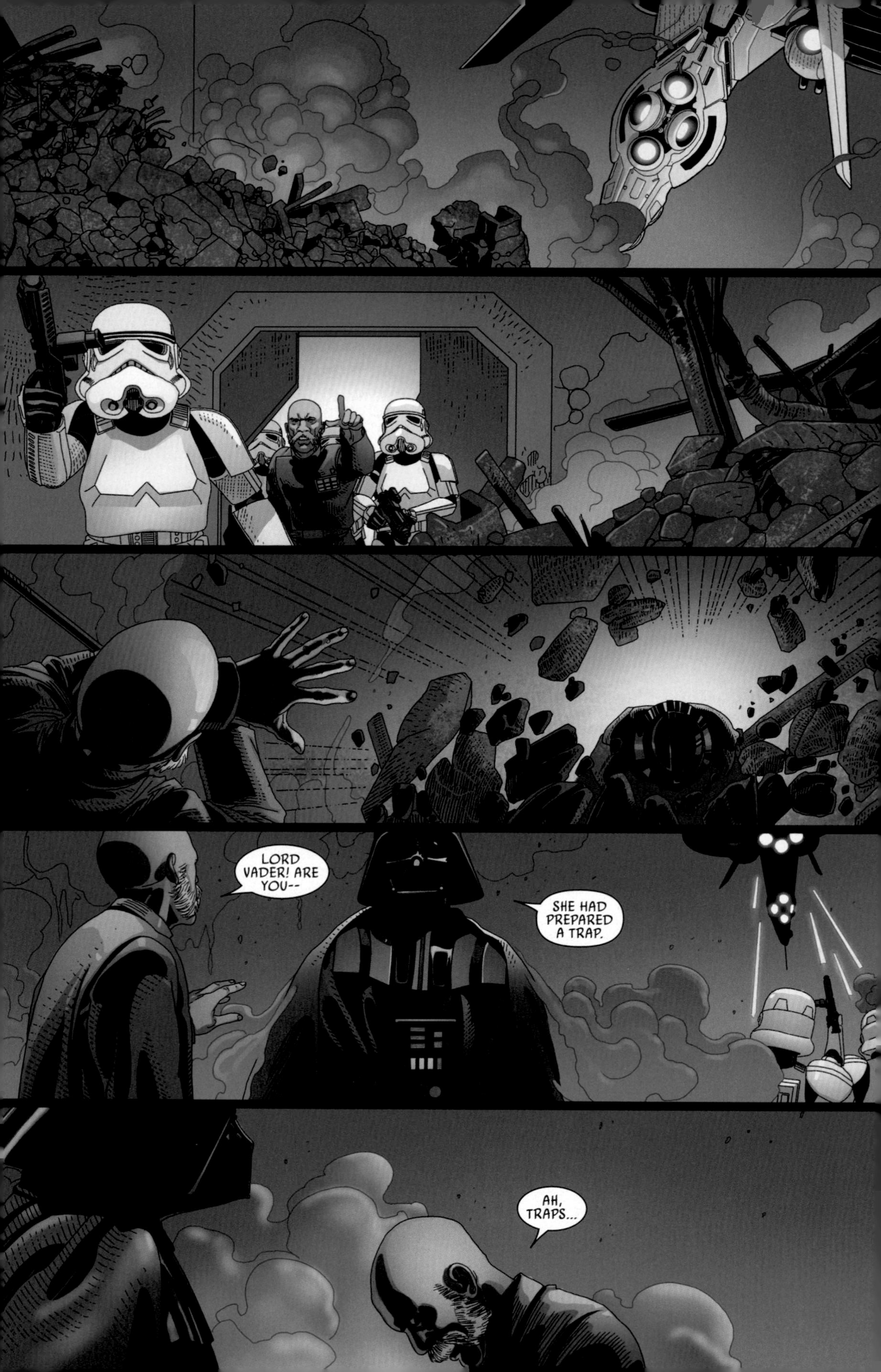
LORD VADER! ARE YOU--
SHE HAD PREPARED A TRAP.
AH, TRAPS...

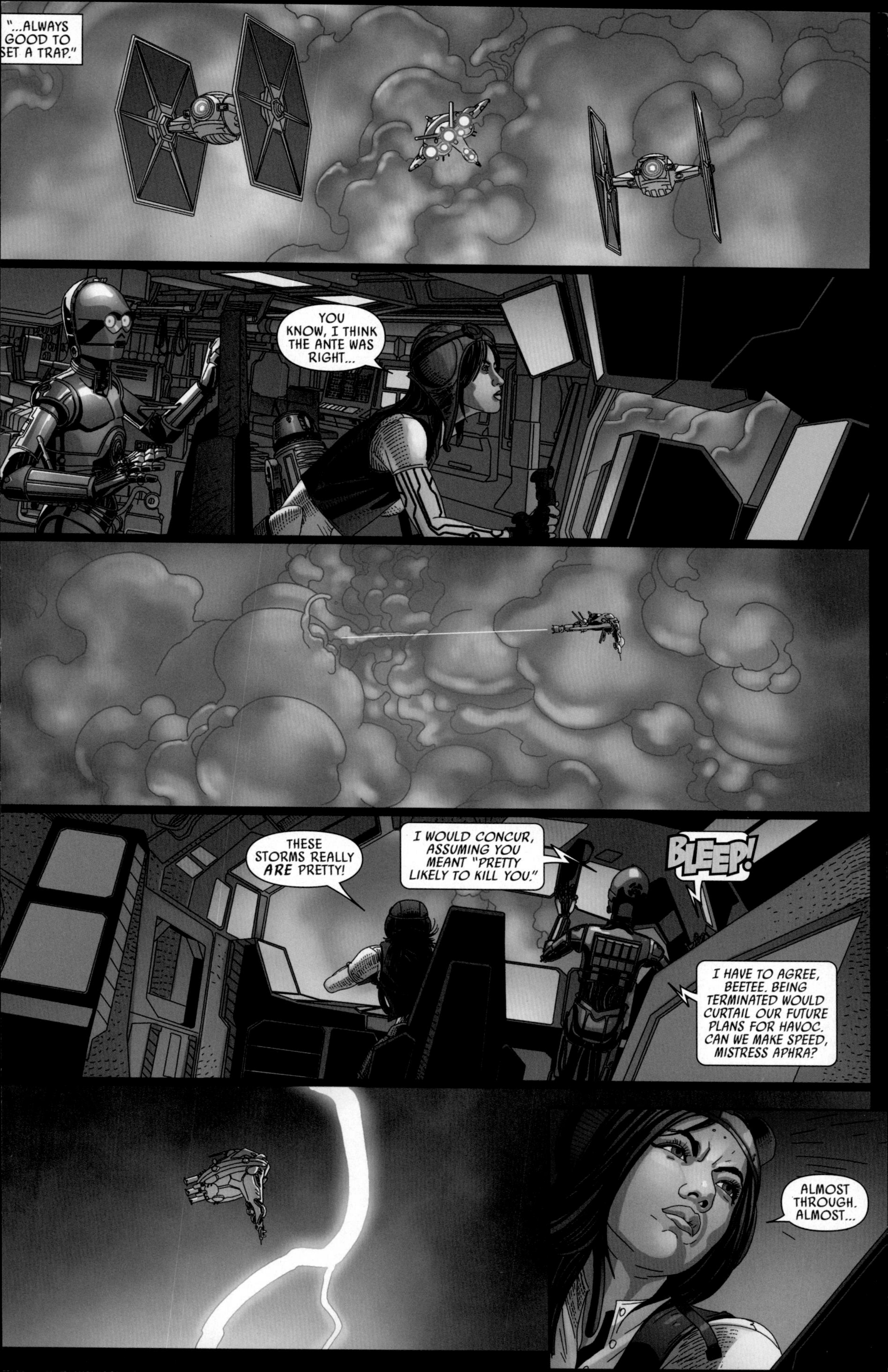
"...ALWAYS GOOD TO SET A TRAP."
YOU KNOW, I THINK THE ANTE WAS RIGHT...
THESE STORMS REALLY ARE PRETTY!
I WOULD CONCUR, ASSUMING YOU MEANT "PRETTY LIKELY TO KILL YOU."
BLEEP!
I HAVE TO AGREE, BEETEE. BEING TERMINATED WOULD CURTAIL OUR FUTURE PLANS FOR HAVOC. CAN WE MAKE SPEED, MISTRESS APHRA?
ALMOST THROUGH. ALMOST...

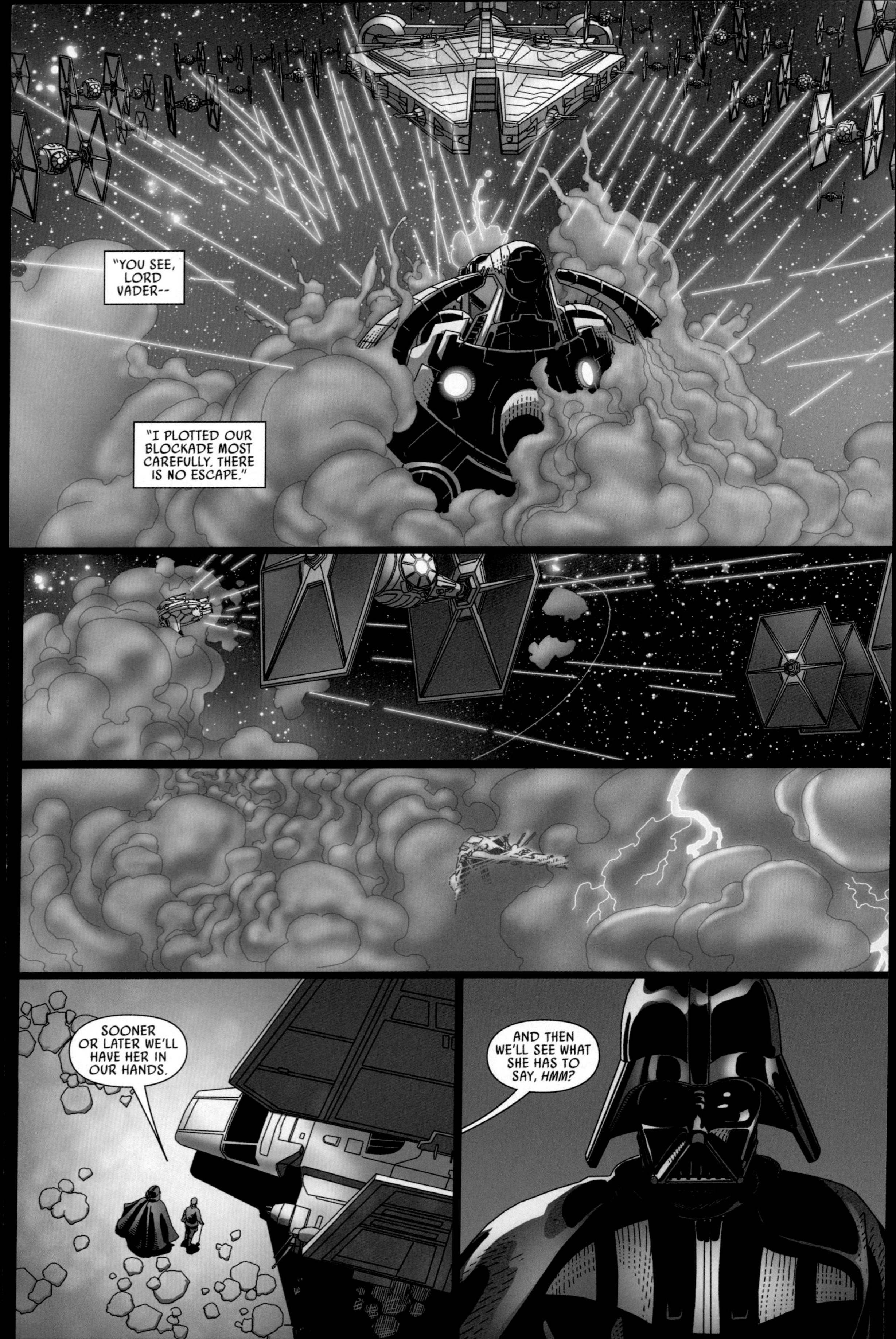
"YOU SEE, LORD VADER--
"I PLOTTED OUR BLOCKADE MOST CAREFULLY. THERE IS NO ESCAPE."
SOONER OR LATER WE'LL HAVE HER IN OUR HANDS.
AND THEN WE'LL SEE WHAT SHE HAS TO SAY, *HMM?*

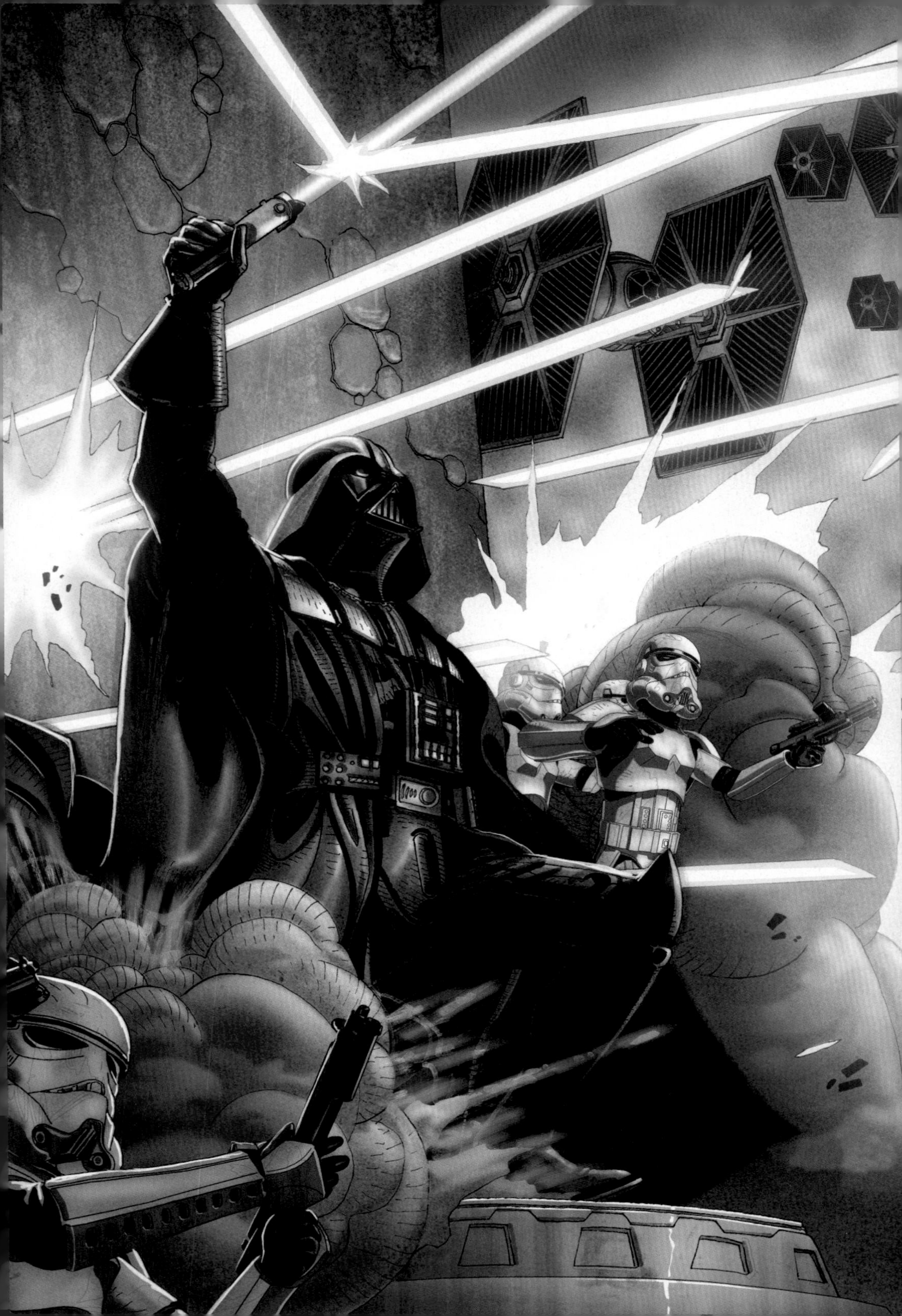

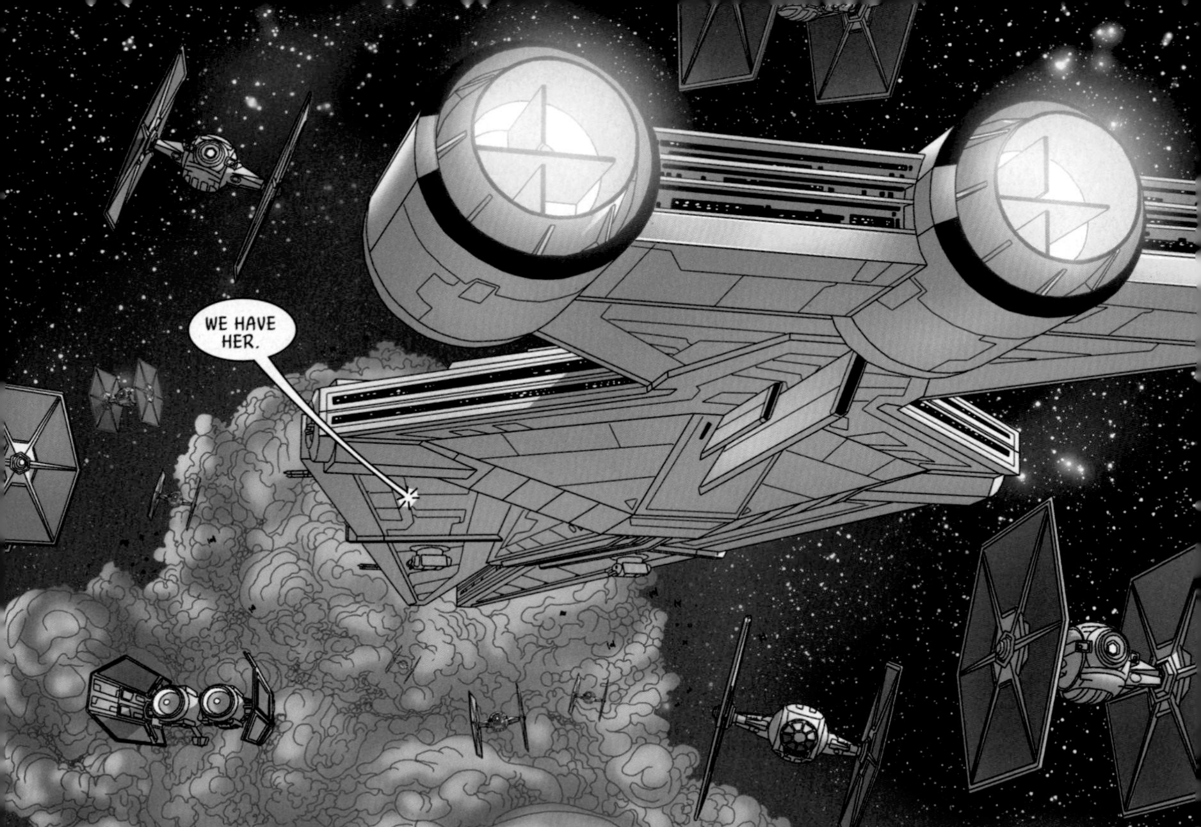
WE HAVE HER.

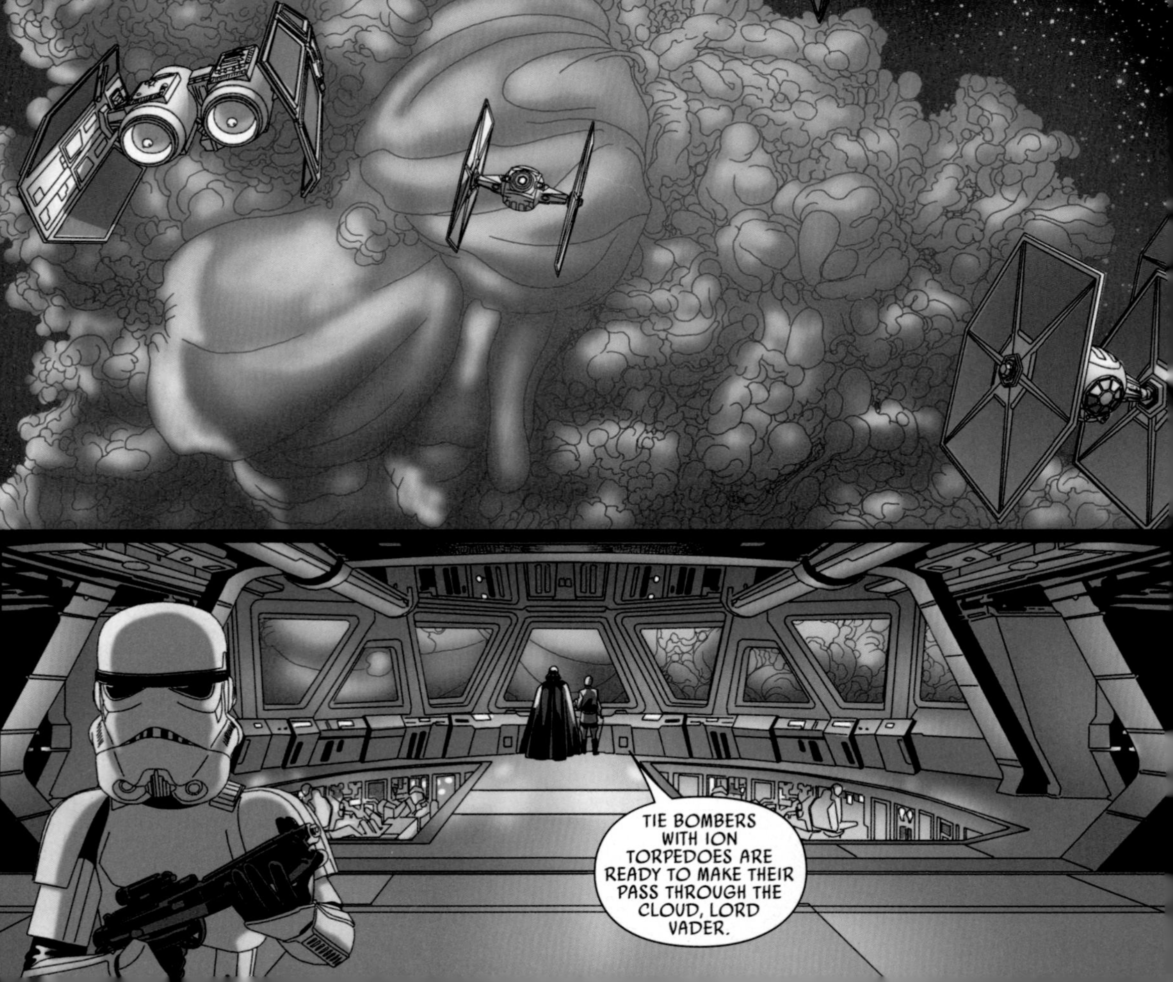
TIE BOMBERS WITH ION TORPEDOES ARE READY TO MAKE THEIR PASS THROUGH THE CLOUD, LORD VADER.

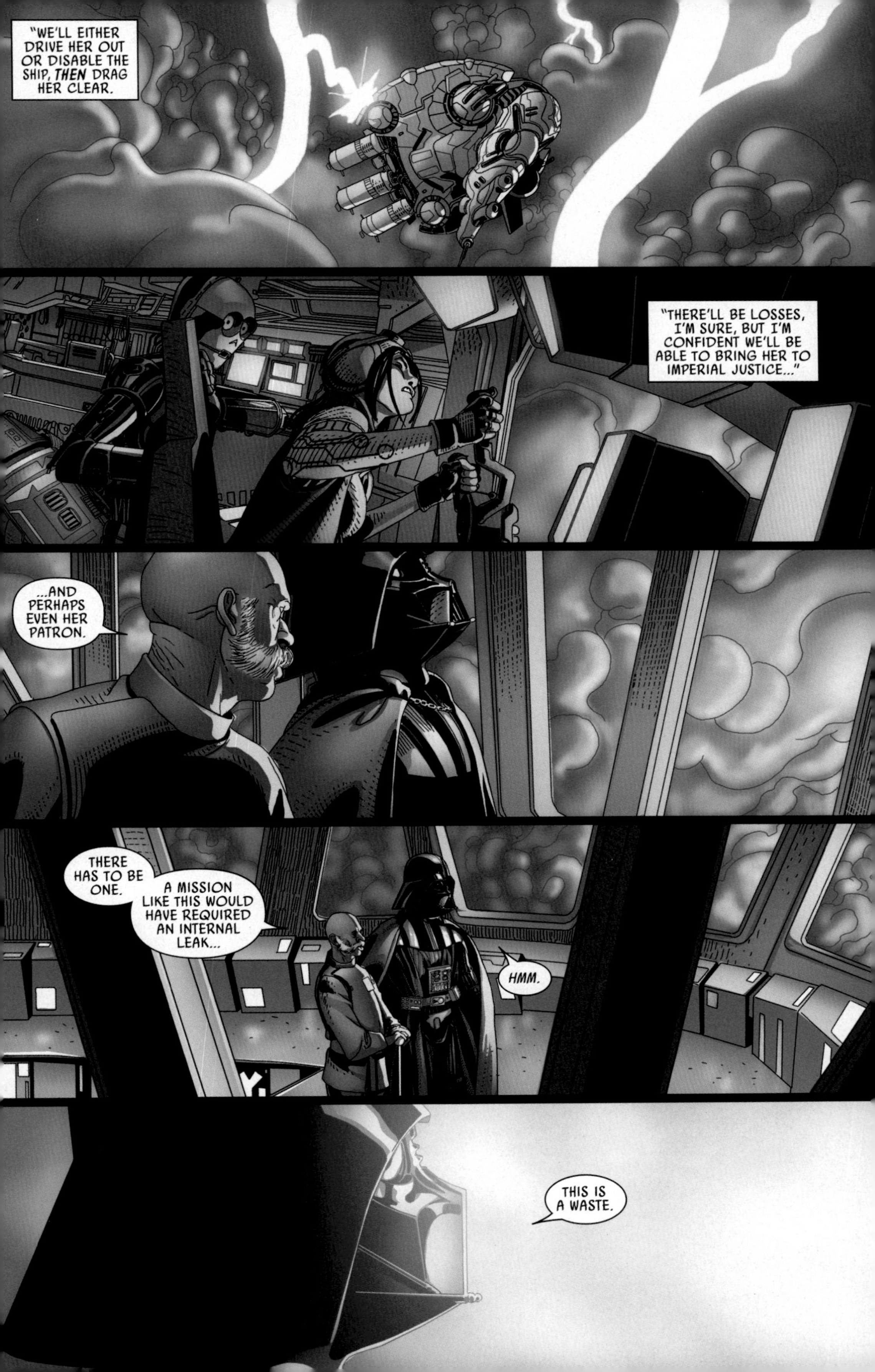
"WE'LL EITHER DRIVE HER OUT OR DISABLE THE SHIP, *THEN* DRAG HER CLEAR.
"THERE'LL BE LOSSES, I'M SURE, BUT I'M CONFIDENT WE'LL BE ABLE TO BRING HER TO IMPERIAL JUSTICE..."
...AND PERHAPS EVEN HER PATRON.
THERE HAS TO BE ONE.
A MISSION LIKE THIS WOULD HAVE REQUIRED AN INTERNAL LEAK...
HMM.
THIS IS A WASTE.

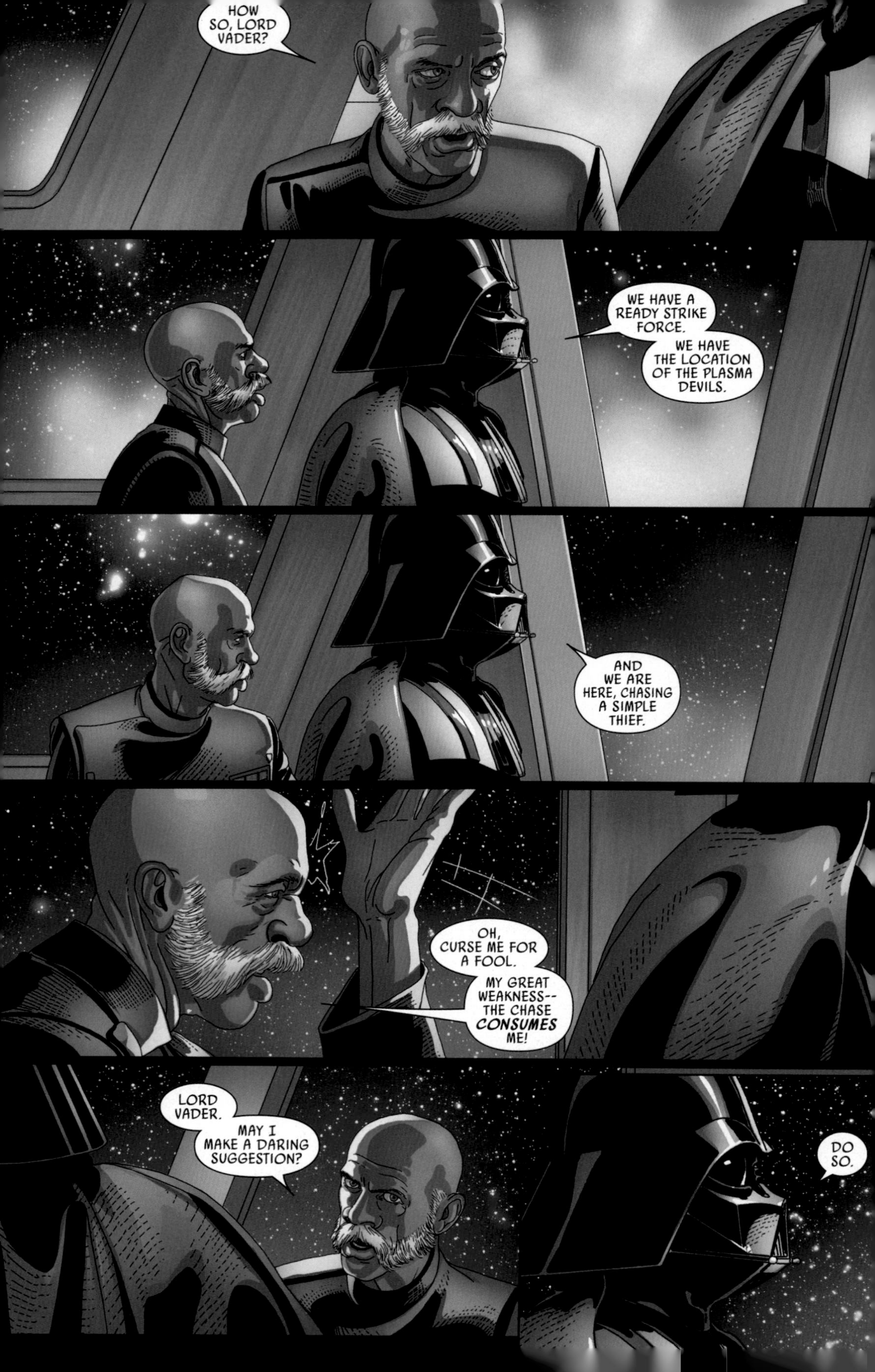
HOW SO, LORD VADER?
WE HAVE A READY STRIKE FORCE.
WE HAVE THE LOCATION OF THE PLASMA DEVILS.
AND WE ARE HERE, CHASING A SIMPLE THIEF.
OH, CURSE ME FOR A FOOL.
MY GREAT WEAKNESS-- THE CHASE CONSUMES ME!
LORD VADER.
MAY I MAKE A DARING SUGGESTION?
DO SO.

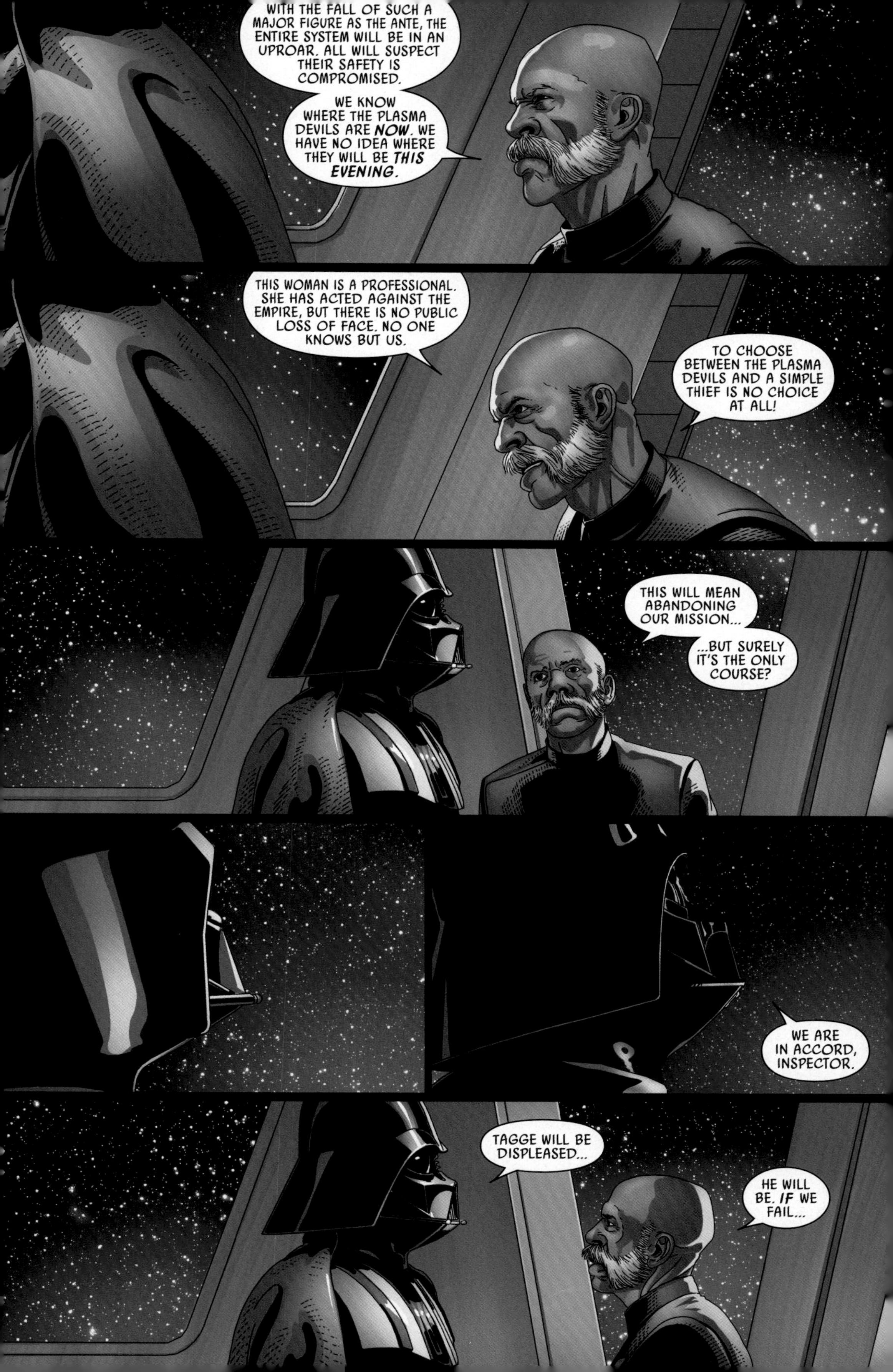
WITH THE FALL OF SUCH A MAJOR FIGURE AS THE ANTE, THE ENTIRE SYSTEM WILL BE IN AN UPROAR. ALL WILL SUSPECT THEIR SAFETY IS COMPROMISED.
WE KNOW WHERE THE PLASMA DEVILS ARE *NOW*. WE HAVE NO IDEA WHERE THEY WILL BE *THIS EVENING*.
THIS WOMAN IS A PROFESSIONAL. SHE HAS ACTED AGAINST THE EMPIRE, BUT THERE IS NO PUBLIC LOSS OF FACE. NO ONE KNOWS BUT US.
TO CHOOSE BETWEEN THE PLASMA DEVILS AND A SIMPLE THIEF IS NO CHOICE AT ALL!
THIS WILL MEAN ABANDONING OUR MISSION...
...BUT SURELY IT'S THE ONLY COURSE?
WE ARE IN ACCORD, INSPECTOR.
TAGGE WILL BE DISPLEASED...
HE WILL BE. *IF* WE FAIL...

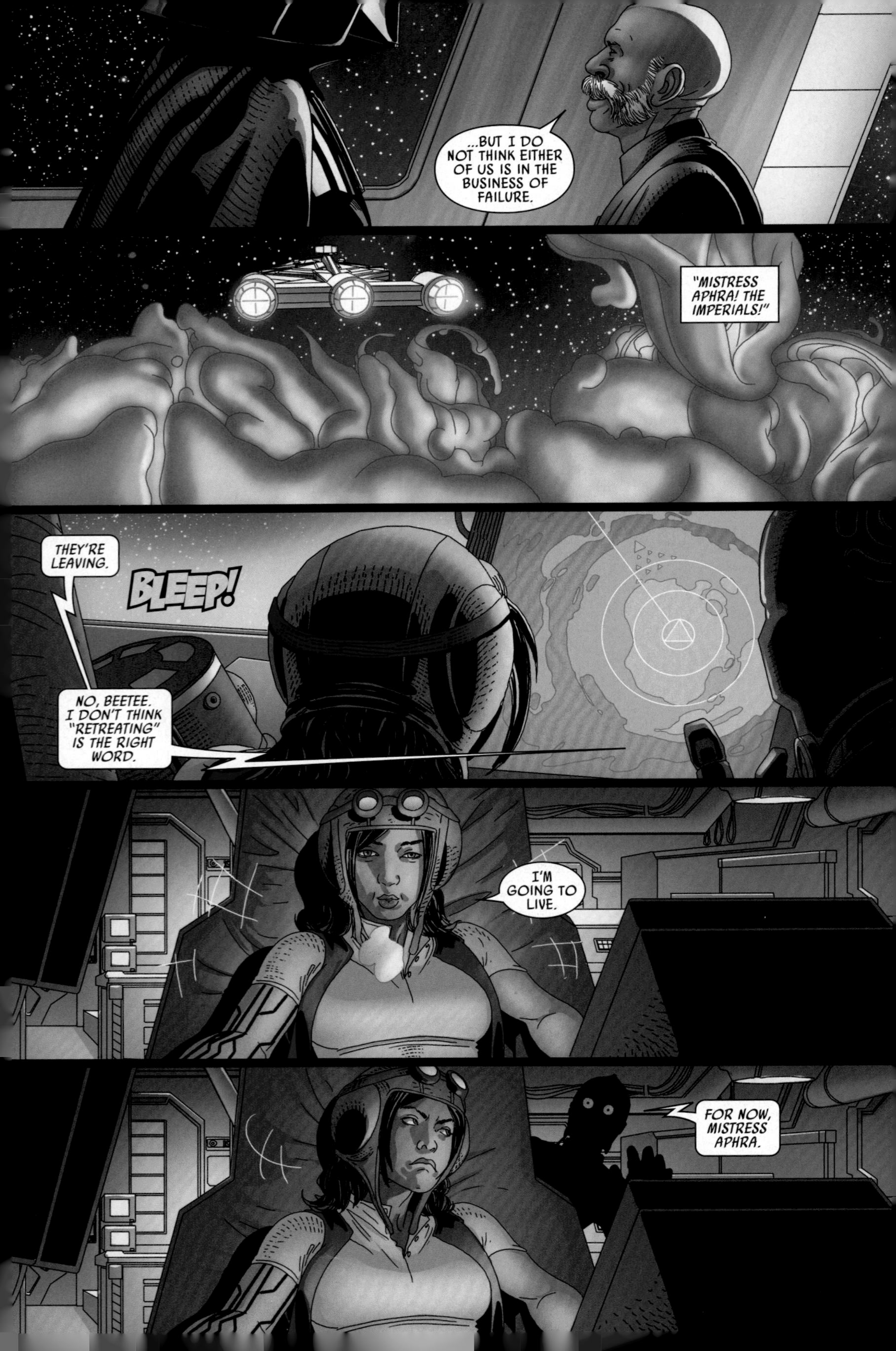
...BUT I DO NOT THINK EITHER OF US IS IN THE BUSINESS OF FAILURE.
"MISTRESS APHRA! THE IMPERIALS!"
THEY'RE LEAVING.
BLEEP!
NO, BEETEE. I DON'T THINK "RETREATING" IS THE RIGHT WORD.
I'M GOING TO LIVE.
FOR NOW, MISTRESS APHRA.

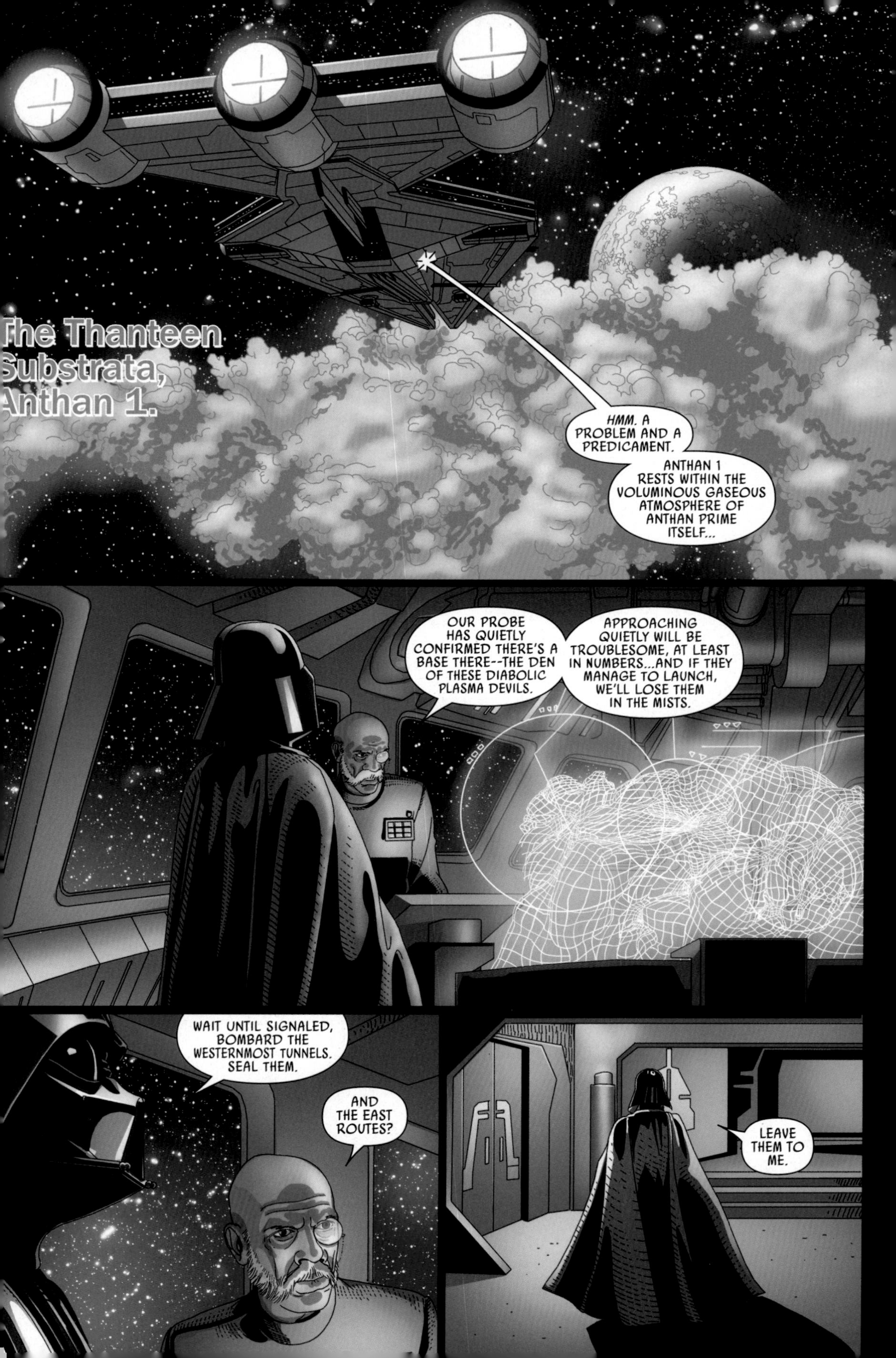

The Thanteen Substrata, Anthan 1.
HMM. A PROBLEM AND A PREDICAMENT.
ANTHAN 1 RESTS WITHIN THE VOLUMINOUS GASEOUS ATMOSPHERE OF ANTHAN PRIME ITSELF...
OUR PROBE HAS QUIETLY CONFIRMED THERE'S A BASE THERE--THE DEN OF THESE DIABOLIC PLASMA DEVILS.
APPROACHING QUIETLY WILL BE TROUBLESOME, AT LEAST IN NUMBERS...AND IF THEY MANAGE TO LAUNCH, WE'LL LOSE THEM IN THE MISTS.
WAIT UNTIL SIGNALED, BOMBARD THE WESTERNMOST TUNNELS. SEAL THEM.
AND THE EAST ROUTES?
LEAVE THEM TO ME.

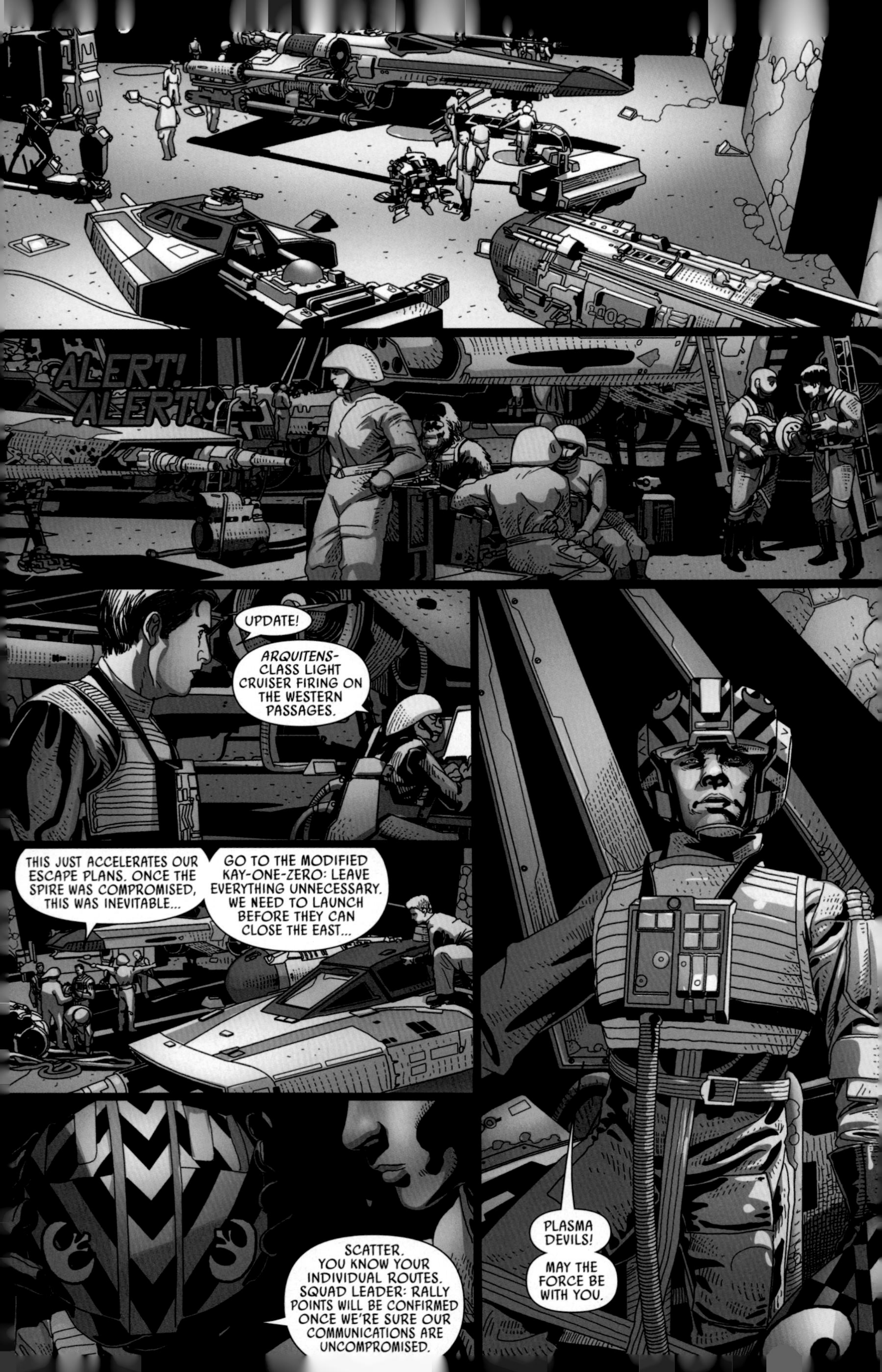
ALERT! ALERT!
UPDATE!
ARQUITENS-CLASS LIGHT CRUISER FIRING ON THE WESTERN PASSAGES.
THIS JUST ACCELERATES OUR ESCAPE PLANS. ONCE THE SPIRE WAS COMPROMISED, THIS WAS INEVITABLE...
GO TO THE MODIFIED KAY-ONE-ZERO: LEAVE EVERYTHING UNNECESSARY. WE NEED TO LAUNCH BEFORE THEY CAN CLOSE THE EAST...
SCATTER. YOU KNOW YOUR INDIVIDUAL ROUTES. SQUAD LEADER: RALLY POINTS WILL BE CONFIRMED ONCE WE'RE SURE OUR COMMUNICATIONS ARE UNCOMPROMISED.
PLASMA DEVILS!
MAY THE FORCE BE WITH YOU.

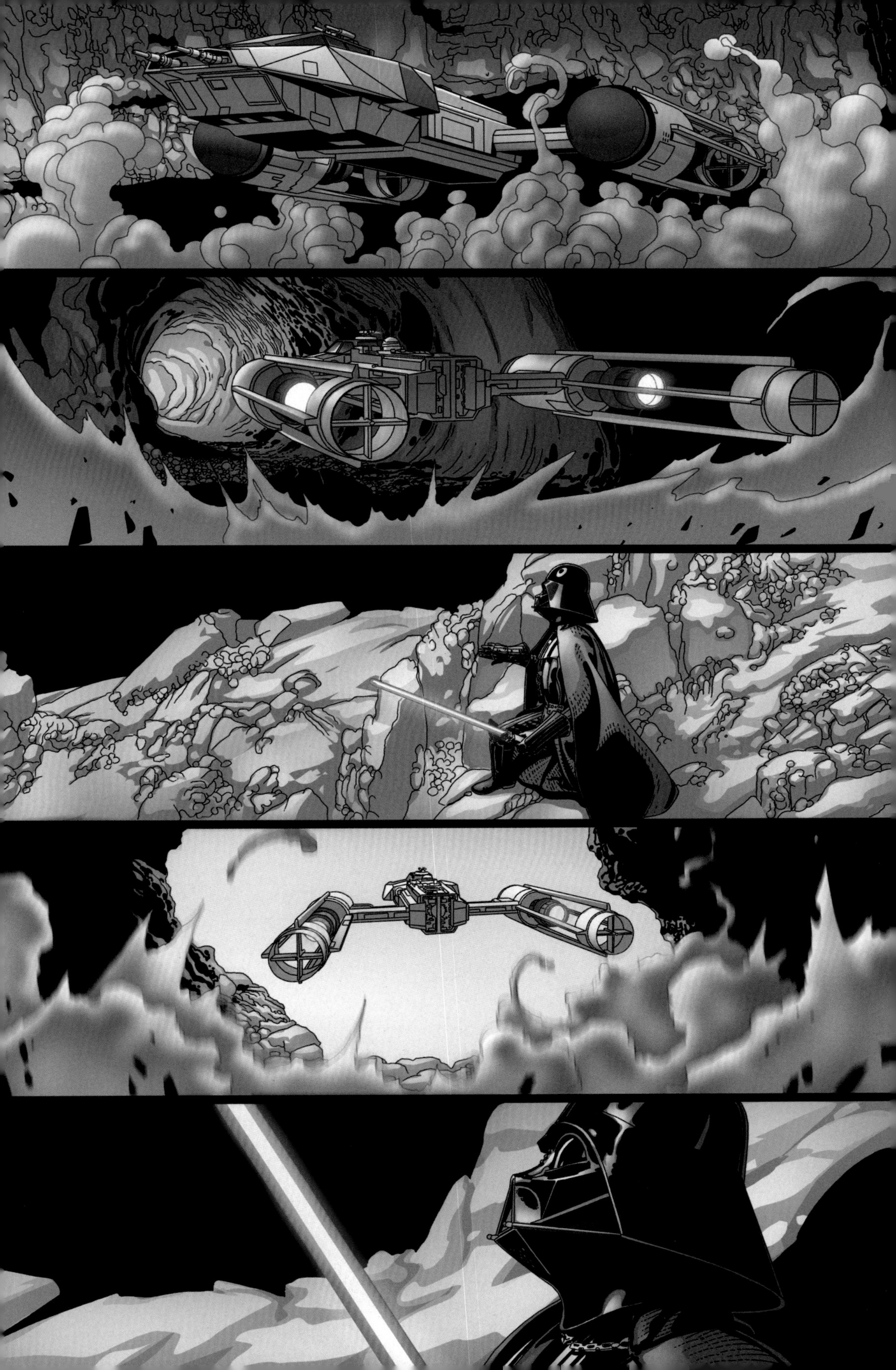

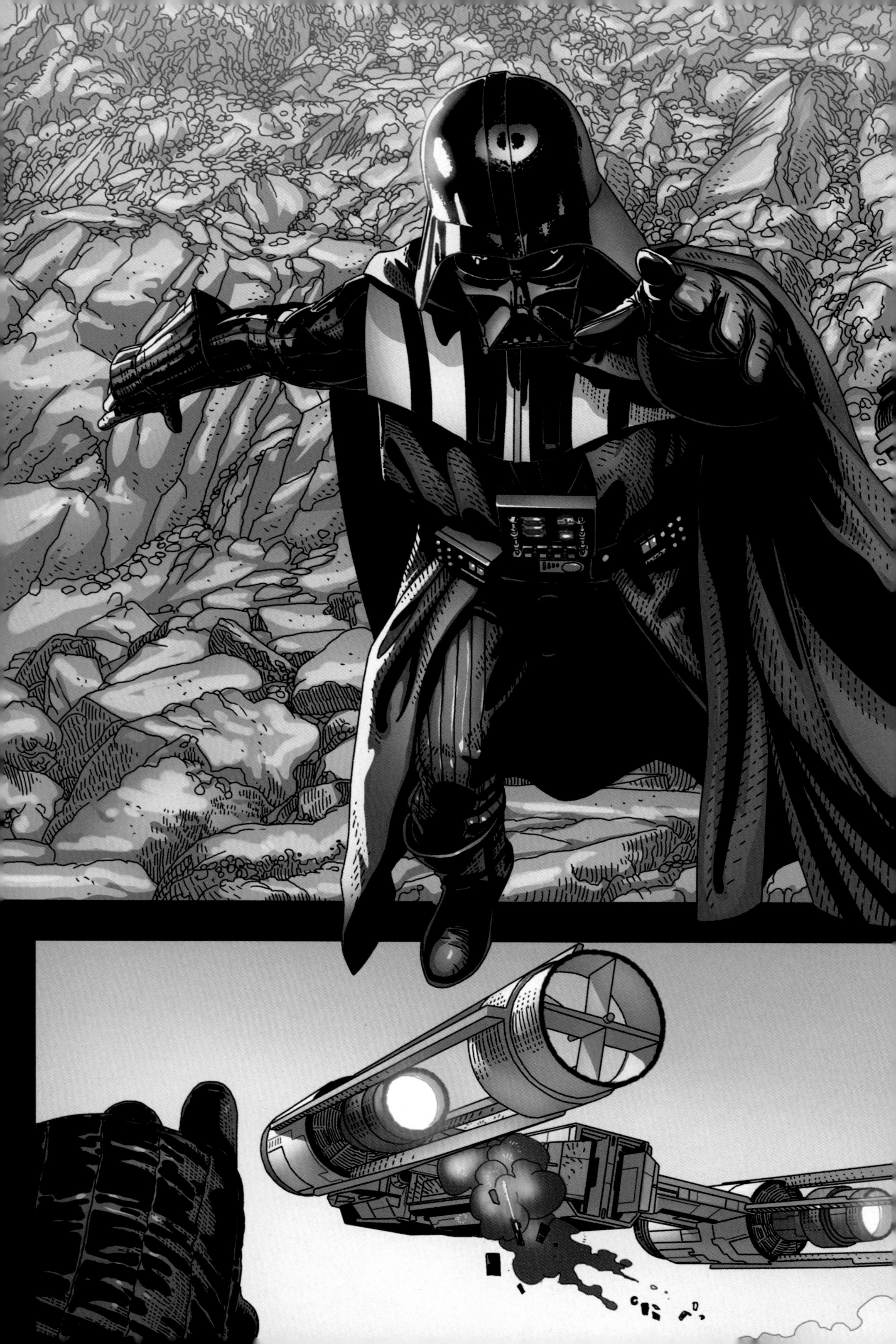

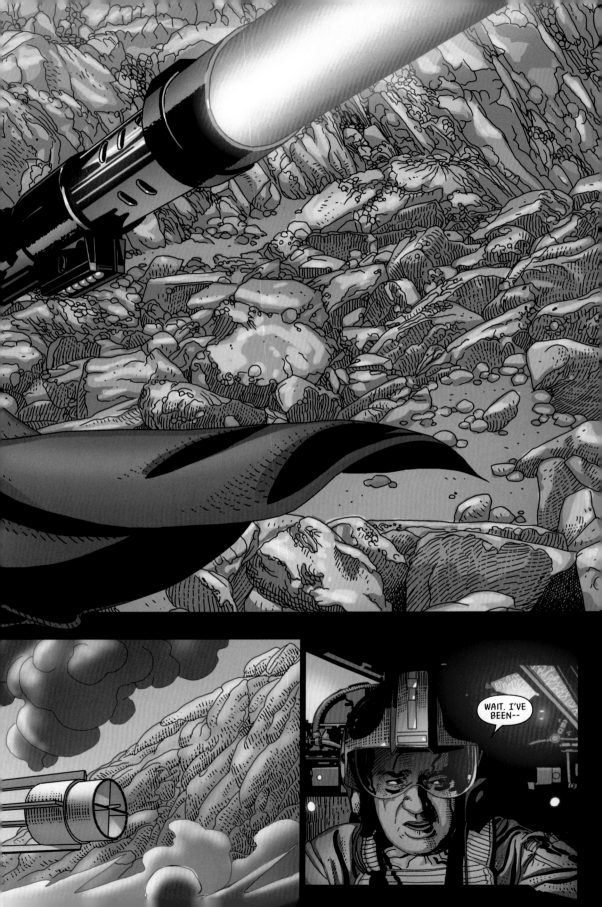

WAIT, I'VE BEEN--

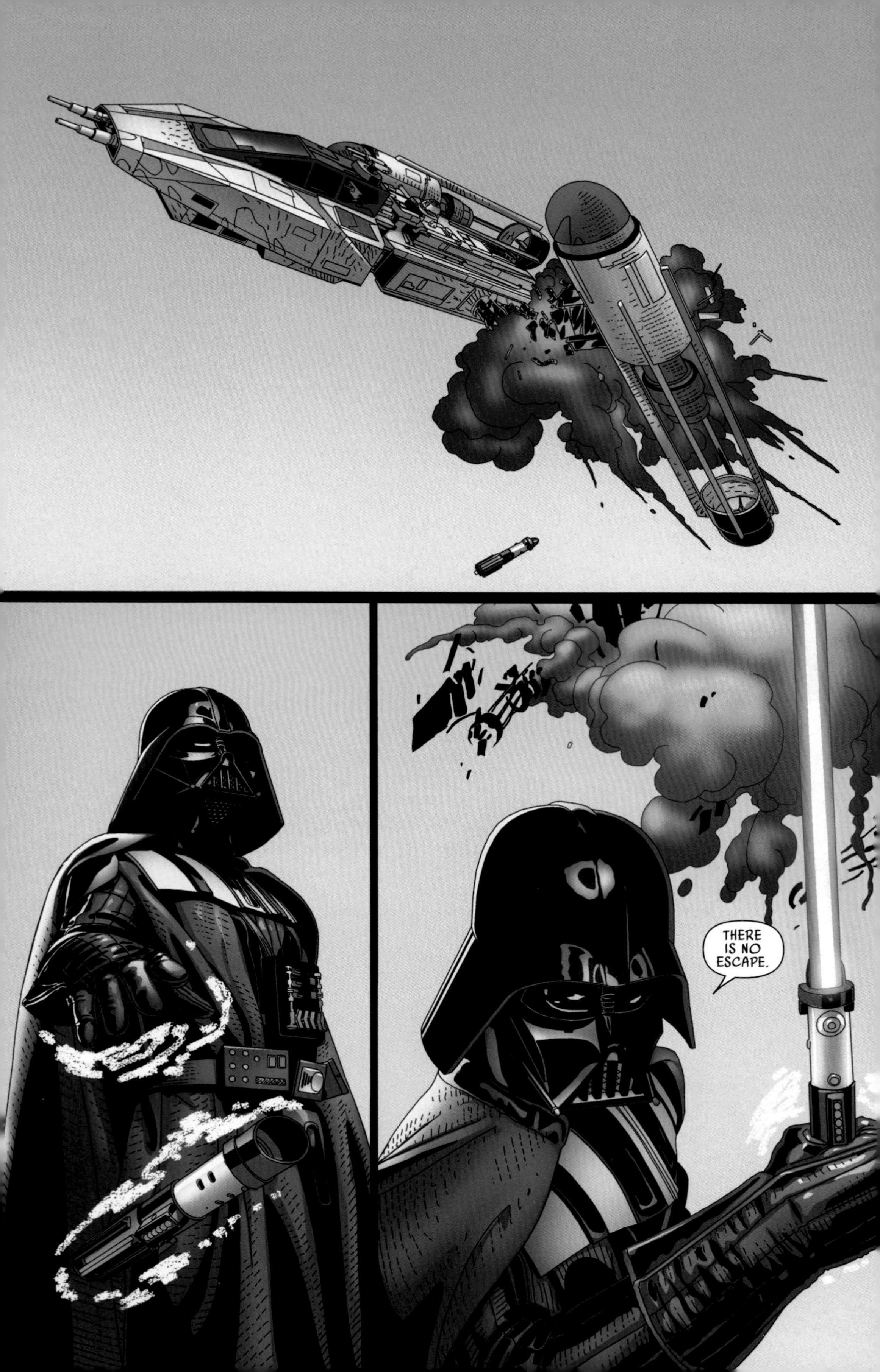
THERE IS NO ESCAPE.

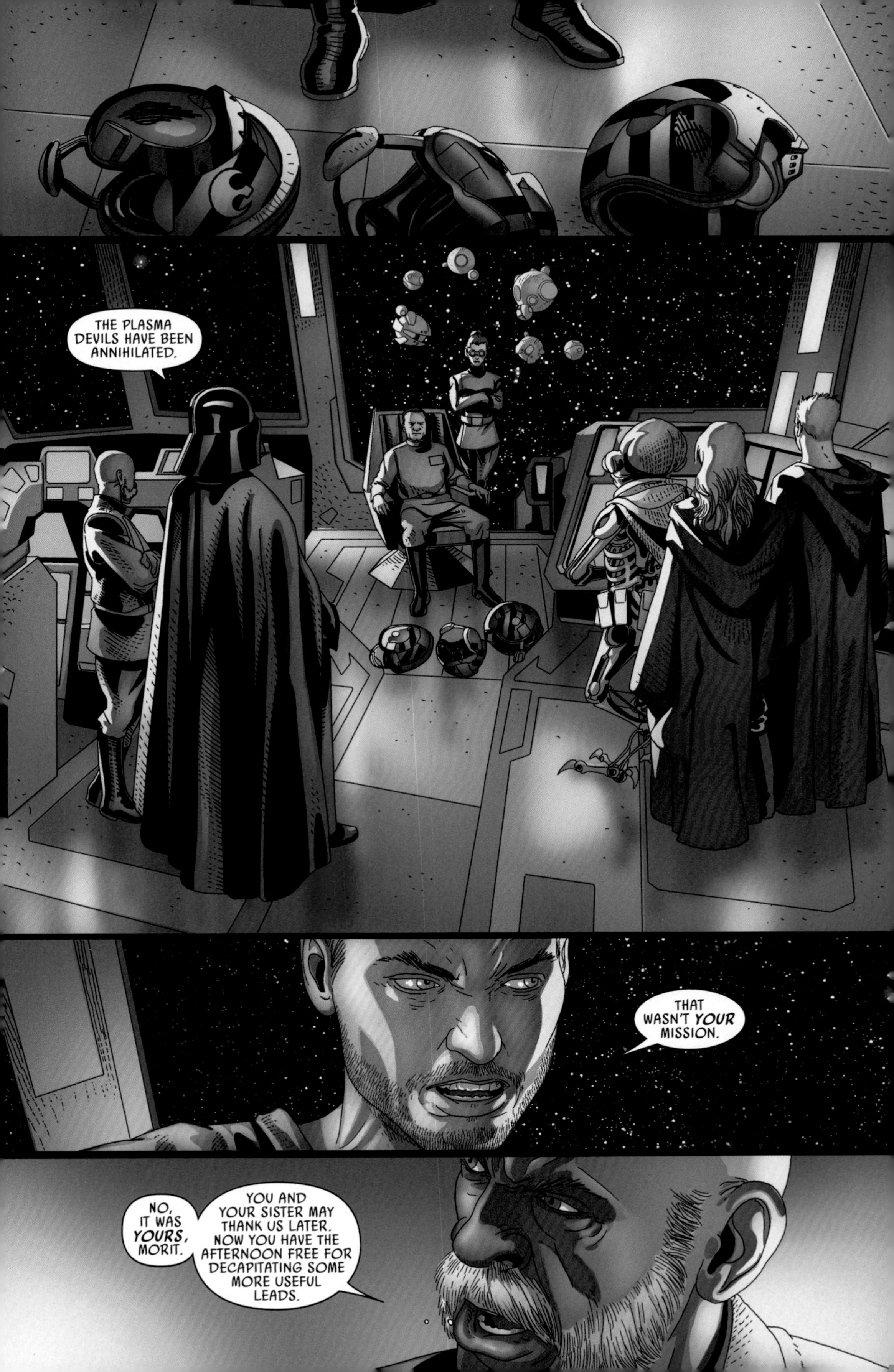
THE PLASMA DEVILS HAVE BEEN ANNIHILATED.
THAT WASN'T *YOUR* MISSION.
NO, IT WAS *YOURS*, MORIT.
YOU AND YOUR SISTER MAY THANK US LATER. NOW YOU HAVE THE AFTERNOON FREE FOR DECAPITATING SOME MORE USEFUL LEADS.

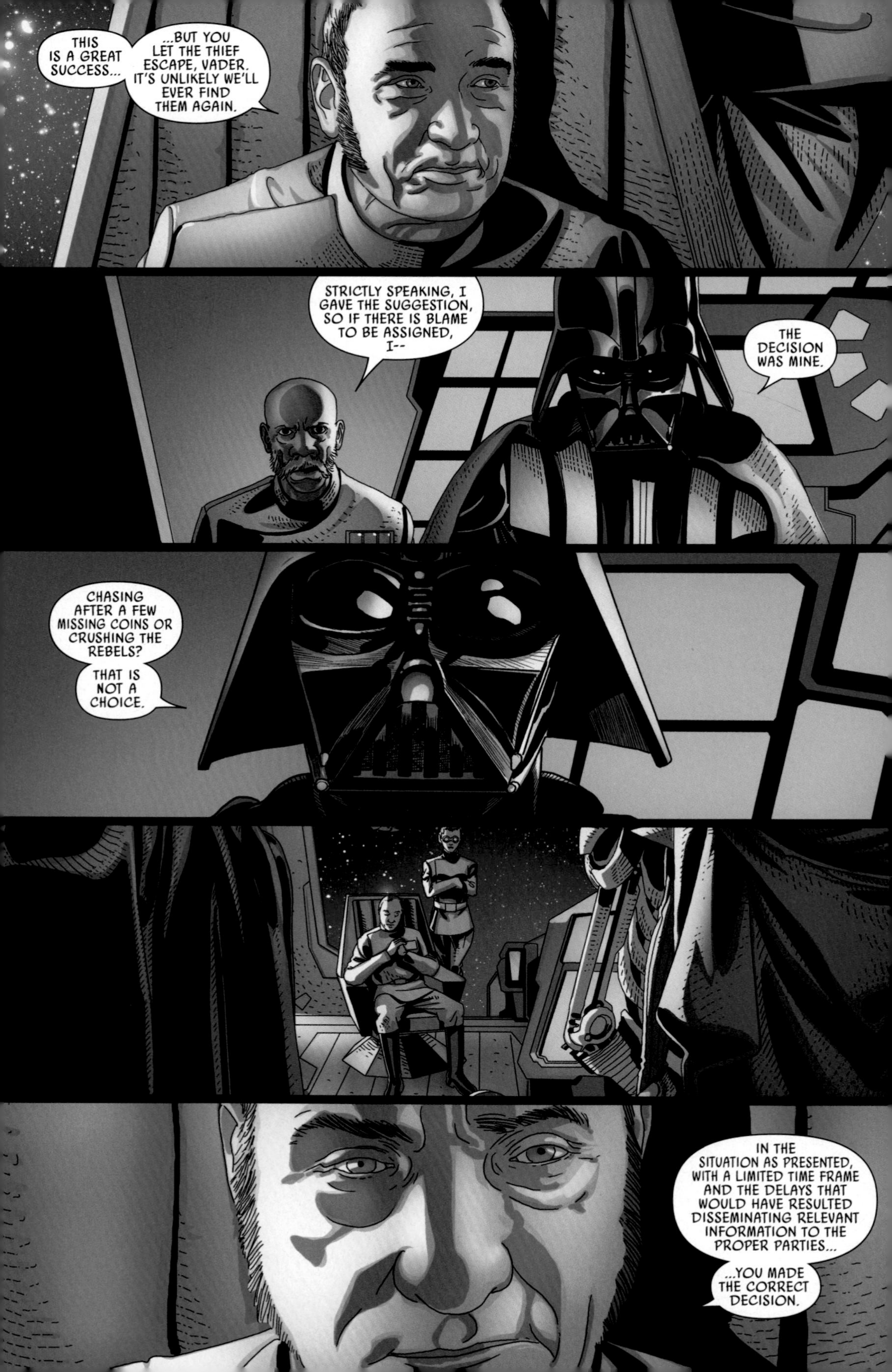
THIS IS A GREAT SUCCESS...
...BUT YOU LET THE THIEF ESCAPE, VADER. IT'S UNLIKELY WE'LL EVER FIND THEM AGAIN.
STRICTLY SPEAKING, I GAVE THE SUGGESTION, SO IF THERE IS BLAME TO BE ASSIGNED, I--
THE DECISION WAS MINE.
CHASING AFTER A FEW MISSING COINS OR CRUSHING THE REBELS?
THAT IS NOT A CHOICE.
IN THE SITUATION AS PRESENTED, WITH A LIMITED TIME FRAME AND THE DELAYS THAT WOULD HAVE RESULTED DISSEMINATING RELEVANT INFORMATION TO THE PROPER PARTIES...
...YOU MADE THE CORRECT DECISION.

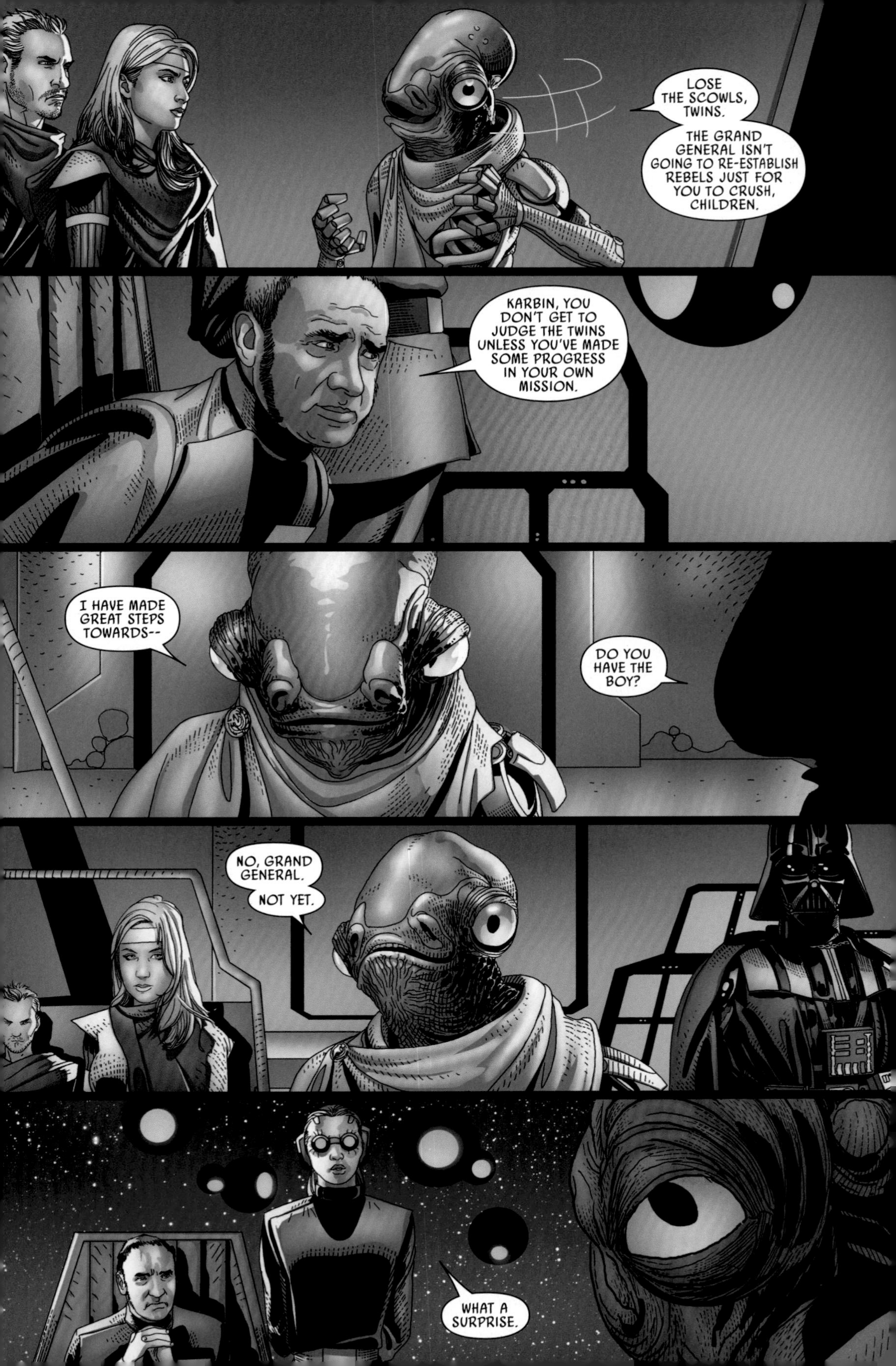
LOSE THE SCOWLS, TWINS.
THE GRAND GENERAL ISN'T GOING TO RE-ESTABLISH REBELS JUST FOR YOU TO CRUSH, CHILDREN.
KARBIN, YOU DON'T GET TO JUDGE THE TWINS UNLESS YOU'VE MADE SOME PROGRESS IN YOUR OWN MISSION.
I HAVE MADE GREAT STEPS TOWARDS--
DO YOU HAVE THE BOY?
NO, GRAND GENERAL.
NOT YET.
WHAT A SURPRISE.

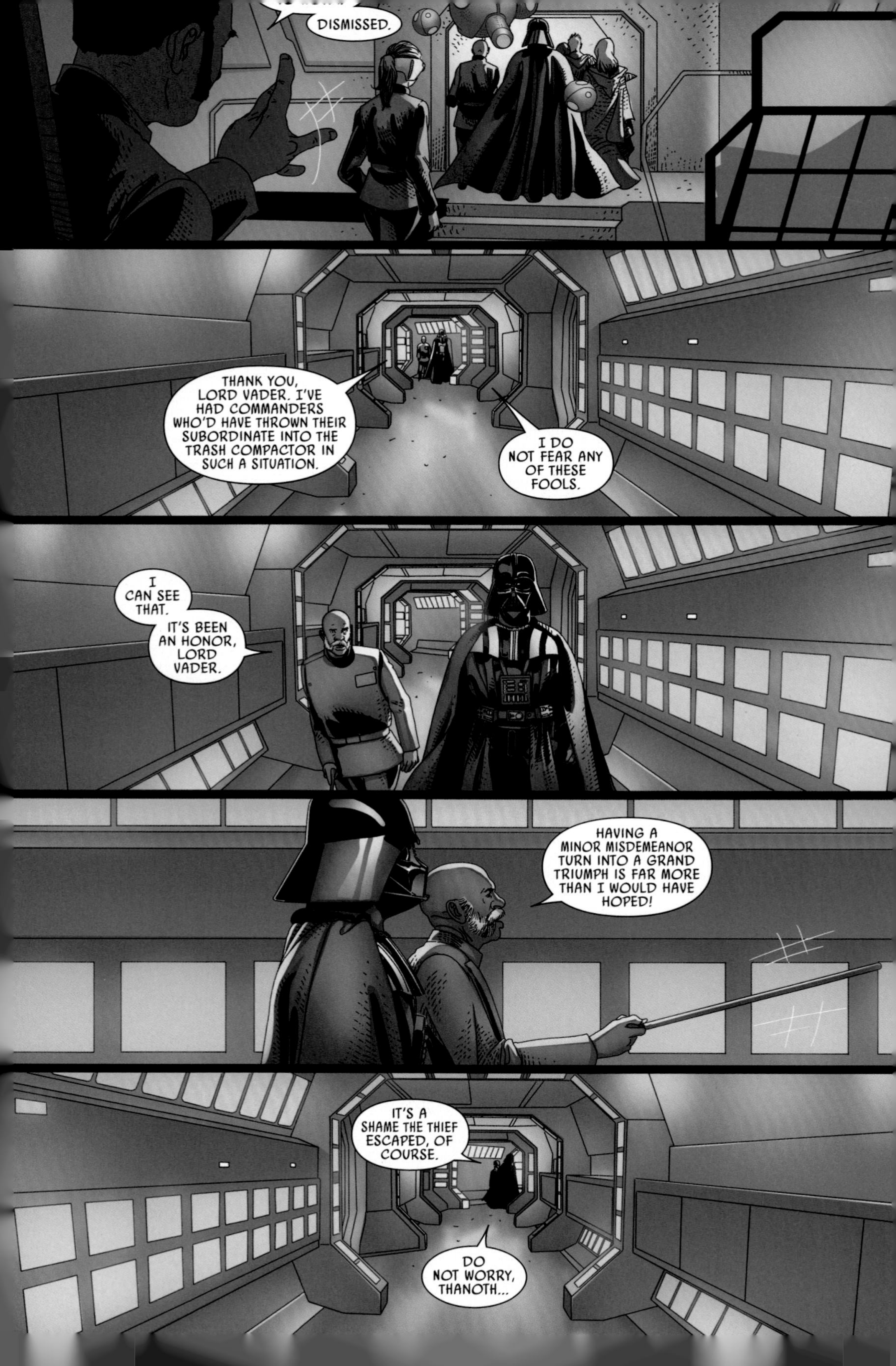
DISMISSED.
THANK YOU, LORD VADER. I'VE HAD COMMANDERS WHO'D HAVE THROWN THEIR SUBORDINATE INTO THE TRASH COMPACTOR IN SUCH A SITUATION.
I DO NOT FEAR ANY OF THESE FOOLS.
I CAN SEE THAT.
IT'S BEEN AN HONOR, LORD VADER.
HAVING A MINOR MISDEMEANOR TURN INTO A GRAND TRIUMPH IS FAR MORE THAN I WOULD HAVE HOPED!
IT'S A SHAME THE THIEF ESCAPED, OF COURSE.
DO NOT WORRY, THANOTH...

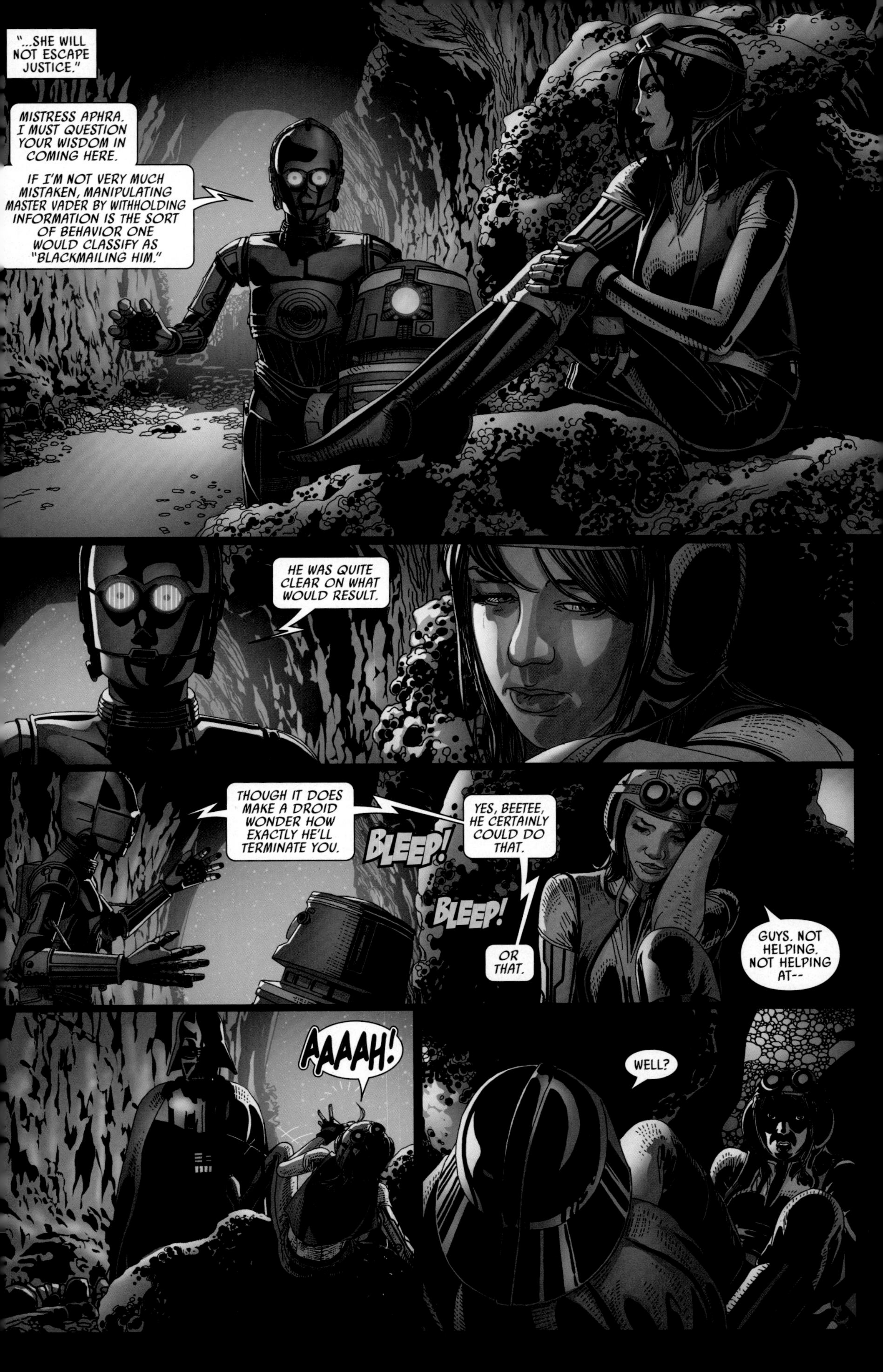
"...SHE WILL NOT ESCAPE JUSTICE."
MISTRESS APHRA. I MUST QUESTION YOUR WISDOM IN COMING HERE.
IF I'M NOT VERY MUCH MISTAKEN, MANIPULATING MASTER VADER BY WITHHOLDING INFORMATION IS THE SORT OF BEHAVIOR ONE WOULD CLASSIFY AS "BLACKMAILING HIM."
HE WAS QUITE CLEAR ON WHAT WOULD RESULT.
THOUGH IT DOES MAKE A DROID WONDER HOW EXACTLY HE'LL TERMINATE YOU.
BLEEP!
YES, BEETEE, HE CERTAINLY COULD DO THAT.
BLEEP!
OR THAT.
GUYS. NOT HELPING. NOT HELPING AT--
AAAAH!
WELL?

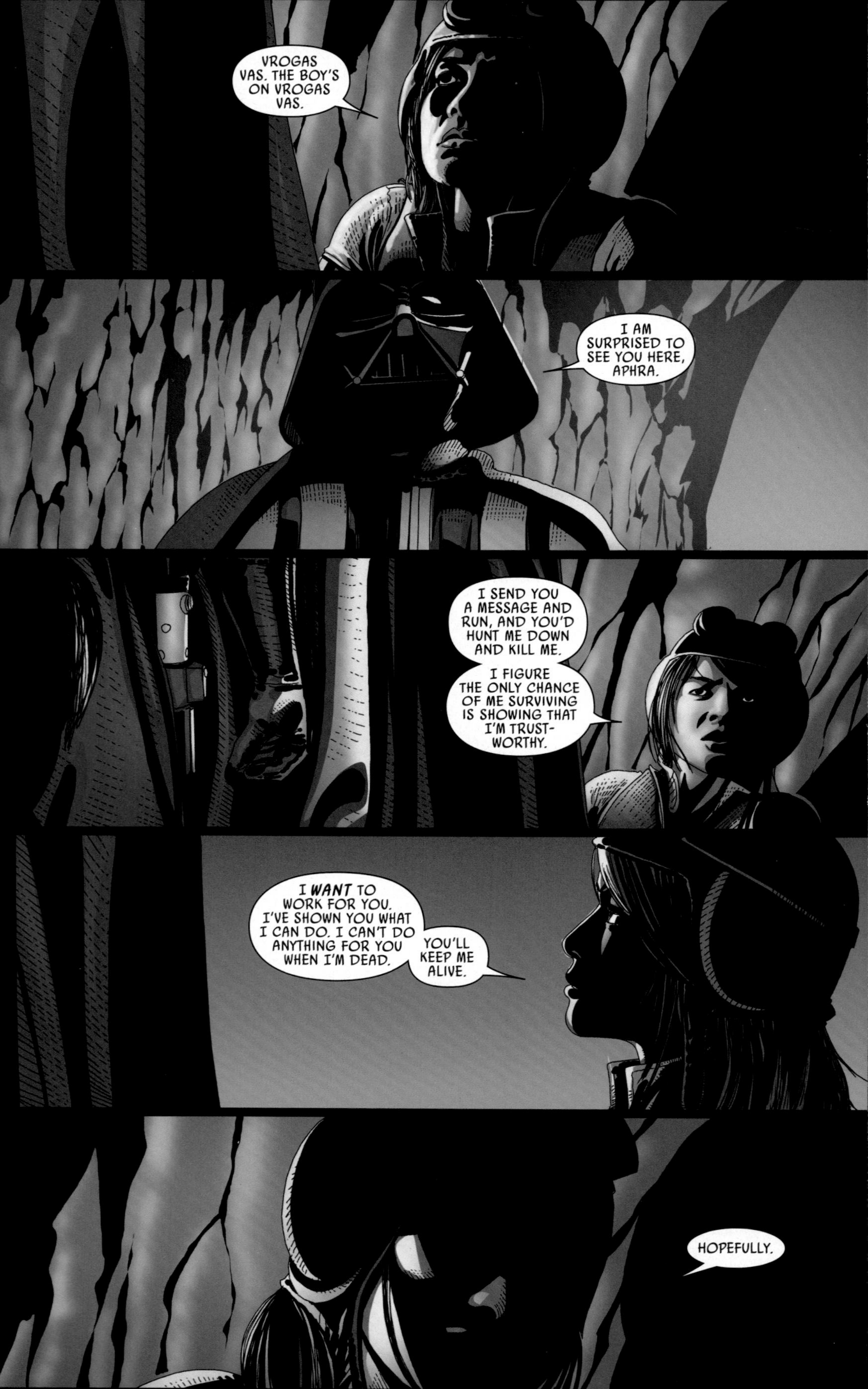
VROGAS VAS. THE BOY'S ON VROGAS VAS.
I AM SURPRISED TO SEE YOU HERE, APHRA.
I SEND YOU A MESSAGE AND RUN, AND YOU'D HUNT ME DOWN AND KILL ME.
I FIGURE THE ONLY CHANCE OF ME SURVIVING IS SHOWING THAT I'M TRUST-WORTHY.
I *WANT* TO WORK FOR YOU. I'VE SHOWN YOU WHAT I CAN DO. I CAN'T DO ANYTHING FOR YOU WHEN I'M DEAD.
YOU'LL KEEP ME ALIVE.
HOPEFULLY.

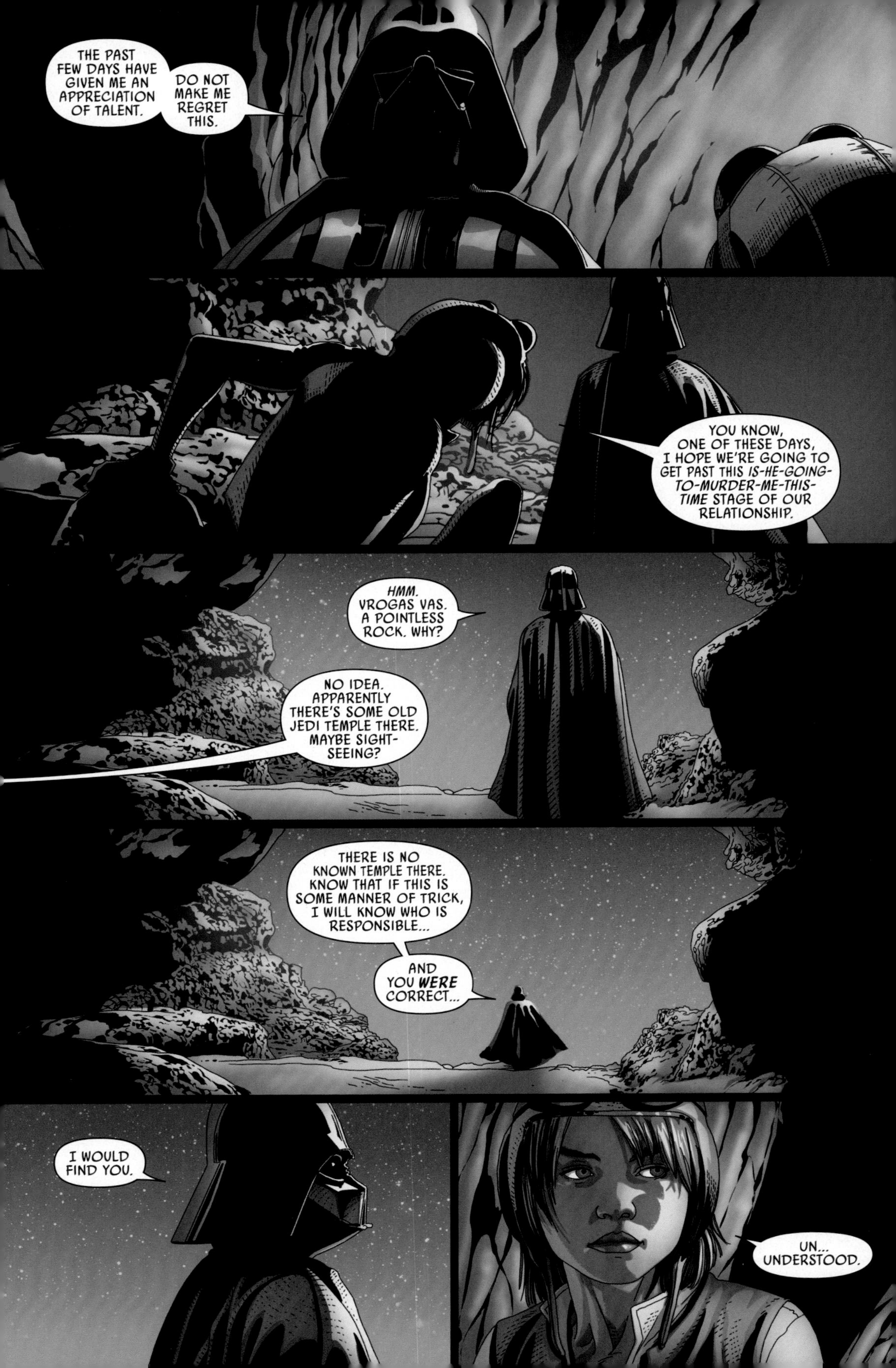
THE PAST FEW DAYS HAVE GIVEN ME AN APPRECIATION OF TALENT.
DO NOT MAKE ME REGRET THIS.
YOU KNOW, ONE OF THESE DAYS, I HOPE WE'RE GOING TO GET PAST THIS *IS-HE-GOING-TO-MURDER-ME-THIS-TIME* STAGE OF OUR RELATIONSHIP.
HMM. VROGAS VAS. A POINTLESS ROCK. WHY?
NO IDEA. APPARENTLY THERE'S SOME OLD JEDI TEMPLE THERE. MAYBE SIGHT-SEEING?
THERE IS NO KNOWN TEMPLE THERE. KNOW THAT IF THIS IS SOME MANNER OF TRICK, I WILL KNOW WHO IS RESPONSIBLE...
AND YOU ***WERE*** CORRECT...
I WOULD FIND YOU.
UN... UNDERSTOOD.

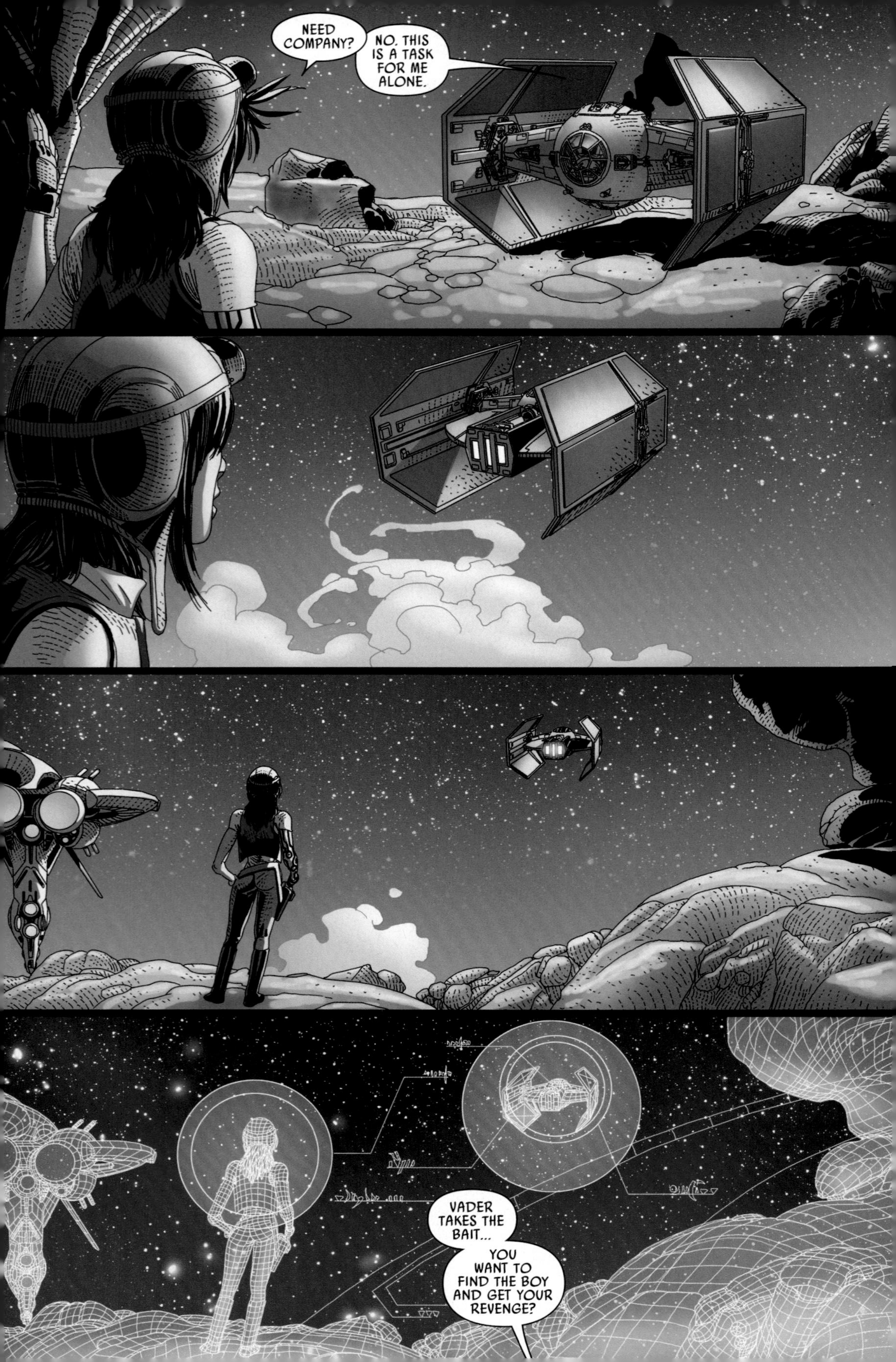
NEED COMPANY?
NO. THIS IS A TASK FOR ME ALONE.
VADER TAKES THE BAIT...
YOU WANT TO FIND THE BOY AND GET YOUR REVENGE?

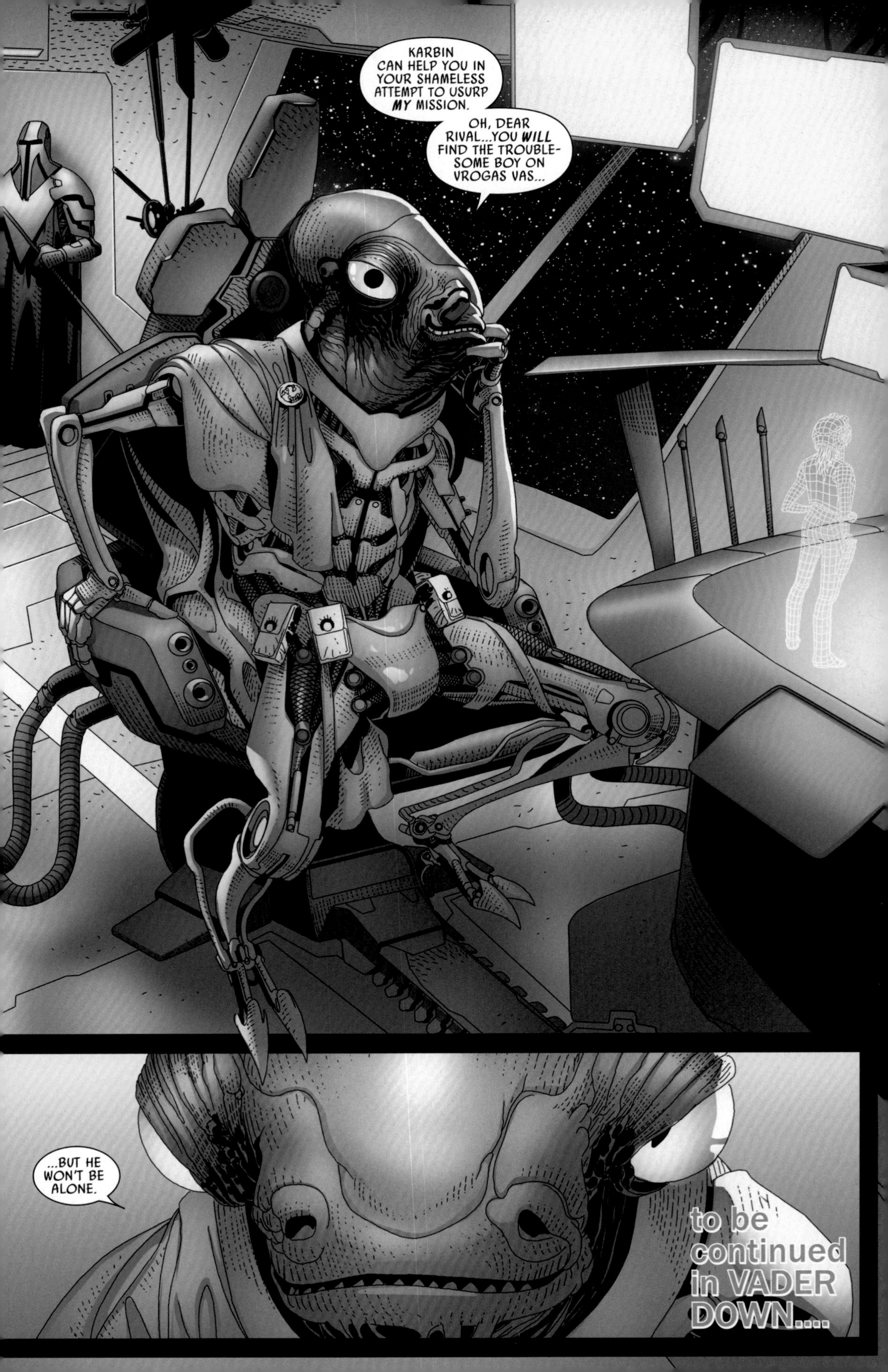
KARBIN CAN HELP YOU IN YOUR SHAMELESS ATTEMPT TO USURP *MY* MISSION.
OH, DEAR RIVAL...YOU *WILL* FIND THE TROUBLE-SOME BOY ON VROGAS VAS...
...BUT HE WON'T BE ALONE.
to be continued in VADER DOWN....

Y FAR, FAR AWAY!
F THE BIGGEST MOVIES IN HISTORY,
ERED INTERIORS!

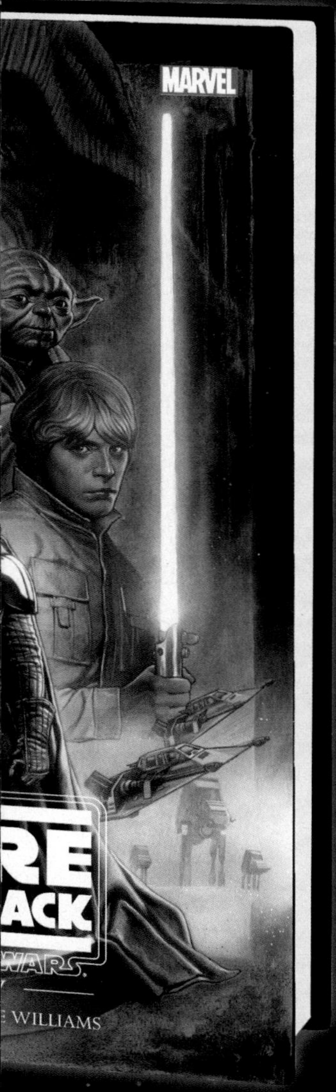
MARVEL
E WILLIAMS

PIRE STRIKES BACK HC

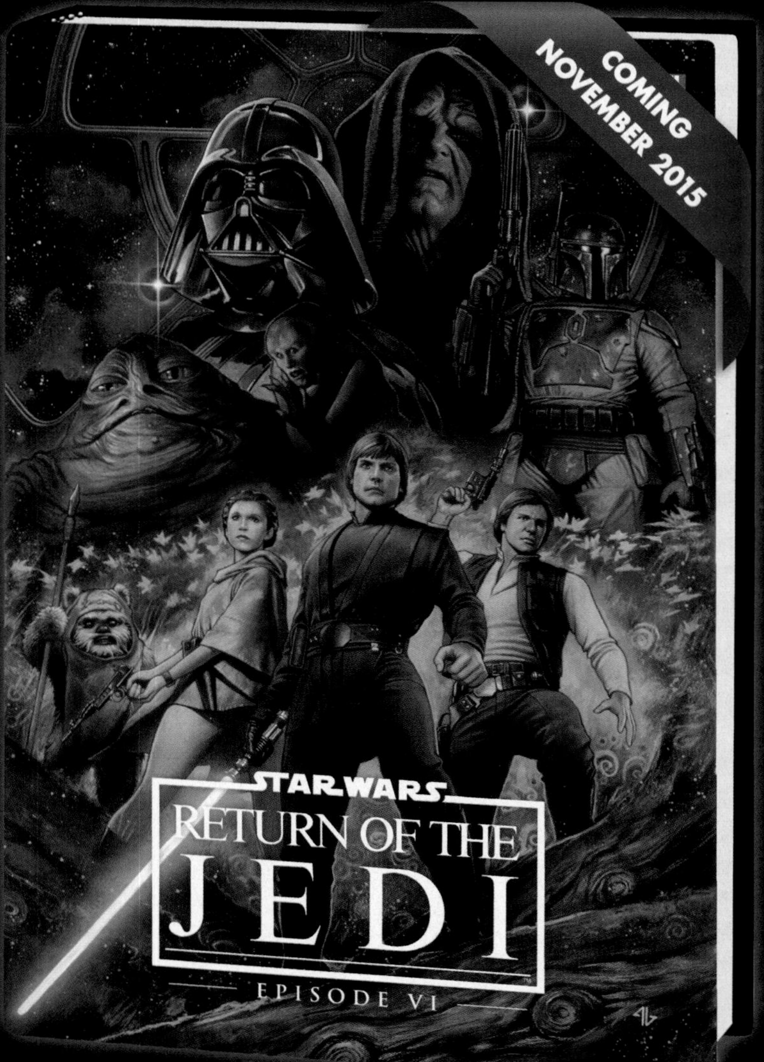
COMING
NOVEMBER 2015
STAR WARS
RETURN OF THE
JEDI
EPISODE VI

STAR WARS: EPISODE VI – RETURN OF THE JEDI HC
978-0-7851-9369-2

AN EPIC JOURNEY FROM THE BEGINNINGS OF THE OLD REPUBLIC TO THE RISE OF THE EMPIRE AND BEYOND!

**STAR WARS LEGENDS EPIC COLLECTION:
THE OLD REPUBLIC VOL. 1 TPB**
978-0-7851-9717-1

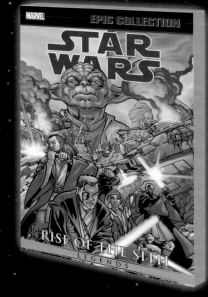

**STAR WARS LEGENDS EPIC COLLECTION:
RISE OF THE SITH VOL. 1 TPB**
978-0-7851-9722-5

**STAR WARS LEGENDS EPIC COLLECTION:
THE EMPIRE VOL. 1 TPB**
978-0-7851-9398-2

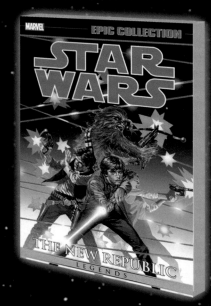

**STAR WARS LEGENDS EPIC COLLECTION:
THE NEW REPUBLIC VOL. 1 TPB**
978-0-7851-9716-4

AVAILABLE NOW WHEREVER BOOKS ARE SOLD